Power Trips and Other Journeys

Power Trips and Other Journeys

Essays in Feminism as Civic Discourse

JEAN BETHKE ELSHTAIN

The University of Wisconsin Press

The University of Wisconsin Press
114 North Murray Street
Madison, Wisconsin 53715

3 Henrietta Street
London WC2E 8LU, England

5 4 3 2 1

Printed in the United States of America

Library of Congress Cataloging–in–Publication Data
Elshtain, Jean Bethke, 1941–
    Power trips and other journeys : essays in feminism as civic discourse /
Jean Bethke Elshtain.
224 pp.   cm.
    Includes index.
    1. Feminism—United States.   2. Women in politics—United States.
I. Title.
HQ1426.E47   1990
305. 42'0973—dc20
ISBN 0–299–12670–6   90–50083
ISBN 0–299–12674–9 (pbk.)   CIP

For my sisters
Patricia Bethke Bing
Bonnie Bethke Stegner
And my brothers
William Paul Bethke
Richard Allan Bethke
To whom brotherhood and sisterhood are not abstractions

Narrative is the art closest to the ordinary daily operation of the human mind. People find the meaning of their lives in the idea of sequence, in conflict, in metaphor and in moral. . . . The narrative mode of thought comes universally to people as, for instance, mathematical or scientific reasoning do not. Everyone all the time is in the act of composition, our experience is an ongoing narrative within each of us.

E. L. Doctorow

Contents

Preface

In 1979 I wrote a play, really a very long-winded dialogue between three female characters, as a paper for a panel at the Annual Meeting of the American Political Science Association entitled, "Towards a Redefinition of Power: Is There a Feminist Contribution?" Everyone agreed there was. But the only way I could enact my sense of that contribution was through the construction of a *mise en scene* that promoted, indeed forced, confrontation and dialogue. My female power players were friends so nobody walked out in a huff. And their evening of "Power Trips and Other Journeys" ended with Paulette, the political theorist of the group, having bid goodnight to her groggy (from too much wine, too much talk, going on too long) companions, turning to the audience and saying:

Words matter. The words with which we characterize our daily lives matter. To subscribe to words that we scarcely believe, words that do not live within, through, and alongside our daily existence, merely in order to be able to deploy them as weapons, useful, perhaps, for beating others over the head, is to traffic in what Dietrich Bonhoeffer called "cheap grace." This imposes a special burden of power and responsibility. Whether one is a feminist or a one-worlder or any of the other bewildering current possibilities, one must shoulder responsibility rather than running amuck, carelessly, through past and present, ransacking what we can "use," defiling what we cannot, and demeaning that which gives meaning to other poor, mortal creatures like ourselves.

Although that play never saw the light of day in the form of publication or, for that matter, production, it helped to frame the ethical and political horizon for themes elaborated within the pages of this volume. I have not had occasion to dispute the closing soliloquy of my character, Paulette, as she brought temporary and only temporary closure to an evening spent in the company of others being human, revealing themselves through speech, yet forging connections to those not present, not heard, not seen. Having derived the title of this book from that decade-old play, I felt a responsibility to be faithful to its spirit and its intent. Thus the reader will find a perspective, arrived at discursively, lurking in the pages to follow. As with many others I don't know what I think until I have written or spoken it. Sometimes my own answers are disturbing, only rarely reassuring, and almost never comforting. I address debates about pornography, child abuse, the meaning of patriotism, among others. These are all vital subjects for civic discourse. But they are also subjects that require independence of mind and an openness to debate, *especially* on the most controversial matters, a commitment to democracy, an understanding of politics as the art of the possible. I am concerned with children and families and communities and not so much with narrow constructions of "women's interests." I am engaged by the relation between rights and responsibilities. I struggle throughout the essays with how to articulate a set of strong claims that do not have the effect of silencing the voices of others.

In my first book, *Public Man, Private Woman,* I evoked the great Wittgenstein in my preface by recalling his words in a letter to a student and friend. Wittgenstein insisted that, as difficult as it was to "think *well* about 'certainty,' 'probability,' 'perception,' " it was "still more difficult to think, or *try* to think, really honestly about your life and other people's lives. And the trouble is that thinking about these things is *not thrilling,* but often downright nasty. And when it's nasty then it's *most* important."[1] As with the words of the fictive Paulette, those of Wittgenstein continue to resonate, to strike home. I find thinking honestly difficult and the temptation to smooth over rough edges, to take shortcuts, to avoid taking up themes or constructing formulations that will draw fire from various and by-now predictable quarters, is at times well nigh irresistible. But I resist, or try to, knowing that fudging and hedging over time becomes habitual and the result is to lose the capacity to "think really honestly."

At the center of all of these essays is conflict, ambivalence, tension, and recognition of and an effort to avoid extremes. A commitment to democratic politics, or the possibility of such a politics, commits one to an imperative to keep debates alive rather than attempting to resolve them definitively by silencing one side to a dispute, such as that over pornography, for example, or just war, or women's power and powerlessness. Debates are embodied in people, concrete human beings living in particular times and places. When I reflect upon my own terms of inclusion and exclusion I try to conjure up images of living human beings and messy human situations, rather than sanitizing matters in line with abstract formulae or rationalized abstractions. Thus it is that, in Hannah Arendt's words, "Those who are on the lookout for representatives of an era, for mouthpieces of the *Zeitgest*, for exponents of History (spelled with a capital H) will look here in vain."[2] Resisting the foolish labeling mania that infects much contemporary political discourse, including feminism, is difficult in an epoch in which we all too often substitute the "politically correct manifesto" for difficult thought and ethically aware debate. But, again, resistance is necessary.

Michel Foucault once proclaimed that the police can see to it that our dossiers are in order—that is not the task of the political intellectual. I will let others worry about whether I "deserve" the name "feminist" or not and, if so, what sort of feminism that might be. I continue to claim the name and the identity and see my work as but one example of the engaged civic discourse that feminism as critical aspiration and moral awareness helps to make possible.

Acknowledgments

For suggestions and criticisms over the years, thanks to Nancy Huston, Sara Ruddick, Catharine Stimpson, Jane Jaquette, Kathy Jones, Carlin Barton, Madeleine Grumet, Jane Humphries, Jane Mansbridge, Sheila Tobias, James Der Derian, William Connolly, Michael Shapiro, David Blankenhorn, Christopher Lasch, Robert Coles, Tom Dumm, Stanley Hauerwas, George Kateb, Eli Sagan, and all those with whom I have debated and discussed the matters elaborated within the pages of this volume.

My husband, Errol L. Elshtain, was supportive in ways that now seem normal but are rather unusual even in this day and age. Gordon Lester-Massman was patient beyond the bounds of decency with the many delays in delivery of this book. He initiated the project and Barbara Hanrahan saw it through to completion. My students, at the University of Massachusetts and now at Vanderbilt University, prodded and poked, challenged and supported. They, and the many questioners whose names are unknown to me, who engaged me at universities and in other settings both in this country and abroad, have played a central role in this discursive and dialogical task. I am indebted to all of them. I am also grateful to Dean Jacque Voegeli of Vanderbilt University for his sustained support.

For permission to reprint portions of a number of the essays between these covers, thanks to *Cross Currents*, *Telos*, *Halcyon*, *Lutheran Forum*, Family in America Research Series and Vakgroep Vrouwenstudies FWS, University of Leiden, and G. Scarre, ed., *Children, Parents and Politics* (Cambridge University Press, 1989).

Introduction

Every veteran of Western education knows what the essay is—the place
where you get to say what you mean.

Reynolds Price

These essays flow from thematic insistencies and political recognitions. Forged over the past six years, they touch on the many faces
and forms of power; on struggles for autonomy as well as deep
commitment to and awareness of human rootedness and sociality; on
the public and the private (yet again and always); on what some call
"individualist versus relational" feminism, though I resist the anti-
nomy; on what others call "equality versus difference" feminism,
though I see no absolute divide there either, at least not a necessary
one. Other debates surface—between contemporary communitarians
and their ultraliberal opponents; between political utopians and
spokeswomen for total struggle, total solutions, and an all-pervasive
politics in contrast to those who, in Karen Offen's words, "practice
politics as the art of the possible."[1] One reason, but not the only one,
that Hannah Arendt's metaphor of natality as "new beginnings,"
including those of the political sort, moves through these essays is the
fact that it conjures up the fragility, mortality, and necessary limited-
ness of all our political efforts. Those whose politics is that of arrogant
overreach cannot tend democratically to the many political concerns
and concepts represented in this volume—whether pornography or
child abuse or power or equality or freedom. I have a long-standing
animus against philosophers and political model builders who disdain our ordinary humanity and who, in their quest for a comprehensive, universal standpoint, wind up, in Martha Nussbaum's
words, making "the humanly possible work look boring and cheap."[2]

Perhaps because I grew up in a small town, reared by morally
serious parents, surrounded by an extended network of kin, yet
bedeviled by the cramped vision and prejudicial parochialism that
surfaced alongside the caring and genuine neighborliness, I have

always seen myself, or placed myself, in the rather odd position of populist intellectual. I am deeply mistrustful of the ministrations of intellectual elites or public policy managers of social problems cut to the cloth of their own knowledge/power site. The need for, or conviction of, a correct and encompassing standpoint, the immediate excitement and visceral satisfaction of theories that make possible scenarios in which the analyst moves in on a given turf, sets up court, and summarily dispenses epistemic and political "justice," is one I eschew and devoutly hope that I avoid.

There are feminist philosophers who have taken upon themselves the role of all-knowing judges. There are categories of feminist analysis that make this will to discursive power possible, for example, the notion of a universal standpoint deriving from the category "woman," to the extent that one has *correctly* recognized and analyzed that category. There are other feminist thinkers who resist dogmatizing and universalizing philosophy and who ongoingly remind us of the fact (in Joan Scott's words) that, "Any unitary concept rests on—contains—repressed or negated material and so is unstable, not unified."[3] This recognition involves the feminist political thinker in an endless series of contests over meaning. This book is part of a wider contestation—a politics of representation that takes place textually, yes, but not in a vacuum. The knowledge generated in and through representational politics circulates, making manifest conflicts, formulating challenges, but, at its best, resisting facile solutions and leaps into empty categories and other substitutes for serious debate.

If one begins with the complex and various social realities in which complex and various women find themselves, one sees quickly that there is no universal standpoint to be found—indeed, a historically situated, concrete location is difficult enough to come by. Instead, one finds the contrasting perspectives of female subjects defining themselves both *with* and *against* the reigning and ready-to-hand identities, public and private, of their own era and social location. If we understand that the world of female subjects, forged within constraints and in and through oppositions, secreted values and imperatives, inspired songs, stories, myths and identities, empowering women at times to act in and on the public sphere, we can better understand both the fears of so-called traditionalists and the qualms of so-called radicals at the implications of the suppression of these concrete and particular identities in favor of what seems an excessively legalistic, abstract personhood.

Take, for example, Section One, "Women for Dark Times." With Hannah Arendt in her *Men for Dark Times,* from which I stole the title for this section and the idea for concerning myself with particular persons, I am drawn to narratives of individual lives that call up wider social, ethical, and historical constraints and possibilities. It was Arendt's conviction that looking at persons, at how particular individuals lived their lives and moved in the world, might offer illumination for "dark times," the "first half of the twentieth century with its political catastrophes, its moral disasters, and its astonishing development of the arts and sciences."[4] Three women—Jane Addams, Simone Weil, and Eleanor Roosevelt—are at the forefront of my concern in part because I responded to what others asked of me ("Will you write an essay for our commemoration of Eleanor Roosevelt's centennial?") and because these women, though vastly different in many respects, nevertheless shared an experience of conflict by chafing against yet shoring up societal and moral norms, by making public what was private via ethical conviction. Their moral commitments prevented their public actions from becoming narrowly self-interested. They sought to act in behalf of others (always a problematic proposition, as each recognized) rather than at the expense of others. Addams struggled throughout her life to balance the family claim and the social claim; Weil strove, tragically and unsuccessfully, for a radical solitarism coupled with an equally radical recognition of the "need for roots"; Roosevelt juggled her identities in a complex way, her private identity as "Mrs. Franklin Roosevelt" making possible but not exhausting her public citizenship. Ironically, the lack of homage—even hostility in some cases—meted out by some contemporary analysts against Addams, less so Roosevelt (and Weil is too much a puzzlement to be "for" or "against")—is rooted in the very reasons that gave their lives purpose and made possible their activism, their moral and religious values. I had the curious experience of citing Addams, at some length, in a presentation for a mixed Political Science–Women's Studies colloquium at a major university and was told in no uncertain terms that Jane Addams did not count as a "gender analyst." My hunch is that this dogmatic conviction derives in part from the fact that what is scandalous for us—lives imbedded in an ethical framework—was essential to Addams—and to Weil and Roosevelt. Much food for thought here.

I recognized, rereading my stories of these women for dark times, that, at times, my own oppositions and affirmations got forged more strongly in light of their stated positions than I think I "really feel." This makes little sense as stated so I will try to explain. My example will be the construction of a strong "social ontology" grounded in human embodiment I bring to bear against Weil's noumenal disembodied ideal. I realize that, were I confronted with a very different thinker, one who located us so deeply inside a strong version of community that no possibility for autonomy or independence of thought or action could emerge, I might call upon Weil to challenge overimbeddedness in the phenomenal realm. My own understandings are ongoingly dependent upon those of others. My politics is an incessant engagement with the demands, claims, and identities of others. Discovering Addams, Weil, and Roosevelt is also discovering oneself, or those aspects of oneself their stories bring to the surface, enact so to speak, and, having appeared, demand critical scrutiny.

Section Two, "All in the Family," keeps me on familiar turf but in less familiar ways than those I have called upon in earlier works. Discussing the family wage, child abuse, the new eugenics, and the relationship of each to wider social forces and political developments, pushed me several directions at once. In the case of the family wage, I found that an earlier, almost automatic endorsement of such a wage as both possible and desirable was problematic in ways I did not foresee when I first tackled the topic. But I also problematize the position of antifamily wage publicists, finding strange, yet finally intelligible, the opposition of self-identified social democrats to a family wage system. I learned that social democrats and socialists may serve as the carriers for a market-metaphorical version of the wage-earning individual(ist). The family in this scheme becomes an aggregate of individuals, no greater than the sum of its parts. The solution to a too predatory individualism, which such arguments help to make possible, is a robust vision of the collective that, all too often, gets construed as management of "social problems" from above via enlightened public policy: hence, for example, calls for sterilization of the feebleminded from many progressive reformers in the 1920s and 1930s.

My discussion of child abuse prompts several no doubt cowardly caveats. To see child abuse as a powerful construction is not to deny its "reality." It is, rather, to examine the ways in which that "reality" is conveyed and identified. What language is available? What sort of "expert knowledge" has more power to define the problem, even to manifest it, than some other? I never resolved the tension in my own position about the ways this society deals with child abuse. No one wants to see children hurt. But who gets to define what counts as abuse?

Historically definitions of "neglect" and "abuse" were all too often weapons in the hands of a more powerful and privileged class against a less powerful and more vulnerable one. In February 1989, the New York State's attorney general, Robert Abrams, called a news conference during which he claimed that most of the "child-protection societies in New York State abuse their police powers and act as vigilantes or perform no function at all."[5] The portrait he painted was of so-called child protectors running wild, with seventeen out of twenty-four societies overstepping their authority. The societies had been authorized in 1875, given peace officer status, and empowered "to make arrests, file charges and take custody of children." Curbing the abuses of such societies signifies no diminution in concern over abuse of children. But it does point to possible abuses by those authorized to stop abuse.

Examining this question and that of pornography in Section Three, I realized how constrained our political options are by the ontologies generated by our political culture and history (individualism versus community, or freedom versus constraint) and by the concepts that have emerged to speak to these ontologies and to replicate them ongoingly. Refusing to think about child abuse and its real human victims, ignoring accusations of child abuse and the victims it generates, is not an option for the engaged political intellectual. Instead, one must explore *how* it is that these questions are put before us and what might be done to criticize insistent, ongoingly reincoded representations. In my discussions of child abuse, pornography, and the new eugenics, I stand in opposition to the hardened categories of current oppositional sides. (Although I am clearly more in sympathy with those who are sounding the alarm about bio-political engineering than with those harmonizing about the wonders of techno-reproduction.) Neither the quest for politically correct sexuality in and through antipornography politics, nor uncritical acceptance of pornography as free speech and unfettered or even radical resistance to established norms, seems to me a position worthy of endorsement. I hope my complete discussion helps to clarify why this is the case.

Finally, in Section Three, "Going Public," I offer a series of related essays written in response to specific requests that, taken together, add up not so much to a program or a platform as to a set of possibilities evoked through how particular issues are constructed, reconstructed, and might in the future be transformed. I try to keep in mind real constraints. I do not forget that there are nation-states that cannot be "politicked" or argued away when one considers war and peace. I remember that most women continue to conceive, to bear, and to nourish infants at some time in their lives. Biological differences do count; the question is how. I track movements from domestic politics to foreign affairs that show the interconnection and mutually constitutive relations between them, in contrast to strong "realist" claims to the contrary. Many of these public pieces, delivered as talks but refined as essays, are cautionary tales. Lots of warning flags go up at various points. But I also express realizable hopes and honor those, like the Mothers of the Disappeared in Argentina, who have taught us, through their desperation and their triumph, about freedom and dignity and what it means to fashion a politics of hope and justice against a politics of defeat and vengeance. Bonhoeffer said, and he was right, "You can't be universal anywhere except in your own back yard." But that backyard sometimes looks out on the world in all its horror and all its beauty. In these essays I try not to turn away when that vista opens up.

Section One

Women for Dark Times

That even in the darkest of times we have the right to expect
some illumination, and that such illumination may well come
less from theories and concepts than from the uncertain, flick-
ering, and often weak light that some men and women, in
their lives and their works, will kindle under almost all circumstances and shed over the time span that was given them on
earth—this conviction is the inarticulate background against
which these profiles were drawn.

Hannah Arendt

1

A Return to Hull House: Reflections on Jane Addams

From a standpoint of jaded modern sophistication, the story of Jane Addams at first seems a tale of old-fashioned do-goodism fired by the charitable impulses of a "lady" who wound up fashioning an overpersonalized approach to social problems. Such naive forms of social intervention, the sophisticate might continue, inevitably gave way to professionalism, social workers who neither require nor need even be aware of the complex inner wellsprings of their own motivation but who act, instead, from the realization that there is a job to be done. The primary question is how most efficiently to do it—to "manage" a "client" population. To see Hull House and Jane Addams simply as an instance of noblesse oblige suited, perhaps, to its day but quickly eclipsed by the welfare state and the abstract demands of justice is not so much to oversimplify—though it is to do that—but to pretty much miss the boat altogether. For Jane Addams was up to something else.

A second layer of distortion that partially obscures Jane Addams's life and work reflects our changing constructions of American womanhood. The chaste and the maternal intermingled in Addams, always Miss Addams, sometimes Queen Jane. Hers was a symbol overtaken in epochs that witnessed, successively, flappers, WACS and Rosie the Riveters, the feminine mystique, feminist protest, sexual liberation, rampant consumerism, demands for "self-actualization" and the (apparent) final triumph of secular and technological world views. A life of unforced chastity infused with a deeply felt maternalism is a combination that we find difficult to understand, even more difficult to respond to. We no longer see the world, as Addams did, through the prism of duty and compassion,

3

social responsibility and witness-bearing: life as a Pilgrim's Progress. Perhaps this as much as anything else dates her and fixes her in our eyes as a remote figure. Having said all this, I shall try, nevertheless, to see her once again, rethinking her as both a theorist and symbol.

Briefly, however, it is worth surveying the received wisdom of Addams as a social thinker. Views of her long ago congealed. Nearly all commentators, with few exceptions, find her work derivative. Allen F. Davis, her most recent biographer, endorses the view that Addams is "more important as a publicist and popularizer" than as an original thinker.[1] Daniel Levine, author of *Jane Addams and the Liberal Tradition*, concurs: Addams is "not an original thinker"; rather, she was a "publicist" alive "to the currents of the day."[2] Addams fares little better in a number of influential social and cultural histories. Henry Steele Commager, in *The American Mind*, mentions her in no capacity.[3] Ralph Henry Gabriel's classic standard, *The Course of American Democratic Thought*, contains one scanty reference to Addams. In his discussion of progressivism, Gabriel gives the progressive kudos for transcending both the agrarian parochialism of the populists and "the humanitarianism of such urban reformers as Jacob Riis and Jane Addams" in the name of a more cosmopolitan, less personally humanitarian stance.[4] In *Age of Reform*, Richard Hofstadter characterizes "The Subjective Necessity for Social Settlements,"an early and important Addams essay, as "fine and penetrating" and Addams herself, he declares, embodies "the most decent stream" in the Progressive moment given her keen awareness of the deracination attendant upon industrialization.[5]

One important exception to cursory notices on Addams is Christopher Lasch's introduction to *The Social Thought of Jane Addams* and his chapter devoted to Addams in *The New Radicalism in America*. Lasch sees Addams as "a theorist and intellectual—a thinker of originality and daring."[6] Though he is critical of the antiintellectualism he finds in some of her work, particularly in those discussions of education that extolled "applied knowledge," Lasch's serious consideration of Addams as a social theorist of continuing importance is instructive, and it is one on which I shall build.[7] I do so in an effort to recover and restore Addams's commitment to an interpretive social theory that bears within it the seeds of cultural and political criticism.

Jane Addams was forty-five years old when she began *Twenty Years at Hull House*, the first volume of her autobiography. Published in 1910, it was to be her most successful book; eighty thousand copies were published during her lifetime. *Twenty Years* stands out among her nearly dozen books and her many essays and occasional pieces as, perhaps, her finest sustained effort.[8] Her gifts as a thinker of rare insight and a writer of unusual descriptive powers are here abundantly displayed. Already a celebrated public figure when she penned her own story, her autobiography sealed that public persona. To her biographer, Davis, *Twenty Years* captures Addams in the self-conscious process of casting her public image in a heroic mold, "at least," Davis equivocates, "acquiescing in the public image of herself as a self-sacrificing saint, and friend of the down-trodden." Davis goes on to scold Addams for refusing to "come clean" about her "administrative talent and her ability to compete in a man's world that actually made her a success"[9]—an injunction wholly out of touch with Addams's own sensibilities and her moral location.

But Davis's judgments, those of a sympathetic but partially debunking observer, show how difficult it is for the sensibilities of the present to get inside the world as Jane Addams understood it. That difficulty is manifest, for example, when the fact that Addams deployed various literary conceits and fictional conventions popular in her era serves as the basis for Davis's additional claim that there is little difference, in principle, between *Twenty Years* and the other tales of the self-made person who overcomes all obstacles to achieve fame and success. If Addams's story were just one more example of the pluck and luck *genre*, we would long ago have ceased to pay it any mind, whether as personal history or as social commentary. These judgments by a biographer highlight a general problem that emerges when our historic hindsights are so finely attuned to contemporary abuses of "publicity" that we blind ourselves to the deeper discursive tradition that—in this case—*Twenty Years* embodies.

What I call to mind here is story-shaped history that aims to edify. "Jenny" Addams viewed her world through the prism of Christian symbols and injunctions, purposes and meanings. These gave her world its shape—a narrative form involving the use of instructive parables in the conviction that the moral life consists in "the imitation of Christ," not in abstract obedience to a formal model of moral conduct. From the book's opening passages, Addams traces her life as a singular narrative, a *particular* story but one that forms as well part of the greater American story. Addams quotes herself (from an 1889 journal entry): "In his own way each man must struggle, lest the moral become a far-off abstraction utterly separated from his active life."[10] Life, she declares, is a quest, and a life of virtue lies within reach if one emulates exemplary individuals. For Jenny, Mr. Lincoln early became her secular saint, a figure with whom she explicitly, self-consciously, and unwaveringly identified until her death. Lincoln was the standard by which she took the measure of her own existence.[11]

Just as she had an ongoing connection to Lincoln, in *Twenty Years* Addams invites her reader into a particular identification with herself. For Addams, each human life was instructive. She evokes the desire of the young girl to please her "handsome father" trying to understand life "as he did," including the sense he conveyed through his attachment to the Italian patriot Joseph Mazzini of the "genuine relationship which may exist between men who share large hopes and like desires, even though they differ in nationality, language and creed."[12] As a child, Addams claims, she recoiled from adult attempts to patronize her by isolating her from life's experiences, being already (at least from hindsight) convinced that ethics "is but another word for 'righteousness,' that for which men and women of every generation have hungered and thirsted, and without which life becomes meaningless."[13]

If the child, from the standpoint of the mature adult, can, through reminiscence, instruct that adult on childhood; if the rebellion of youth is forged and shaped so long as there "is something vital to rebel against"—adults revealed with their flaws but their dignity intact—the social bond is strained but unbroken and the power of empathetic reflection is affirmed. "Even if we, the elderly," she writes, "have nothing to report but sordid compromises, nothing to offer but a disconcerting acknowledgement that life has marked us with its slow stain, it is still better to define our position."[14] *Twenty Years* is her attempt, mid-life, to define and to clarify her own position so that others might emulate or challenge written in the conviction that "truth itself may be discovered by honest reminiscence."[15]

In this sense *Twenty Years* represents the culmination of Addams's early social thinking and sets the agenda for her work to come.[16] All the characteristics of her philosophy are present: her repudiation of abstract systems in favor of a social theory open to experience; her sense of moral seriousness and struggle; her rejection of "feverish searches" after culture that cultivated a life of pale aestheticism in favor of a life of action, for "action is the only medium man has for receiving and appropriating truth."[17] To this one must add her powerfully conveyed image of human solidarity, "which will not waver when the race happens to be represented by a drunken woman or an idiot boy."[18] That was the starting point from which she derived a politics whose end was social change through the ever-deepening processes of social democracy.

Several apparent paradoxes in Addams's thought come to the surface—double convictions that set her apart from unambivalent celebrants of the progressive faith. One such double commitment lies in her battered but never repudiated belief in progression towards more inclusive and pacific social forms, on one hand, and her equally unwavering recognition and depiction of the pathos of those lives swept up, as so much human debris, by imperious waves of industrialization, on the other. When Addams celebrated progress she did so as an expression of liberal faith and given a particular reading of history. But when she told the story of history's victims she did so from the point of view of those victims, from inside their despair, their often stupefied not-being-at-home in a strange new world that forced many into silence, madness, or self-destruction.

Addams's ambivalence about the world industrialization had wrought is rooted in her social morality and compelled as well by her commitment to a social theory anchored in the detailed consideration of particular cases. No social abstraction has authenticity, she argued, unless it is rooted in concrete human experience. Her immersion in the particular, her ability to articulate wider social meaning through powerful depictions of individual suffering or joy, hope or despair, sets her apart from all who write abstractly about experience. One example must suffice to evoke the human suffering the early wage-labor system trailed in its wake and to illustrate Addams's descriptive powers. Addams pens an unforgettable word portrait of a single suffering woman, one human story beneath—or beyond—the facts of the matter. She writes:

With all the efforts made by modern society to nurture and educate the young, how stupid it is to permit the mothers of young children to spend themselves in the coarser work of the world! It is curiously inconsistent that with the emphasis this generation has placed upon the mother and upon the prolongation of infancy, we constantly allow the waste of this most precious material. I cannot recall without indignation a recent experience. I was detained late one evening in an office building by a prolonged committee meeting of the Board of Education. As I came out at eleven o'clock, I met in the corridor of the fourteenth floor a woman whom I knew, on her knees scrubbing the marble tiling. As she straightened to greet me, she seemed so wet from her feet up to her chin, that I hastily inquired the cause. Her reply was that she left home at five o'clock every night and had no opportunity for six hours to nurse her baby. Her mother's milk mingled with the very water with which she scrubbed the floors until she should return at midnight, heated and exhausted to feed her screaming child with what remained within her breasts.[19]

Addams's project, with this vignette, is a task at once ethical and political. Her theory of morality opposed abstract appeals and the repetition of formulae. It was her conviction that only a tug upon our human sympathies and affections could draw us into an ethical life and keep us there. This life has no final fixed reference point but evolves as an ongoing engagement with competing human goods and purposes. "Pity, memory, and faithfulness are natural ties with paramount claims,"[20] claims run roughshod over in the preceding story. To override these claims, those Addams called "the family claim," or in some manner to reconstruct and transform the terms and boundaries of moral life, powerful countervailing forces, "the social claim," must be at work.[21] The tragedy of the scrubwoman is that she has no choice at balancing out these competing claims: She is simply forced against her will into ill-paid labor by economic necessity, compelled to deny the needs of her child but denied as well the opportunity to make her way in the larger scheme of things.

A human ethic, then, is embedded in life as lived. Because that life is complex, not simple; because human motivations are a dense thicket, difficult to cut one's way through; because one often has to choose between two goods, not between a clear-cut case of good versus evil, our ethics must be similarly complex. What spares Addams from a slide into thorough-going relativism or, alternatively, a leap into high-handed moral preachment, is her dual commitment to empathetic understanding as the surest route to social truth and to a compassion that eschews judging human beings by their "hours of Defeat."[22] These two—understanding that demands of the social observer a sympathetic attempt to convey the nature and meaning of the experiences of others, and a compassionate awareness of our human tendency to "backslide"—lie at the core of Addams's social theory and her apostleship of nonviolent social change.

Human nature being "incalculable," there can be no final, fixed human definition—neither fallen man, nor economic man, nor any other one-dimensional substitute for infinitely varied human life. What staves off anarchy and flux is that rootedness provided by Addams's social ontology, the ground of her discourse. She gives prescriptive force to a human solidarity that links us, across societies and through time; that has its base in "widespread and basic emotional experience" central to a human condition but allowing a wide berth for individual particularity and cultural diversity. As individuals and societies we can come to know ourselves, Addams suggests, *only* to the extent that we realize the experience of others. Cultures as well as individuals would fall into stagnation and dullness without the terms of perspicuous contrast offered by those different from themselves.

This brings us, in a sense, to the starting point—to the establishment of Hull House itself. That experiment was never intended primarily as a charitable institution or as a possible solution to the assorted evils of uncontrolled industrialization. Addams's "subjective necessity" compelled the genesis of Hull House and precluded any simple account of its purposes or her own. Hull House aimed explicitly to meet the needs of Addams and others like her to put their beliefs into practice, to lead lives of action. She and her comrades needed Hull House and that is why it was created—to open up a life of humanitarian action to young women "who had been given over too exclusively to study."[23] To serve but in serving to reveal oneself. Without an understanding of this double edge, Hull House cannot be seen for what it was: an attempt to put into practice "the theory that the dependence of classes on each other is reciprocal."[24] This reciprocity "gives rise to a form of expression that has peculiar value."[25] "It is not," she declared, "philanthropy or benevolence, but a thing fuller and wider than either of these, as revelation that, to have meaning, to be made manifest, must be put into terms of action."[26]

Placed alongside Addams's rich exploration of her own complex motives, the prose of the Hull House charter sounds remarkably prosaic: "To provide a center for a higher civic and social life; to institute and maintain educational and philanthropic enterprises, and to investigate and improve the conditions in the industrial districts of Chicago."[27] She and her companions learned quickly "not to hold preconceived ideas of what the neighborhood ought to have, but to keep ourselves in readiness to modify and adapt our undertakings as we discovered those things which the neighborhood was ready to accept."[28] "Those things" were diverse, and Hull House quickly turned into a social space, a particular sphere, that encompassed drama classes, play groups, music societies, well-baby clinics, nutritional courses, day nurseries, and an immigrant arts and crafts museum to reveal the skill and pride of immigrant parents and grandparents to Americanized children often ashamed of them. To this one must add the "Working People's Social Science Club" and Hull House's own social scientific investigation of conditions in the district ranging from housing to hygiene, medicine to transportation, employment to child care, prostitution to truancy. In *Twenty Years*, Addams details this diversity and an exhilarating sense of shared adventure. She resisted attempts to structure Hull House rigidly or to homogenize its many activities. The firmness of her commitment to social interpretation, to politics as the chief way people in a complex, heterogeneous society reveal themselves to one another, shines through. But what also emerges is the tension between providing a forum where immigrant cultural diversity and dignity could be displayed and preserved and studying this population or that through the methods of the new social science and in the sure conviction of historic progress.

We, from our standpoint, are aware of the decline of the Hull House model as the state has taken over more and more benevolent functions and we are immersed, in a way Addams was not, in a social era that is almost totally dependent on officials and experts. Given this, our assessment of Addams and her "subjective necessity" will depend in part on our approval or dissent from our own era. Whatever that assessment, there is great poignancy in Addams's summary of the idealistic convictions that dignified Hull House: "At that time I had come to believe that if the activities of Hull House were misunderstood, it would be either because there was not enough time to fully explain or because our motives had become mixed, for I was convinced that disinterested action was like truth or beauty in its lucidity and power of appeal."[29]

Criticism of the progressivist spirit and faith that Jane Addams shared, if not uncritically, is by now well known: the stress on social hygiene and "more wholesome" pursuits; the promotion of better methods of "social adjustment," wavering, in Addams's case, between bitter indictments of a brutal industrial order and efforts to make that society work better by smoothing over some of its roughest edges and helping people to adjust to industrial machinery and to a social world indifferent to their welfare.[30] With other progressives, Addams turned to the state to ameliorate social distress, to embody a social-wide commitment to compassion, constituting the state as a Hegelian embodiment of the highest ethical imperatives. But Addams's suspicions of the state grew after World War I, and she eventually concluded that any state founded on nationalism and militarism was incompatible with genuine social progress, perhaps even with democracy. She also held apparently contradictory views on play and pleasure as well, celebrating play as free and spontaneous, on the one hand, and calling for its organization and control on the other.[31] There are tensions embedded in her celebration of the settlement as "a place for enthusiasms," an attempt "to interpret opposing forces to each other," and her stress upon adjusting these same individuals to industrial life. The lacunae in her thinking often leave one stranded; paradoxes and tensions threaten to implode her arguments from within. But in *Twenty Years* she holds it all together, grasping firmly to the thread of empathetic understanding made manifest in her potent characterizations of the plights and purposes of others.

The honesty of this early vision shows us Addams at her best. This is an Addams concerned with the kind of story America will tell the world. Will it be a tale of power and conquest through arms? Or will it be the story of a decent and free industrialized democracy? Will there be room for many diverse stories or will one grand narrative swallow up all "lesser" tales? Perhaps even Addams's politics of class cooperation is less disingenuous than it appears at first glance. We all know the problem: How can there be class reciprocity and mutual recognition in the face of vast disparities of power and privilege? Given that Addams was no advocate of quiescent social suffering, what did she have in mind by repudiating politics as preeminently a power struggle? It is clear that disparities of power *and* the politics that flow from a power-grounded obsession concerned her. Within such a power system, the politics available to those least well placed often results in romantic, suicidal gestures or a smoldering resentment that sees politics as the means to get what "they" have now got. As an advocate of nonviolent social change, Addams urged face-to-face (or arbitrated) debate, even confrontation, so that each side could see and hear the other. What to us sounds hopelessly naive may, in fact, offer a compelling alternative to power politics-as-usual. Whether we are open to Addams's arguments will turn, in part, on how we evaluate later movements for nonviolent social change and what space, if any, we see for moral suasion, for the power of disinterested moral action to touch and to persuade people—even one's adversaries.

There is, then, much to question and to challenge in Addams's social thought but there is also much to learn, particularly about how to do social theory from the "inside out." But *Twenty Years at Hull House* also retains its freshness after more than seventy years because it invites us to reflect on welfare state liberalism, on the difference between Addams's participant-interpreter and the bureaucratic case worker; between a social science that views the world through the lens of functionalist givens and an interpretive approach alive to the sights, sounds, and smells of everyday human existence. That a "Jane Addams" is unlikely to come into being in our society at this time tells us much about ourselves. It signifies how deeply we are sunk in instrumental reason and technocratic bureaucracy. It indicates how entrenched is the conviction that nearly all constraints on the pursuit of personal pleasure are unacceptably limiting. For Jane Addams recalls another world. The fact that contemporary America would not provide the social soil to nurture her points to our loss of a particular civic culture and the ideal of that culture. Paternalistic, hypocritical, and stifling as that world could be, especially for young women, it nevertheless instilled in many of its young the conviction that a *human* life is one lived with purpose, dignity, and honor.

To see in the dissolution of the way of life that sustained such beliefs and practices *only* our collective liberation from irrational constraints is no longer tenable. Jane Addams helps us to take the measure of what we have lost as well as what we have gained. We cannot simply call up or go back to the civic culture of an earlier time, whether through individual will or social polity. But we can at least try to understand what forms of community make lives such as Jane Addams's possible. Rereading Jane Addams renews our acquaintance with a writer of great clarity, one gifted with the capacity to convey deep human emotion without mawkishness or cheap sentimentality. In this way she deepens our empathies and stirs us to an awareness of human limits and vulnerabilities.

Though Jane Addams has had her day, she has yet to receive her due.

2

The Vexation of Weil

Simone Weil is a vexation. An intellectual in the French Cartesian tradition who bore witness to her experience of Christ's presence (in November 1938); a radical who called "the destruction of the past . . . perhaps the greatest of all crimes"[1]; a left-winger who penned trenchant critiques of Marxist thought and state socialist practice; a social theorist who condemned human collectives as a Great Beast yet yearned for a working class movement from below; Weil defies the usual categories. Embracing the role of outsider, she charted an almost perversely lonely course. Certain facts of her life, her mysticism, her apparent devotion to Catholicism (to which she never converted), a harsh asceticism that figured in her early death, prove stumbling blocks to many.

From the standpoint of bourgeois common sense, Weil seems morbid, a perturbed spirit haunting the terrible history of our century. To orthodox Marxists, she is an apostate. In 1936, Trotsky articulated the orthodox position on Weil when he claimed that she had deserted "our cause," lost "faith in the proletariat and in Marxism," and begun "to write absurd idealistic-psychological articles" defending "the idea of individuality." "Perhaps," he mused, "she will turn left again. But what's the use of talking about this any longer?"[2] To Staughton Lynd, writing in 1981, Weil is a thinker whose brave condemnation of Soviet repression and clear critique of Marxist messianism paved the way for "other non-conformist members of the left," including Albert Camus, C. Wright Mills, and E. P. Thompson.[3]

That the broad contours of Weil's discussion of bureaucracy and statism are familiar to us offers tacit recognition of how deeply the analysis she and other nonorthodox members of the French Left proffered in the 1930s permeate our universe of political discourse. In three densely reasoned essays, "Are We Heading for the Proletarian

13

Revolution?" published in 1933, and "An Analysis of Oppression" and "Sketch of Contemporary Social Life," both published in 1924, Weil launched a blistering critique of Soviet state socialism in particular and modern bureaucratic society in general:[4]

"Instead of genuine freedom of the press, there is the impossibility of expressing free opinion, whether in the form of a printed, typewritten or hand-written document, or simply by word of mouth, without running the risk of being deported; instead of free play between parties within the framework of the Soviet system, there is the cry of "one party in power, and all the rest in prison"; instead of a communist party destined to rally together, for purposes of free co-operation, men possessing the highest degree of devotion, conscientiousness, culture, and critical aptitude, there is mere administrative machine, a passive instrument in the hands of the secretariat."[5]

To appreciate this broadside, one must recall the context—the vacillations and bad faith within a broad segment of the French Left on the matter of Stalinism.[6] Weil stripped away the euphemisms by which some were able to delude themselves as to the nature of the Soviet order. She remarks: "To call a state a workers' state when you go on to explain that each worker in it is put economically and politically at the complete disposal of a bureaucratic caste sounds like a bad joke."[7] Refusing the false solace embraced by some—that the Soviet Union was going through a temporary deformation en route to the socialist transformation and the completion of the revolutionary promise—Weil argued that Stalin's regime was no temporary derangement but "a different social mechanism."[8]

Weil parted company with mainstream liberal anticommunism, however, by insisting that the "social mechanism" that drew her ire could also be found, in less virulent form, in Western capitalist societies. We face "a new species of oppression, oppression exercised in the name of management."[9] Antidemocratic at base, the bureaucratic machine "tends, by its very structure to concentrate all power in itself," threatening individual liberty and values, "the very existence of everything that still remains precious for us in the bourgeois regime."[10] One finds this dynamic at work, for example, in the spread of Taylorism, "scientific management" of production developed in the United States but adopted enthusiastically by Lenin for factory production in the Soviet Union. By breaking the productive process into minute parts in order to speed up and pacify workers as well as increase productivity, Taylorism erodes human dignity no matter who owns the productive forces. Both Marxists and capitalists adhere to this cult of productivity. Man is more and more an appendage of the machine; exhausted and demeaned, the worker is more likely to submit than rebel.

The *particular* aberrations of Stalinism highlight in dramatic form general forces at work—the "emancipation" not of human beings but of productive forces; growing control by management and engineering elites; the reduction of workers to more and more passive roles; the uprooting of peoples and the destruction of traditions. "We are living in a world in which nothing is made to man's measure; there exists a monstrous discrepancy between man's body, man's mind and the things which at the present time constitute the elements of human existence; everything is disequilibrium."[11]

Weil's analysis of bureaucratic domination yields an extreme antistatist stance. She rejects all modes of analysis and political doctrines that look toward the state or some "future perfect" vision of one for the completion or initiation of their agenda. In her view, there are no good and bad centralized states: any bureaucratically structured centralized state is a powerful means of coercion that fills up and absorbs more social space as human lives are planned, coordinated, and rationalized.[12]

Weil does, at times, distinguish between societies that preserve room for individual dissent and political liberty and those that quash all such notions and possibilities. But she fears that one day the state, whether socialist or capitalist, will have flattened out all intermediary institutions and severed all noninstrumental social bonds. Facing the collective alone, the citizen will be compelled to reach for the state for there will be nothing else. "The state," she writes, "is a cold concern, which cannot inspire love, but itself kills, suppressing everything that might be loved; so one is forced to love it, because there is nothing else."[13] Inevitably, it will come down to this: in a society dominated by a state, the main task of administration and coordination will eventually devolve into war preparedness. A self-reinforcing dynamic will operate, for "every increase in the state's grip on economic life has the effect of orienting industrial life yet a little farther towards preparation for war; while, conversely, the ever-increasing demands occasioned by preparation for war help day by day to bring the all-round economic and social activities of each country more and more into subjection to the authority of the central power."[14]

Weil no doubt overstates her case and underplays historic and cultural variations in statist orders. But her negative critique retains much of its force in an age—our own—in which rationalization and social engineering have grown apace. The potential for disciplinary control inherent in this top-heavy edifice draws into sharp focus those forces that Weil witnessed coalescing in the 1930s.

Although Weil's antistatist blasts resemble anarchist critiques of centralization of power, her theory differs from anarchism for she has no antagonism to authority (political, spiritual, cultural) as such. Indeed, she explicitly endorses hierarchism, order, and obedience—as well as liberty, equality, and freedom of opinion—as intrinsic "needs" of the human soul and bases of social life—a mix anarchists would find contradictory. Weil's position has nothing sentimental about it; she had no illusions that human beings might create a social order that is perfectly democratic and self-administering.

While liberals might indicate some measure of agreement with Weil's fears of centralized power, they could not share her argument's deep structure. For she proposes a powerful alternative to the classical liberal view that portrays tyrannical traditional authority giving way to free consent. Having gotten rid of the authority of kings and priests, and having broken the shackles of "irrational" modes of authority in all its forms, liberalism, through consent, gives birth to a civil society in which legitimate authority inheres in the majority and is no longer lodged in specific persons. Weil finds the fruits of this project problematic. Rather than flourishing republics, we face an abstract society, justified by tacit consent, governed increasingly by what Hannah Arendt once called "no-body": authority without a human face.

An argument along Weil's lines—that bureaucratic forms and the centralized state corrode other social institutions and relations and eviscerate political entities beneath the level of the state—can take radical or conservative directions. Radical and conservative analysts often concur in a general description of the features of statist society yet differ in their explanations of the emergence of that society and in their political prescriptions for treating sophisticated forces of normalization. There is grist for a number of theoretical mills in Weil's indictment. Antistatism does not fall neatly into a Left-Right divide. It is likely that both conservative restorationists and radical democrats would find support for particular features of their respective positions in Weil's dismantling of bureaucratic centralization.

Holding that the nodal point of state centralization signifies, by its very existence, a collapse in the proper order of things, Weil insists that the whole problem of politics comes to this: to find, "in conditions as they are, a form of society that would conform to the demands of reason."[15] What those demands are, and what reason requires, should come into focus as I proceed. At present, Weil insists, modern man inverts the moral order by proclaiming as universal and eternal that which is conventional and in flux. God is supplanted with abstract schemes for earthly justice, and we worship that which we have become: Plato's Great Beast, the social collective. Our love for this collective is another perversion, a falling away from supernatural love. Increasingly, we conform ourselves to the "enormous animal," the Beast. Weil's formulations here may put one off, but they do suggest that her alternative order will be one that reflects and is open to emanations of supernatural truth and justice. This aesthetic ideal is Platonic in its broad force and in its cosmological inspiration.

Weil contrasts her Platonic vision sharply to the hope proffered by Marxist doctrine. Although Marxism proclaims itself the final solution to our present derangements, in fact it is a powerful symptom of the disorder. Marx—and Marxism—are not exempt from the "most ill-founded superstitions" of the day, including "the cult of production, the cult of big industry, the blind belief in progress."[16] The scientism and historicism through which the Marxist faith enunciates its truths are, in fact, "superstitions." Truth, for Weil, is available to us only if our souls are in their proper relationship to that God whose grace is the singular source of authentic value.

If one takes up the question of human work—its current degradation and its possible transformation—the difference between Marxism and Weil's theory comes into clearer focus. The wage labor the Marxist calls alienated, Weil construes as desacralized, hence stripped of meaning. The worker, as a result, loses the dignity that is a value of the spiritual order. Crushed and manipulated by great social forces, he becomes part of the Beast. Marxism only deepens this disorder when it proclaims its abstract proletariat and promotes the notion that the workers as a collective have a scientifically certified historic task. Nothing changes in work-life, she continues, but workers are caught in fluctuations of arrogance and disillusionment the false promises of revolution promote; moreover, this collective, this massified "we," undermines the possibility that workers might, *from themselves,* as a community and not a collective, become a force for change in the direction of more cooperative social life. This latter hope, in contrast to the apotheosis of the collective entailed in the category "proletariat," *must* begin with an *a priori:* an affirmation of the inherent and inalienable dignity of the human soul as a transcendental value. For Weil, this project is a concrete option available to each individual subject.

It may be well, at this point, to remember that Weil also finds capitalist and liberal society grounded in a reversal of the right order of things. Capitalism, too, constitutes individuals as a consuming and producing collective and unleashes social desires and hopes it cannot fulfill. The inevitable disillusionment that follows may require further tightening of the noose of social control and an extension of the sway of administration. In this way, the false gods before whom we bow down increasingly threaten to crush us. Presaging Foucault's depiction of the carceral society, modern life as a tangled web of surveillance and control mechanisms, covert and overt, Weil tells a tale of the history of force rather than singing a song of progress. Repudiating the Marxist belief that each epoch gives way to its own suppression and that a victory over domination is (at some point) certain, Weil's is a stringently disillusioned view.

Weil portrays early man "handed over weak and naked to all the blind forces that make up the universe." Over time, "the power which keeps him on his knees has been as it were transformed . . . to the human society of which he is a member."[17] Man cannot escape definition by that which enslaves him. Reaching for a theory of power that does not require a *bete noire*, a universal group of oppressors holding sway over a universal group of oppressed, Weil repudiates the category of oppression itself as it is usually understood. She writes: "The notion of oppression is, in short, a stupidity. . . . And the notion of an oppressive class is even more stupid. We can only speak of an oppressive structure of society."[18] Power, in her view, is not a top-down relation but an immanent force. In a world of force, man becomes means and power supplants all other ends. The victim of force is complicit in his or her degradation; hence, there can be no assurance that he will "use force justly if it is put into his hands."[19] Weil's picture of the power system is so total there seems little or no space for renewal or dissent. After all, she cannot call to arms a reserve army of the Weltgeist, having rejected the proletariat and, by implication, all other collective visions of a historic subject. Yet, the very idea of an oppressive system entailing, as it does, notions of imposition, domination, and constriction presupposes the possibility of (greater) freedom. Weil's alternative is unpersuasive.

Within the web of her remorseless logic, the (socialist) revolution emerges not as the historic alternative to capitalism but as its double. Each requires the other. The revolution, brought into existence by capitalism, shares its historic and conceptual ground, thus offering no genuine hope for a rightly ordered social world. Weil writes:

> It is often said that the situation is objectively revolutionary, and that all that is lacking is the "subjective factor"; as if the complete absence of that very force which alone could transform the system were not an objective characteristic of the present situation, whose origins must be sought in the structure of our society! That is why the first duty the present period imposes on us is to have enough intellectual courage to ask ourselves if the term "revolution" is anything else but a name, if it has any precise content, if it is not simply one of the numerous lies produced by the capitalist system in its rise to power.[20]

Revolution is a *façon de parler*, lacking substance. Renewal, if it is to come, must involve a radical relocation of the self in relation to the supernatural and social deformations signified by the wholesale delivery of humanity over to a vast "machine for breaking hearts and crushing spirits."[21] This social machine cannot "stop grinding . . . no matter in whose hand" it may be. State socialism and bureaucratic capitalism are the Tweedledum and Tweedledee of uprootedness, oppression, and disequilibrium.

Where, then, is the space of hope? Weil contends that those who function as parts of the machine, assimilated to history and production, might yet become a source for change, not as a collective but as Kantian subjects open to pure noumenal reality. Weil's "essentially active" subject is not the human being in all his or her aspects but in a "faculty of self-determination" and an abstract intelligence she privileges. This faculty, having transcendent status, cannot be renounced or destroyed save through death; hence, every victory by force or power "contains within itself the germ of a possible defeat."[22] Power may go so far as to exterminate the subject, but this is self-defeating, wiping out its own object. Power cannot, by definition, eliminate the transcendental dimension of the subject. Human rootedness, the alternative to modern dislocation and alienating force, can only grow from an affirmation of our noumenal being that shatters the false realm of appearances. Weil locates the ground out of which social transformation might emerge solely on the spiritual plane. "Rootedness lies in something other than the social,"[23] she decrees. "We must be rooted in the absence of a place."[24] We must, in fact, uproot ourselves from our location in unreal appearances in order to open ourselves to the reality of unchanging truths. True Justice—capitalized—is a supernatural virtue that descends from God to human beings in moments of grace.

The notion of uprooted rootedness may appear impossibly paradoxical, but it flows directly from Weil's prior commitment to a cosmology that is essentially Platonic, an epistemology indebted to Kant's phenomenal-noumenal split and a severely Manichean metaphysic.[25] I cannot trace her argument in detail. But what is most striking about Weil's positive vision is her failure to draw the earthly and the divine, *physis* and *nomos*, freedom and necessity, together in any compelling way. Her dualism severs the human from the divine and the body from the spirit so starkly there is no way, within this frame, for human beings to locate themselves in particular bodies, or as a social body, in history. In line with her Gnostic repudiation of the material world, matter is maligned. The human body is a stumbling block, a barrier to be overcome, an alien entity to be chastened until such time—death—as it is cast off and the pure fragment of the transcendent soul alone remains to enjoy an ongoing existence.

Weil's political theory mirrors her metaphysic, including a theism in which God sits at the *point d'appui* of an aesthetically ordered cosmology. Wholly outside historic time (an implicit rejection of incarnational doctrine), God is Good. He is also absent, far removed from the lowly stuff of created matter. "There is every degree of distance between the creature and God. A distance where the love of God is impossible. Matter, plants, animals. Here evil is so complete that it destroys itself."[26] From her early Cartesian formulas that proved God's existence through geometrical theorems, to her mature view of a God absent from the world, Weil's theism is terribly abstract and pure. Weil's theism takes this Gnostic form—with God placed "at an infinite distance"—because she must "conceive of him as innocent of evil" and the material world itself embodies evil.[27] The world is given over to necessity. Human beings, cast into time and space, are separated from unity with God. Yet this abstract God does intervene in the souls of thinking beings insofar as the eternal part of the soul may mingle with transcendence. The irrational or lesser aspect of the soul is noneternal and doomed to nothingness.

In common with a Platonic metaphysic, then, God as the Good and necessity are infinitely separated. In line with Gnostic doctrines, the created material universe is disparaged. What emerges is an aesthetic order unsullied by corporeality at its apogee, lowly and evil at its base. This metaphysic yields a vision of a subject who breathes air far too rarefied to sustain a life lived among others. For example, Weil insists that all bonds of affection and necessity between human beings must either be transformed "supernaturally" into friendship or remain impure and of a lower order. Weil disassociates her affirmation of the subject sharply from the experience of human life as lived, of what it means to be in a social location, not as a member of a spiritual elite but as an imperfect human being in a concrete place. Hobbled by a rupture between the earthly and the spiritual, Weil cannot constitute any ground for social being. Instead, she posits a radically solitary vision of a self severed from constitutive attachments to concrete others, a place, a history.

In her posthumously published *L'Enracinement* (the English title is *The Need for Roots*), Weil sets forth dogmatically, if unsystematically, her picture of the roots of human condition and the good to which human societies might aspire. She aimed to recover for her people their identities as French men and women insofar as France could be said to embody supernatural values. At the same time, she severs the ordinary citizen from any duty or obligation to the collective. She rejects nearly all forms of association. Yet she calls upon workers to seek change from below, through cooperative participation. Only in community (as opposed to collectivity) is it possible for transcendent meaning and purpose to be instantiated as each worker recognizes, in a radically autonomous sense, each other as a Kantian end-in-himself. This, she insists, is a prior step to forging a community.

But what makes the worker who he is—his ties to family and place, the markers of his particular regional and occupational identity, and so on—are for Weil, a stumbling block to radical autonomy. Staughton Lynd is correct to appreciate Weil's insistence that democracy requires a powerful affirmation of the person and of individual dignity. But Weil's understanding of the human subject disassociates this affirmation so sharply from lived experience that her wider political vision is derailed before it even gets on the track.

The problem here is not, as some would have it, Weil's embrace of mysticism or her theism per se, but the substance of her theology. An appreciation of Weil's theism and the particulars of her mature metaphysic help us to make sense of her social and political judgments and, at the same time, demonstrate the inadequacies of her project for contemporary critical discourse and democratic politics. What is striking is how heavily Weil is indebted to classical philosophic anthropology, a hierarchy on top of which is perched the rational soul, and to later Gnostic disparagements of the body, and how little she draws upon early Christian theology and doctrine. She bypasses the anthropological presumptions that flow from the doctrines of creation, incarnation, and the resurrection of the body—and which created a conceptual Copernican revolution in their time—in favor of both older formulations and newer Manichean dualisms. Thus, she cannot draw together the spheres of freedom and necessity or link the human community to the divine.[28]

The point here is to suggest that there are modes of thought that offer possibilities for grounding human social rootedness Weil rejects, although she is not often clear about the depth of her repudiation of alternative anthropologies and the very different social and political evaluations they yield. My criticism is another of the many footnotes to the long history of discourse pitting Plato against Aristotle, Augustine against Aquinas, Kant against Hegel and Marx. It also helps us to make sense of Weil's flirtation with Catholicism—a relationship that was never consummated. Weil's antimaterialism and dualism created an unbridgeable gulf between her metaphysics and that of Catholicism; as well, her radically solitary personalism is at odds with Catholic communalism. Her attraction to Catholicism seems to have been primarily aesthetic. This is evident in her advice to teachers on how to discuss Christianity with children: "It is so beautiful that it must surely contain much that is true."[29]

Weil's too-lofty spiritual subject must be brought down to earth and embodied. For the human subject is always a corporeal being in a particular place and time and none other. The basis of an alternative to Weil's radical "I-Thou" metaphysic lies in a social ontology that forges links (or allows us to) between and among human beings. Recognition of our essential sociality (i.e., that for a being to be, indeed to become human, he or she cannot be posited outside the frame of a human network) becomes, in turn, a basis for the solidarity and communality Weil desires but can neither attain nor sustain. The ordinary social world, in this non-Weilian view, is not a Great Beast but the ground of our being, for better or worse.

Weil's project of human dignity is better served by a theory that enables us to see the divine in the human, the spiritual in the material, the transcendent in the immanent. This runs counter to Weil's view that divine reality or spiritual force can "never be identified with the human."[30] Weil's asceticism, which forced her into a repudiation of the body not required by Christian social thought, is very much in line with neo-Platonist and Gnostic formulations.

By severing the subject from his or her embodiment, and the individual from a social body, Weil paradoxically constitutes us as beings more, not less, subject to demands from an importunate bureaucratic order. Robust social loyalties and affections, an untidy but flourishing body political and social, are loci for resistance over time. Individual acts of heroism and supererogation leave behind repositories of courage and idealism, but, if individuals are to claim their dignity and to situate it in social forms, they must do so as a community. In the beginning is the body, not the Word. We are never not our bodies. What body is Weil denying? The argument, then, both to reclaim Weil and to criticize her, is that when the body is denied, when the appetitive part of the soul is repudiated altogether, one suppresses part of one's self. Perhaps more important, Weil denies the procreative female body. Yet, if the terms of our politics and discourse are to shift from the necromancy Weil so unerringly signals to a vision that promises hope and action, one alternative metaphor is that of natality.

Hannah Arendt argues that Greek antiquity, worshipped by Weil and celebrated by Arendt herself, nevertheless ignored "two essential characteristics of human existence"—faith and hope. Yet, Arendt continues:

The miracle that saves the world, the realm of human affairs, from its normal "natural" ruin is ultimately the fact of natality, in which the faculty of action is ontologically rooted. It is, in other words, the birth of new men and the new beginning, the action they are capable of by virtue of being born. Only the full experience of this capacity can bestow upon human affairs faith and hope. . . . It is this faith in and hope for the world that found perhaps its most glorious and most succinct expression in the few words with which the Gospels announced their "glad tidings": "A child has been born unto us."[31]

Weil recognized the need for roots yet left her subject peculiarly unrooted. Drawing upon her recognition of the destructive pain of uprootedness, one can construct an alternative that builds upon her insights. Weil reminds us that human beings are always vulnerable and that they can be destroyed. Against the statist idols of her time, she hurled the challenge of a meticulous conscience. That Weil is so difficult a figure—a vexation—may be because she just does not fit. That most of us most of the time do, quite comfortably, represents (she would say) both individual tragedy and historic triumph. But her way out leaves far too many behind.

3

Eleanor Roosevelt as Activist and Thinker: "The Lady" and the Life of Duty

Written originally to be delivered at Vassar College for its centenary celebration of Roosevelt's birth.

Eleanor Roosevelt's career was made possible, in part, by her self and social definition as a *lady*—a role and identity we see as inherently limiting if not altogether stifling. Yet the *lady* could, if she chose, enter into social life and defined forms of action without sacrificing her female identity. This made of the ladies of Eleanor Roosevelt's era beings very different from the later housewives of the feminine mystique. We do not have ladies anymore in this sense and it seems appropriate to remember, even as we find much to criticize, that particular cultural and historic form and its political implications.

As I began my reflection on Roosevelt I mused on why she has not figured centrally in contemporary feminist theorizing or served as inspiration for a life of social activism for my generation or for those younger than me. A number of explanations as to why this is the case suggest themselves. The intersection of Roosevelt's life with profound alterations in the fabric of American social and political culture make it more difficult for us to see her sympathetically. She was wholly opposed to the therapeutic mode that now dominates American culture and she didn't think much of sexual liberation. She is out of touch with sensibilities deeply immersed in that therapeutic culture and with a reigning ideology that dictates that sexual constraint is "repression" by definition and a very bad thing indeed.

Perhaps she is undervalued because she was strongly devoted to the notion that women and men are different and because she can be seen as piggybacking off her husband's career. Surely the more general loss of women's history is implicated in why Roosevelt's story is one schoolchildren do not learn. These are matters for speculation. But it seems likely that the revival of interest in Roosevelt comes when it does in part because of the force of the feminist "third wave," an argument for equality that respects difference rather than requiring the homogenization of male and female roles and identities across the board; in part because focus on the so-called gender gap raises explicitly political distinctions between men and women and their attitudes toward, among others, matters of war and peace, a subject on which Roosevelt had a lot to say; in part because many of us now recognize that the theoretical formulations and categories with which we have been working, or with which we have been saddled, are not up to the task of helping us to develop nuanced, rich visions of social life.

One brief example: social and political theorists have inherited binary models of oppression and power. That is, we presume a category of oppressed and a category of oppressors, or a category of powerful and a category of the powerless. If we are locked into this binary deadlock, we will find it impossible to see and thus to understand the many faces and forms of power and authority, including those traditionally available to women. The new women's social history and feminist inspired cultural anthropology teach us that women have often been both constrained *and* empowered by potent clusters of typical figurations concerning maternal or feminine ideals. More and more we realize that the thesis of universal male dominance blinds us to the *actual* exercise by women of social authority. Peggy Reeves Sanday, a cultural anthropologist, argues that we—we members of modern, bureaucratic statist societies—tend to equate power with official public leadership. Karen Sacks, another anthropologist, adds that to view male and female authority in societies like the Iroquois, for example, where women wielded great power, as *unequal* rather than *different* reflects a "state bias in Western anthropological interpretation of prestate politics."[1]

What has this to do with Eleanor Roosevelt? Precisely this: by seeing Roosevelt as one who exercised power or influence only insofar as she was the wife of her husband, we not only reinforce rigid views of power and authority, we downgrade her considerable contribution. We perpetuate a view of the world that leaves women in epochs prior to or different from our own in the shadows. A supple approach open to the power of moral suasion and to the potency of leading through example helps us to take the measure of Eleanor Roosevelt as lady and activist. I begin with her struggle to achieve a sense of self—a struggle with and against the identity of lady and the way in which she made use of the concept of duty and the need to serve to steer a course that took her further and further away from a limited and constrained vision of her proper place. Second, I argue that one cannot, as Wittgenstein might put it, "find one's feet" with Eleanor Roosevelt unless one understands the depth of her Christian conviction, her determination to serve and to bear witness, and her clearly articulated position that "Democracy . . . is based on the possibility of a Christ-like life."[2] Finally, I tie the life and career of Roosevelt to that of another great and, at least at this point in time, underrated activist and thinker, Jane Addams.

ELEANOR ROOSEVELT AS LADY: *SIC ET NON*

It is a remarkable journey—from the miserably unhappy young woman ill at ease in society and the world of young ladies "coming out" to the public figure known as "First Lady of the World." Through it all Eleanor Roosevelt remained a lady, repudiating much of the mandate that status trailed in its wake even as she stretched other features beyond recognition.

The lady has a long and ambiguous history. In 1938, Emily James Putnam assayed, *The Lady: Studies of Certain Significant Phases of Her History*, concluding that the "lady is proverbial for her skill in eluding definition" but, at least for the purpose of Putnam's study, the lady "may be described merely as the female of the favoured social class."[3] Putnam also determined that the lady must be a virgin or a lawful wife and that religion has given the lady her "strongest hold." Abigail Addams's early plea to her husband to "remember the ladies," and to grant them the franchise, was argued on classic civic republican line—that women were the future educators of male citizens and republican mothers alike.[4]

Anne Firor Scott, in her study of *The Southern Lady*, found progressive women in the South cherishing a "ladylike aspect" and being "modest about their achievements." The "power of the image," she continues, "also helped to explain the kinds of women who appeared in southern reform movements: those of impeccable antecedents and secure family positions."[5] Wives of mill workers and Negro servants could not be ladies by definition. But ladies by the score entered politics via the women's club movement and found themselves involved with topics—especially those that touched on race—that "ladies were not supposed to even know about."[6] These activist women used their status as ladies as a way into public service and politics. This is true in Eleanor Roosevelt's case as well given her experience in the women's club movement—and Scott argues further that the ladies reinforced their status continuously, reminding "each other of the importance of being ladylike," reassuring people that they were "gentle, beautiful, feminine" even as they stalked the halls of legislatures.[7] As well, southern women could work and remain ladies after the war if the war had left them widowed or responsible for permanently disabled husbands.

To understand how the identity of lady played itself out in Roosevelt's life one must appreciate what the lady had become in northern high society. The lady was simultaneously a being called to service of a circumscribed sort and a being constituted as the symbolic representation of a particular aestheticism. A very sharp distinction between politics—the world of public man—and service—the world of private woman—had evolved. Though these lines were always blurred, arguments in behalf of keeping them separate revolved around visions of the woman as a "beautiful soul," one above the sullied affairs of the world yet one who concerns herself with the victims of the world's ways in a benign, *noblesse oblige* manner.

The tradition of *noblesse oblige* took the existence of distinct social classes for granted and presumed what Tamara Hareven calls the "lasting superiority of the upper class."[8] "For ladies to feel and express sympathy was permissible," writes Duncan Crow, "for them to *take* action beyond parlour charity was not . . . those who did were denounced as having cast off the refinement and delicacy of their sex."[9] Franklin Roosevelt's mother, Sara Delano Roosevelt, for example, once characterized her charity work as delivering baskets of food to the poor, flowers to hospitals, and taking part in sewing circles. But her own circle grew until one day its members no longer did the sewing themselves but sent it out to be done by needy women! Sara Roosevelt also served on boards of charities for mental patients and the handicapped, activities Eleanor Roosevelt later came to see as patronizing, turning on a stance of pity for, rather than identification with, the suffering of others.

Despite these constraints, many women in the decades after the Civil War broke through the bonds of merely charitable ladyhood to make other sorts of arguments and to engage in actions that strained the *noblesse oblige* tradition. In addition to the Suffrage movement, by the end of the nineteenth century and into the early decades of the twentieth, women progressives worked to *eliminate* the distinction between the domestic arena and the world of politics. The women's reform movement, empowered with a notion that women had a distinct and potent contribution to make given their life experiences and social consciousness, played a key role in setting the terms for urban reform movements and policies. A major source of inspiration came from religious and moral beliefs translated as central political imperatives. There was much that was radical and much that was ameliorative in this politicization of several generations of activist women. But overall it meant that the young woman of society could go a number of different directions depending upon her sense of social conscience; on how powerfully she had internalized the concept of duty and how far she saw her duties extending; and on how confined she remained by the lady bountiful tradition and the dictates of society itself.

Roosevelt came of age in a period of stuffy conformism *and* change. Archibald MacLeish overstates the case when he proclaims that "nothing in history has been more banal that the provinciality of the lives of the rich and well born in the New York of Eleanor Roosevelt's girlhood. Eleanor Roosevelt had no desire as a young girl but to belong to that world. . . . She was, in short, not only a child of her class and place and time, but a child of her class and place and time who asked for nothing better than to win its approval—and who failed."[10] That is only part of the story. In the often traumatic complexities of her childhood lay varying possibilities. Her beloved father, though a scandal to both the Roosevelt and Hall families, was a nonconformist and adventurer of sorts. Joseph Lash writes that her father "gave her the ideals that she tried to live up to all her life by presenting her with the picture of what he wanted her to be—noble, brave, studious, religious, loving, and good."[11] Roosevelt's identification with him, one that lasted throughout her life, worked to block immersion in the dour severities she associated with her Grandmother Hall and with her own mother's life. Her admiration for "Uncle Ted" and the reformist, public-duty ethic of the Roosevelt mode of social activism also created ballast against the mode of leisure society as did Roosevelt's education in Mlle. Souvestre's school for young ladies in England.

But the best teller of this tale is Roosevelt herself. In *This Is My Story*, Roosevelt describes her Grandmother Hall as a "beauty and a belle" who was treated like a cherished but somewhat spoiled child. She was expected to bring children into the world and seven were born, but she was not expected to bring them up. "My grandfather told her nothing about business, not even how to draw a check, and died without a will, leaving her with six children under seventeen years of age, a responsibility for which she was totally unprepared." As Roosevelt continues the narration, she paints a picture of the old lady as one both publicly and privately inept—as one kept in the dark and treated like a household plant. She uses words like "rigidity in conforming to a conventional pattern which had been put before them as the only proper existence for a lady." She writes: "In that society you were kind to the poor, you did not neglect your philanthropic duties in whatever community you lived, you assisted the hospitals and did something for the needy. You accepted invitations to dine and to dance with the right people only, you lived where you would be in their midst. . . . In short, you conformed with the conventional pattern."[12]

"Ladies wore long dresses . . . that trailed in the dust unless they were held up" (thus making one's arms and hands useless for any other purpose, Roosevelt might have added though she probably did not need to make the point so explicitly) and "I seem to remember [her] generally [in] tight-fitting bodices of the day."[13] As a young child, and this is a tale oft told so I will only remind us of it, Roosevelt was painfully aware of her lack of beauty and thus of the fact that she, unlike so many other neophyte ladies, would neither attract attention nor get admiration and that was a good bit of what being a lady was all about. Although Roosevelt rejected this piece of society rather early on, long before she successfully broke the mold of the lady bountiful tradition, she remained "haunted by my upbringing and believed that what was known as New York Society was really important."[14] Sometimes part of the haunting, sometimes a cluster of inchoate glimmerings of something else, Roosevelt's "painfully high ideals" and "tremendous sense of duty" pushed her into service activities and, after her marriage, into "a fairly conventional, quiet, young society matron" way of life.

She was torn—wanting to be independent, "beginning to realize that something within me craved to be an individual"—yet still living "under the compulsion of my early training" with "duty . . . the motivating force in my life."[15] Duty as her daimon, the driving force in her life, never disappeared. But the scope and the sphere of her duty grew to encompass the entire globe. This fascinating extension of a few heartfelt moral principles is the key theme in her tale of ambivalent acceptance and simultaneous repudiation of the lady identity and image. The point of rupture comes when the duty Roosevelt does is not that laid down for her by others but that dictated to her by her own demanding conscience. The specifically Christian features of Roosevelt's duty will be explored later. For the moment I shall home in on the particulars of her pilgrimage *away* from a confining ladyhood to an expansive understanding of that status.

Roosevelt's journey from lady to lady—radically transforming the possibilities internal to that linguistic and cultural form—is a fascinating one. As Shane Phelan notes, Roosevelt evolved over time but she downplayed many of leaps she had made. Perhaps this was done in the interest of good taste—ladies were rather modest about their achievements.[16] According to Lash, Roosevelt loved and frequently recalled a passage from Stephen Vincent Benet's "John Brown's Body", which described the lady of the plantation: "She was often mistaken, not often blind/And she knew the whole duty of womankind; To take the burden and have the power/And seem like the well-protected flower."[17] Certainly this underplaying of identity shifts in her writing and bears witness to the stubborn fact that she found it easier to deal with public activities if they were placed in a framework in behalf of, or alongside of, her husband.[18] Thus she frequently couched her own involvement in politics—as compared to service—as part and parcel of a wife's duty to be interested in whatever interested her husband. For example: in 1924 she wrote FDR that she was "only being active till you can be again," adding that once he was up and about she would "fall back into habits of sloth quite easily!"—an unbelievable statement to anyone familiar with even the merest sketch of her life.

Her story is one of stretching and reshaping the boundaries of traditional concepts and obligations. In so doing, she necessarily failed to meet the expectations of those who wanted ladies of the old-fashioned "pastel and mauve tradition." For example, Hareven cites an outraged letter from a proper lady to Roosevelt that reads, in part: "Instead of tearing around the country, I think you should stay at home and personally see that the White House is clean. I soiled my white gloves yesterday morning on the stair-railing. It is disgraceful."[19]

The markers of Roosevelt's personal journey, her consciousness raising in feminist language from the 1970s, are many. In the winter of her nineteenth year she became involved with the Consumers

League and visited garment factories, sweat shops, and department stores firsthand. Like Jane Addams, she learned from experience— from the evidence of her own eyes, ears, and reactions. It had not occurred to her that girls might get tired standing behind counters all day, with no seats provided should they wish to take a short break. She had no idea that the air was foul and conditions unsanitary in dress factories. Writes Lash: "Now she saw misery and exploitation on a scale she had not dreamed possible, and pleas for legislative reform were more compelling to her because she saw the conditions to which they were addressed."[20] Roosevelt granted these and other experiences authoritative weight; thus, the good deeds of ladies bountiful and systemic injustices grew more disproportionate the more she learned. Roosevelt never indicted good deed doing— her whole life makes sense in terms of good works—but she did distance herself from the patronage-client nexus of the high society tradition.

A hiatus occurred in the early, childbearing years of her marriage. She was not a reluctant bride: her curiosity about life and desire to be part of its stream propelled her into wifehood. But she felt contained by the society matron tradition, held in in terms of her own deepest emotions, particularly towards her children. Her crusading spirit was dampened "because I had been told I had no right to go into the slums or the hospitals, for fear of bringing diseases home to my children."[21] In later years this, and more, rankled because convention also dictated that the mother turn child rearing over to nurses, a habit that Roosevelt later criticized. One other feature of her pre–World War I existence was the ritual of social visiting by wives of public officials. As the conscientious wife of the undersecretary of the navy, Roosevelt went about in her white gloves, sallying forth on appointed rounds: "Mondays the wives of justices of the Supreme Court, Tuesdays Congress, Thursdays Cabinet, Fridays Diplomats. Wednesday would be the day she received."[22]

Interestingly, as First Lady she singles out this sort of social obligation for scarcely muted scorn. In *This I Remember,* the second volume of her autobiography, Roosevelt describes a group of cabinet wives politely going along with her and Elinor Morgenthau to observe conditions in the Washington alleys and slums but declining to get out of the cars to take in things firsthand. "They were busy with the social life of Washington and they did not feel they could undertake any work of this kind, and besides their husbands would not approve. I never made any further effort to work with the cabinet wives but our joint social duties. They were most cooperative in that field, which they felt was safe and correct."[23]

Roosevelt ceased being safe and correct when two earth-shattering events—one private, one public—intervened. Her husband's affair with Luci Mercer shook her womanly confidence and seems to have jolted her into a far tougher, perhaps even hard, stance regarding where and how she would deploy her concern. More important to her public career was World War I. When the war came many women wanted to be more directly involved than tradition allowed. There is an interesting interlude when her brother enters the air force over her grandmother's objection—she wonders why he can't buy a substitute as gentlemen did in the Civil War. Eleanor responded angrily that gentlemen owed the same duty to their country as other citizens. To which she might have added: ladies do too. A later advocate of full citizen mobilization in service to the country, in this earlier period the war provided Roosevelt with a field for action unlike any she had previously known. No one could gainsay war work. She began to learn to do things by herself and developed a hardy self-reliance. Even learning to sew was a triumph—it seems not much to us but for Roosevelt this bit of self-help signified growing independence.

Contenting herself with war-work in this country, though she yearned to go to England, Roosevelt writes of how her priorities changed and how she gained "a certain assurance as to my ability to run things."[24] The war made her a more competent person and, she insists, a "more tolerant" one. Her imprisonment in society slowly dissolved. "The war," she writes,"was my emancipation and education."[25] The glimmerings of that loyalty to the truth and to oneself came slowly but surely into focus—as part and parcel of a generous patriotic duty to one's nation. Women participated in every aspect of the war effort save actual combat. Roosevelt herself ran canteens, made clothing, tended the wounded, and set up services for soldiers, an apparently exhaustive list of particulars.

After the war she fought the male political machine—in the period of her husband's convalescence—and felt blocked by male hostility when she engaged in tireless organizing of women in New York State. She recognized the paternalism in the standard male attitude that evoked love and honor for the ladies but then urged them back to their charities and to their houses, leaving business and politics to the men. She became close friends with, and political allies of, a remarkable group of activist women who furthered her self-education and her shift away from a stifling ladyhood. Her chief fear when Franklin was elected governor of New York and, later, president was that she would have to conform to the expectations of others as to what a First Lady must be. The fears never left her and she never conformed.

In her writings, Roosevelt redefines many of the terms by which she herself felt demeaned and constrained. The claustrophobic society of young ladies of her adolescence is recharacterized in her 1933 volume, *It's Up to the Women*—addressed to all women but especially to housewives—to mean "the big society of all men and women and each of us in our own little sphere."[26] The rigid sex markers of her own upbringing, which left nearly all household tasks to male and female servants, are forsaken and in their place Roosevelt insists that boys along with girls learn to put "bedclothes to air even if he does not have to make a bed." Not only little girls but young boys should learn how to be parents: "There should be no real reason why a boy should not be taught the underlying principles of the proper way of feeding a baby," and so on.[27]

Linking together private child tending with public virtue, Roosevelt evokes that civic republican tradition marked by Abigail Adams and detailed by Alexis de Tocqueville when she proclaims that giving the child proper sleep, food, and exercise "can be tied up with the child's understanding of patriotism and love of country," a nonchauvinist love of country that will not launch destructive wars if there is any way they can be prevented. Mothers, in this scheme of things, overthrow the old regime of the lady and the tyranny (for Roosevelt experienced it as such) of nurses and watchful mothers-in-law and take child care into their own hands, making it something of a civic mission and an exercise in greater sexual equality. But she still finds herself, in 1933, pleading with "Mr. Man" to be understanding if his wife decides to work, telling this generic Everyman, though the vision is surely class-bound, that in the long run his wife will be a "better helpmate" and their lives together happier if he does not block her route to self-development.

Roosevelt's ambivalence about the lady never left her. Nor is there any reason why she should have restored it in some clear-cut ideological way. She cherished her hard-won individuality and warned of the loss of individuality, of the rise of pressures to conform, in the last years of her life. She knew firsthand the costs of sullen conformity. She cherished the honorific title, "First Lady of the World," even as she surely approved a statement by a journalist during her tenure as First Lady that she was "the strongest argument that could be presented against those who hold that by entering politics a woman is bound to lose her womanliness and her charm."[28] Although she disliked excessively masculine women—and politics— she nonetheless called upon women to "deliver the goods" if they would hold power and disabuse "their male competitors of the old idea that women are only 'ladies in business'." For Roosevelt, being a lady and being tough was no contradiction in terms—none at all—and her explicit fusing of the two turned older understandings inside out.

ELEANOR ROOSEVELT AND "A CHRISTLIKE WAY OF LIFE"

Eleanor Roosevelt's deeply devout and intensely felt religious con- viction, her determination to bear witness and to serve as Christ did, and her unabashed openness about all of this, is more of a scandal to us than to her contemporaries. They were more perturbed by a lady breaking traditions,but they understood what a life of service was all about. We, however, are far less shocked by tradition breaking and far more shocked by open evocation of religious ideals. For example, in a collection of essays on Roosevelt's life and career (*Without Precedent*, published in 1984), every aspect of that life and career is covered save her faith. Fortunately, Lash's definitive study treats this theme with the depth and seriousness it deserves if we are to achieve any understanding of the sources of meaning and the roots of action in Roosevelt's life.

For Roosevelt, moral values—specifically Christian values—lay at the basis of her own life's work and formed the foundation for American democracy. In a little cited work, *The Moral Basis of Democracy*, published in 1940, Roosevelt articulated a simple but moving vision of what democracy consists, whence it came, and what must be done to preserve it. American democracy, she declared, had its "roots in religious belief" and "the life of Christ was based on principles which are necessary to the development of a Democratic state."[29] Christ's divinity was less important to her than "His life" as a "shining example of what success means." Success lies in service, in loving thy neighbor as thyself, in living up to one's beliefs and carrying them out in everyday life. There is hope for our future only insofar as we "base it on the Christian way of life as lived by church."[30]

All of this makes us uncomfortable. We have grown far more cynical and far less certain of our ideals—or *any* ideals. How did

Christian ideals operate in Eleanor Roosevelt's life? Here things might have gone several directions. Lash notes that in the Roosevelt household "religion was seen as the affirmation of love, charity, and compassion; in the Hall household . . . it was felt that only a ramrodlike self-denial was acceptable to God. Religion was also used to justify domestic tyranny."[31] As she was to do with the concept and identity of lady, Roosevelt tilted towards the love and compassion pole of her inherited religious possibilities, chastening the dour self-denying features of her Hall background even though she remained a Prohibition advocate and teetotaler throughout her life.

She was not alone in using religion as a springboard into a life of active service. Professor Vida Scudder of Wellesley urged young women into a "new Fransiscanism," appealing to them to go among the poor and to staff settlement houses.[32] Overflowing with the need to serve, Roosevelt came to associate Christ-likeness both with a near pacifism, with God's call coming in particular to women of the world to proclaim, "No, you shall no longer kill your fellow men,"and with a vision of social justice that operated from compassion, calling her to service and mercy, not pity and contempt. Lash describes the many injunctions and reminders Roosevelt carried with her in her purse. For example: to Henry Van Dyke's prayer "The Footpath to Peace" she added the words "with oneself." Lash writes: "Among the prayer's injunctions were to think seldom of your enemies, often of your friends, and everyday of Christ; she had circled the phrase about Christ. . . . As completely as she could,she wanted to live according to Christ's teachings."[33]

Lash writes of Roosevelt's "logic of love" and counterposes that to a "logic of power and governance." It is hard for us to take the measure of such a love. We think it must turn sickly and finally sour. Yet love combined with tough-minded, canny activism to achieve goals dictated to Roosevelt by empathetic identifications with the poor, the outcast, the segregated, the abused. She seems to have been genuinely capable of real solidarity with those not of her class or race, a *compassion* unlike both paternalism (or maternalism) and a vanguardist stance of leading others where we have determined they would want to go if they only knew enough. Perhaps, in fact, she was working on a new understanding of power—moving away from *realpolitik* to some more fully realized vision. Empowered herself by a "seemingly inexhaustible spring of human sympathy," she sought to enliven others, to give them hope. Though not a self-conscious political theorist, Roosevelt would agree with Hannah Arendt that hope is the wellspring of action. "I think there is a tremendous energy in the psychology of hopefulness," she wrote in a letter.[34]

Holding that it never hurts to be kind, she preferred to be sinned against rather than sinning and tended to take everyone at his or her word. Operating from an overflowing of what the early Christians called *agape*, she could give to others without any fear of depleting herself. She suffered when she saw abuses being committed in the name of her own beliefs—especially when Christ's name got used in vain. For example: she could not comprehend how a German friend could claim to be a Christian and support Hitler. For Roosevelt this was an irrationality, a blindness, a horrible inconsistency, for only Christ's teachings, completely at odds with Hitler's, can save us, she wrote.[35] Similarly, she found racial abuse and Christianity at odds, praising a southern woman, "a Christian who believes in all Christ's teachings, including the concept that all men are brothers" who, on her own and in a situation where "white southern women are so often used as a pretext for lynching," went forth to investigate and to expose lynchings.[36]

True Christian belief should animate a civic capacity and gear it in particular directions. Roosevelt was primarily an activist, not a theorist, so she spelled out her ideas in a down to earth and sketchy way, most often as homilies, anecdotes, and stories pointing to a moral truth. She made no sharp distinction between "private beliefs" and "public actions"—indeed such a disjuncture would have made no sense to her at all. (She would find much of the current church-state debate peculiar, for some advocates of the "wall of separation" go much beyond the antiestablishment clause to insist that our "private" beliefs should carry no explicit weight at all with regard to our public policy determinations.) But if her beliefs were more fully spelled out I think they would add up to something akin to Archbishop Oscar Romero's address on "The Political Dimension of Christian Love," delivered at the University of Louvain shortly before his assassination by right-wing death squads in El Salvador.

Romero begins by stating that the Christian faith has always had socio-political repercussions—has always had influence, for good or ill. But the "essence of the church," to the extent it is faithful to that essence, is to "act in solidarity with the hopes and the joys, with the anxieties and with the sorrows, of men and women."[37] The "world which the church ought to serve," he continues, "is the poor," and it is the poor who tell us what the "polis is, what the city is, and what it means for the church really to live in that world."[38] The church must opt for the "real, and not the fictitious poor" that sometimes populate the pages of abstract analyses and dry theories. "The political dimension of faith is nothing other than the church's response to the demands made upon it by the real socio-political world in which it exists."[39] This world should teach us what the nature of "Christian love is, a love which certainly seeks peace but which unmasks false pacifism—the pacifism of resignation and inactivity."[40]

Roosevelt never viewed persons as isolated bundles of absolute (or nearly so) rights but as beings who exist within a communal fabric and whose rights can only be the counterpart of duties. She had little patience with the self-absorbed and no patience at all with the unconcerned. In the present debates about religion and politics, she would be scandalized that we are scandalized by the open embrace of religious ideals as the basis for political life and thought. That signifies just how much times have changed. It is much easier to see Roosevelt as a lady in at least partial revolt than a Christian fully devout. But if we ignore this dimension of her life, we promote a shadowy Roosevelt, one disarticulated from the self-proclaimed wellspring of her identity, most important her need to serve and to bear witness.

ELEANOR ROOSEVELT AND JANE ADDAMS: TAKING THE MEASURE OF TWO GREAT AMERICAN LIVES

Roosevelt considered Addams her great teacher. "Through their example of personal devotion and service, the settlement workers convinced her [Roosevelt] that the individual's responsibility to his community was as important as legislation."[41] Addams and Roosevelt shared the fact that they were private citizens with powerful public influence. And they have suffered a similar fate. They were not feminists in a way that reassures, and they were both religious in ways that trouble. Moreover, Roosevelt as lady and Addams's embrace and use of a maternal identity, though she was herself not a mother, strike us as reinforcing restrictive views of womanhood. So Roosevelt "has vanished into the background, to be remembered only as a benevolent lady or as a busy body."[42] Addams in turn, has come in for some rough treatment by historians. For example, Jill Conway links Addams to a defunct "stereotype of the female."[43]

Two brief points: First, the real quarrel some have with Roosevelt and Addams is that they were great amateurs, generalist citizens. Roosevelt and Addams both had great trust in people to govern themselves, and it is, alas, true that many members of our educated and professional elites have no such faith at all. Second, Roosevelt and Addams embody a feminist alternative at odds in many respects with the liberal feminism that dominates our discourse. For both held that women were different from men—but equal—and saw in this no paradox.

Addams and Roosevelt were progressive reformers first, and feminists second. They integrated their feminism with a wider vision of social change. Both went through highly intense personal struggles for independence and were sensitive to patronizing attitudes and policies—whether within families or from governments. Both "used their belief in women's traditional contribution to society as a standpoint for critiquing the selfishness and privatization of their society, and envisioned a future in which commitment to others . . . came to characterize society as a whole."[44] Conway's dismissal of this program as a delusion is startling and harsh. She makes no attempt to get inside the world views that animated Addams (her specific target) and propelled her into a life of activism and keen social thought.

What Roosevelt and Addams share is a commitment to self-development that repudiates the old paternalism without advocating a new atomism, a female version of that mythic being, the self-made man. Both were attuned to the delicate filiations of social life and the way we are implicated one with the other. Both were storytellers, using biography to teach and to edify, giving the world its shape through narratives that involved the use of instructive parables in the conviction that moral life consists in the "imitatio Christi," not in abstract obedience to formal models of conduct. Both held inclusive visions of the human community and evoked solidarity. Both rejected lives of pale aestheticism in favor of lives of action.

There are gaps, lacunaes, and problematic features in the public careers of both women and the great movements—Progressivism and the New Deal—with which each is linked. But that is not my concern here. My concern is why we find it so difficult to see them for what they were. Here I shall throw down my first gauntlet: We live in world of experts and managers. We believe that those who *know* ought to instruct and *manage* those who do not. Even dissidents who want to change our social order frequently set themselves up as experts with a plan or scheme designed to propel others to ends they seek. We talk about democracy but do we really believe in it? The thrust of Conway's attack on Addams is that her "pathetic stereotype" grabbed the public imagination more completely than the newer models of female professionalism that were then emerging. Conway valorizes the "professional expert or scientist" and thinks it a pity that the image of the female "sage or prophetess" (a demeaning way to characterize what Addams and others were about), took center stage: "The woman as expert did not captivate the popular imagination."[45]

But Jane Addams confronted the question of the expert head on in a number of astute essays and vignettes pitting middle-class, educated reformers against poor, often desperate, non–English speaking immigrants. She showed the ways in which these worlds were incommensurable—or nearly so—and why the social worker should be humble, nonintrusive, and aware of the fact that she, too, is implicated in a human social relation that instructs and challenges her received ideas. Addams's capacity for empathetic indentification, and her ability to think like a sophisticated cultural anthropologist, kept her from sliding into either an arrogant maternalism or into evocation of a reign of experts to do for others rather than to help them do for themselves projects of their own choosing. She criticized the progressive "expert [who] believes that the people must be made over by 'good citizens'."[46] Addams learned from stories of immigrant women, mothers, and grandmothers, from what she called "the long road of women's memory." This is no occultish prophetess mode but an act of political and narrative imagination.

Similarly, Roosevelt sought a new meaning for politics through the leavening women might provide if they brought their life situations and experiences to bear. With Addams, she worried about loss of what she called "that personal touch" as machines took over and unaccountable experts and bureaucrats gained control over people's lives. As First Lady she was famous, notorious to some, for the adroit ways she cut through bureaucracies or went around them to get things done. Democracy, for Addams and Roosevelt, required much from its citizens—it demanded a high level of participation. One begins from one's own community, with its streets and schools and recreation centers, with its complex, often troubled souls, and then moves on to national commitments, for this latter commitment must begin in a concrete place.

In Roosevelt's words: "My interest or sympathy or indignation is not aroused by an abstract cause but by the plight of a single person whom I have seen with my own eyes. It was the sight of a child dying of hunger that made the tragedy of hunger become of such overriding importance to me."[47] Both Addams and Roosevelt were gradualists in opposition to revolutions as well as to a deadly and destructive status quo. Their opposition to sudden and violent revolution flows directly from their belief in democracy. Reforms must be gradual and subject to ongoing revision. People must have a hand in making changes in their capacities as citizens. The story of violent revolution is, too often, the overturning of one set of rulers for another—that, at least, was their joint conclusion, just as their opposition to bureaucracy and the reign of experts stemmed from their democratic faith, from minds "open . . . to currents of air and to light from all sides."[48]

A second major barrier in the way of understanding the lives and world of Addams and Roosevelt is their commitment to equality *and* difference. Addams was a strong believer in equal rights for women. But she was convinced that women might add something of importance to political debate and discussion, drawing upon their varying experiences and life worlds. Feminism for her made sense only if it was linked to repudiation of a world "governed solely by physical force." Her arguments on this score are sophisticated, and she is aware of the difficulties of translating the peace-minded proclivities that might flow from women's activities (not from some female essence) into public action and debate.[49]

One paradox of Roosevelt's career is the fact that a war had first liberated her energies—as it did those of many other women, she claimed—but, finally, "it's up to the women" to make the strongest case for peace. She believed in ideals of womanly service but she also believed in women who lived and worked independently. She did *not* want women singled out as some special category or target for reform, holding that women are included in any definition of a people—a stance that now seems naive or inadequate to many. For Roosevelt, "women constituted"—or could—a democratic "vanguard for social change" for women have yet to realize their full political strength.[50] Proclaiming women historically a "tremendous power in the destiny of the world," she wanted that power made explicit and directed, above all, towards the cause of peace—also the great and overriding passion of Jane Addams's public life. Women must educate their children into the adventure and excitement of peace—away from the predominant excitement of war. With Addams, she sought ways to tap youthful devotion to a cause for militantly pacific purposes.[51] All this was part of their social feminism, a position now out of favor, which aims to integrate feminism with other social reforms and to empower ordinary women to that end—women who care about their families and their communities and whether or not they will have a future.

The will to peace must supplant a will to power. This supplanting "will have to start with women" who must become the crusaders on this question, men being too immersed in the old will to war. Roosevelt saw no incompatibility between her embrace of difference and her advocacy of equality. Need we? Too often we drive a sharp wedge between difference and equality and demand homogeneity as a vision of equality. There *are*, as well, feminist visions that celebrate difference and say very little about, or are hostile to, equality. But perhaps Addams and Roosevelt suggest an alternative. They suggest that one need not create some new "other" (the vision of the male as an incorrigible brute in some versions of radical feminism), or eliminate difference *en route* to sex equality (as do some celebrations of androgyny). Neither Addams nor Roosevelt wanted the new woman to be an updated version of the old man. Both were empowered by a generous spirit, idealist but not cloying, that looked to a future in which each one of us could dream individual dreams, but the greatest dream of all remained the dream of democracy.

Section Two

All In The Family

Heat, noise, lights, looks, words, gestures, personalities,
appliances. A colloquial density that makes family life the
one medium of sense knowledge in which an astonishment
of heart is routinely contained.

Don DeLillo

4

The Family and Civic Life

Democratic politics and families have always existed in tension with one another. Capitalism and families have always existed in tension with one another. Socialism and families are not a happy mix. Perhaps this tells us something about families. Michael Walzer, in *Sphere of Justice*, suggests that attempts, whether from defenders or opponents of the market or the state, to restructure the family in order to make it "fit" neatly with some abstract scheme of total justice or some overarching, systematic theory are always problematic, even disastrous.

Perhaps a few examples of just how problematic are in order. Consider Plato, the Plato of *The Republic*. As with all subsequent totalizing attempts to control every aspect of social reality and to define it in line with an overarching schema, Plato must eliminate the family if the ideal city is to come into being. The ruler-philosophers must take "the dispositions of human beings as though they were a tablet . . . which, in the first place, they would wipe clean."[1] Women must be held "in common." A powerful, all-encompassing bond between individuals and the state must be achieved such that all social and political conflict disappears, discord melts away, and the state comes to resemble a "single person," a fused, organic entity. All private loyalties and purposes must be eliminated.

Plato constructs a rationist meritocracy that requires that all considerations of sex, race, age, class, family ties, tradition, and history be stripped away in order to fit people into their appropriate social slots, performing only that function to which each is suited. Children below the ruler class can be shunted upward or downward at the will of the Guardians for they are so much raw material to be turned into instruments of social "good." A system of eugenics is devised for the Guardians. Children are removed from mothers at birth and placed in a child ghetto, tended to by those best suited for the job. No loyalties of any kind are allowed to emerge. No child knows who his or her parents are. What is all this for? What is it a defense against? Plato claims his moves are required to eradicate motives for discord. Private homes and sexual attachments, devotion to friends, dedication to individual or group aims and purposes militate against single-minded devotion to the city. Particular ties are a great evil. Only those that bind the individual to the state are good.

Rather extreme, the reader will surely cavil. Who would try to implement such an ideal, with all its frightening consequences, anyway? The answer is: subsequent totalitarians of all stripes, social engineers of various hues, revolutionaries of several flavors, and a small army of contemporary philosophers. Here are several examples, drawn from feminist politics and philosophy. Shulamith Firestone's radical feminist "classic," *The Dialectic of Sex,* depicts a world of stark lovelessness in which pervasive force, coercion, manipulation, and crude power roam undifferentially over the landscape, suffusing society unto its innermost parts. The family is totally pervaded by the domination of the "female sex-class" by the "male sex-class" and must be destroyed. In Firestone's scenario for the future test-tube babies will replace biological reproduction and every aspect of life will rest in the beneficent hands of a "new elite of engineers, cybernetricians."[2] The child, with no need to be "hung up" by authoritarian parents (parents having pretty much melted away), is "free" to bargain for the best deal in contracted households.

Firestone's vision has been attacked as a nightmare by many feminist critics in the past few years because "it rests on conceptual foundations that have much in common with the presuppositions of researchers and policy-makers who would . . . support technological intervention for the sake of the monopoly of power it would make possible. . . . Both see human biology as a limitation to be overcome—for Firestone, because she takes the relations of procreation to be . . . the source of women's oppression; for those who would support 'a brave new world,' because the diffusion of power among women and families threatens their own power hegemony."[3]

Despite these and other critiques, the philosophic drumbeat continues: the feminist future must be radically family-less world. Indeed Alison M. Jagger, in her widely hailed volume, *Feminist Politics and Human Nature,* even foresees the elimination of *males* and *females* in her ideal future order. She calls for an "ultimate transformation of human nature at which socialist feminists aim," one that goes much

beyond liberal tampering, for this transformation is an actual biological reformation of the human species. She continues, "This transformation might even include the capacities for insemination, for
lactation and for gestation so that, for instance, one woman could
inseminate another, so that men and nonparturitive women could
lactate and so that fertilized ova could be transplanted into women's
or even men's bodies. These developments may seem farfetched, but
in fact they are already on the technological horizon." What is
technologically possible is politically and ethically desirable so long as
these new means of control are controlled by women. For women are
oppressed by "having to be women."[4]

The historic animus of philosophers and revolutionaries to ordinary
human lives and ties and meaning continues unabated. Rather than
continue to proliferate these and dozens of other examples, I am
going to do something different. First, I will offer a brief interpretation of *why* totalists of all stripes must move aggressively to undermine or destroy family relations. Second, I will pose questions that
help to situate the reader so that he or she has a strong sense of those
considerations that constitute the horizon for my own arguments
concerning the family and civic life. Finally, I will make a case for the
family—mothers, fathers, and children—that is not only *not* at odds
with democratic civil society but, more now than ever, required for
that society to function. I do not move to eliminate all tensions, to
create some overarching ideal of *the* family and *the* democratic order.
Rather, I aim to preserve the necessary and fruitful tension between
particular and universal commitments that the family constitutes and
that democratic society cannot flourish without.

Martha Nussbaum, in her remarkable work, *The Fragility of Goodness*, offers a knowing and wise discussion of why Plato had to wreck
the family. Plato's urge in this direction is linked to his animus against
the poets and tragedians who, you will recall, must be banished from
his ideal city. For families and tragedies and poetic visions stir up
strong emotions, they rouse pity and fear, longing and love. Plato
aspired to "rational self-sufficiency." He would make the lives of
human beings immune to the fragility of messy existence. The ideal of
self-sufficiency was one of mastery in which the male citizen got
imbued with a "mythology of autochthony that persistently, and
paradoxically, suppressed the biological role of the female and
therefore the family in the continuity of the city."[5] (I trust the irony of
late twentieth-century feminist philosophers embracing this anti-
body, antifemale model is not lost on the reader.) Moral conflicts, for

Plato, suggest irrationalism. One must be "discarded as false." If one cannot be loyal both to families and to the city, loyalty to one must be made to conform to the other. For Plato and subsequent Platonists of every variety, including Marxist, "Our ordinary humanity is a source of confusion rather than of insight . . . [and] the philosopher alone judges with the right criterion or from the appropriate standpoint."[6] Hence the ascetic plan of *The Republic,* which aims to purify and to control by depriving human beings of "the nourishment of close ongoing attachments, of the family, of dramatic poetry."[7]

Subsequent grand universalists take a similar track. I have pointed to several feminist examples already. What ties all these attempts to undermine familial ties and loyalties together is the conviction that all relationships that are not totally voluntary, rationalistic, and contractual are irrational and suspect, that the traditional family is the example *par excellance* of imbedded particularity; that the world will attain an ideal of justice and order only when various radical proposals to "wipe the slate clean" have been implemented and human beings are no longer constrained and limited by special obligations and duties to specific familial others.

Finally, it seems, we must choose. We must choose between visions of total order and rationalistic harmony or an open, complex, conflicted receptivity to "the rich plurality of values that exist in the world of nature and of history." Diverse families contribute to that plurality of values in a way no other social institution can. But this takes me ahead of my story. Let me now move to those framing questions I noted previously and to some rough-and-ready notion of my own philosophical "method," although that is no doubt too grand a way to put it.

Here are a few questions that are constitutive of my discourse and my argument: In what ways is the family issue also a civic issue with weighty public consequences? What is the relationship between democratic theory and practice and intergenerational family ties and commitments? What ideal of the human person is imbedded in contrasting visions of intimate life? Do we have a stake in sustaining some visions as compared to others? What do families, composed of parents and children, do that no other social institution can? How does current political rhetoric militate against expressions of family obligations and downgrade what was once construed as the moral vocation of parenting?

These questions animate the argument that follows. As to method, it is one of interpretive complexity grounded in a strong set of moral commitments. I am interested in the problems any way of life creates and how human beings deal with them. If the political thinker is not to be arrogant and lofty, contemptuous of the values and judgments people make and the attachments and ties they have, she must attempt a way of philosophizing that comes close to the complexity and content of our actual beliefs and actions rather than performing desimplifying philosophical surgery in the hope that political life may one day be brought into line.

DEMOCRATIC POLITICS AND THE FAMILY: THE CONSTRUCTION OF A DILEMMA

The suspicions democrats have and have had about traditional authority, lodged in kings and chiefs, in popes and lords, are easily understood. For democracy requires self-governing and self-regulating citizens rather than obedient subjects. Being in a position of authority in democracy is the temporary holding of an office at the sufferance of those who delegate powers to the office holder.

The background features of democratic authority and its exercise emerged unevenly over several centuries as late medieval and early modern cosmologies faltered.[8] The features I have in mind include the principle that citizens possess inalienable rights. Possession of such rights empowers citizens to offer authoritative assent to the laws, rules, and practices that constitute democratic politics, including those procedural guarantees that afford them protection against abuses of the authority they have themselves authorized.

Equality between and among citizens was assumed from the beginning on the part of liberals and democrats; indeed, the citizen was, by definition, equal to any other *qua* citizen. (Not everyone, of course, could be a citizen: another ongoing dilemma.) Liberal and democratic citizenship required the creation of persons with qualities of mind and spirit necessary for civic participation. This creation of citizens was seen as neither simple nor automatic by early liberal theorists, leading many to insist upon a structure of education tied to a particular understanding of "the sentiments." This education should usher into a moral autonomy that stresses self-chosen obligations, thereby casting further suspicion upon all relations, practices, and loyalties deemed unchosen, involuntary, or natural.

Within such accounts of civic authority, the family emerged as a problem. For one does not enter a family through free consent; one is born into the world unwilled and unchosen by oneself, beginning life as a helpless and dependent infant. Eventually one reaches "the age of consent." But in the meantime one is a child, not a citizen. This vexed liberal and democratic theorists, some of whom believed, at least abstractly, that the completion of the democratic ideal required bringing all of social life under the sway of a single democratic authority principle.

The historic period most critical as backdrop for our current conflict over politics, democracy, and the family is rooted in the sixteenth- and seventeenth-century shift from patriarchal to liberal-contractarian discourse. Patriarchalist discourse in its paradigmatic form (I have in mind Robert Filmer's *Patriarcha*) was preeminently about authority, construing a tight case for authority as single, absolute, patriarchal, natural, and political. In Filmer's world there is no drawing of distinctions between public and private, family and politics; indeed, there is no private sphere—in a sense of a realm demarcated from political life—or political sphere—in the sense of a realm diverging from exigencies of the private world—at all. Power, authority, and obedience are fused within the original grant of dominion by God to Adam at creation. Within Filmer's unitary theory of authority there are only subjects, save, perhaps, for the divine right monarch alone. Each father lords it over his wife, his children, and his servants in his own little kingdom. But he, in turn, is subjected to the First Father, the lordly King.

Countering the strong traditional case for God-given patriarchal authority proved relatively easy for liberals and democrats where their visions of civil society were concerned but was trickier by far where their transformed notions of authority seemed to challenge the family. Was a familial form dominated by patriarchal presumptions, however softened in practice, suitable or legitimate within a civic world framed by presumptions of consent? If liberals sought to end a condition of perpetual political childhood were they required to eliminate childhood itself? A strong version of the liberal ideal, "free consent" from birth, was deeply problematic given the nature of human infants.[9] Liberal contractarians were often cautious in carrying their political principles into domestic life, some contenting themselves with contractarianism in politics and economics, traditionalism in families but not, however, without considerable discursive maneuvering.[10] Filmer's caustic query to his liberal interlocutors concerning whether people sprang up like "so many mushrooms" and his incredulous insistency, "How can a child express consent?"

continued to haunt liberals in part because they shared with Filmer the presumption that authority must be single in form if a society is to be coherent and orderly.

John Locke, more subtle than many early liberal thinkers, softened demands for relentless consistency in social practices and norms, arguing instead for the coexistence of diverse authoritative social forms and practices. Conjugal society must come into being through consent on the part of two adults. But "parental" or "paternal" power within the family (Locke recognizes both but privileges the latter) could not serve as a model for the liberal party any more than the norms constituting civil society could provide an apposite model for families. Locke strips the father-husband of patriarchal absolutism by denying him sovereignty, which includes the power of life and death. That prerogative is reserved *only* to democratically legitimized public authority. A father's power is "conjugal . . . not Political" and these two are "perfectly distinct and separate . . . built upon so different Foundations and given to so different Ends."[11] The child's status is that of not-yet-adult, hence not part of the consensual civil order. But the education of the child into moral sentiments is vital to that wider order. Locke avoids the seductions of the patriarchal authority principle as an all-encompassing norm by refusing to launch a project that mirrors patriarchalism. That is, he does not substitute an overreaching liberal authority principle that turns the family into an explicit political society governed by the same principles that prevailed in liberal public life.

The lack of perfect congruence between political and familial modes continued to vex post-Lockean liberal and democratic thinkers. Whether because the position of women, who, having reached the age of consent, could enter freely into a marriage relation only to find future consent foreclosed or because the family itself was a blemish to those who foresaw the ultimate triumph of rationalism and contract in all spheres of human existence, liberals returned over and over to relations between the family and politics.

This culminates in the nineteenth century when John Stuart Mill, in contrast to Locke, insists that familial and civic orders be drawn into a tight mesh with one another. For Mill, the family remained a despotic sphere governed by a "law of force" whose "odious source" was rooted in preenlightened and barbaric epochs. By revealing the origins of family relations, thus bringing out their "true" character, Mill hoped to demonstrate that the continued subjection of women blunts social progress. He proposed a leap into relations of "perfect equality" between the sexes as the only way to complete the teleology of liberal individualism and equality, to assure the promise of progress.

In his tract, *The Subjection of Women,* Mill argued that his contemporaries, male and female alike, were tainted by the atavisms of family life with its illegitimate, because unchosen, and prerational male authority, and its illegitimate, because manipulative and irrational, female quests for private power.[12] The family will become a school in the virtues of freedom only when parents live together without power on one side or obedience on the other. Power, for Mill, is repugnant: true liberty must reign in all spheres. But what about the children? Mill's children emerge as rather abstract concerns: blank slates on which parents must encode the lessons of obedience towards the end of inculcating authoritatively the lessons of freedom. Stripped of undemocratic authority and privilege, the parental union serves as a model of democratic probity.[13]

Mill's paean to liberal individualism is interestingly contrasted to Alexis de Tocqueville's concrete observations of family life in nineteenth-century America, a society already showing the effects of the extension of democratic, and the breakdown of patriarchal and Puritan, norms and practices. The political fathers of Tocqueville's America were fathers in a different mode, at once stern but forgiving, strong but flexible. They listened to their children and humored them. They educated as well as demanded obedience. Like the new democratic father, the American political leader did not lord it over his people. Citizens were not required to bend the knee or stand transfixed in awe. The leader was owed respect and, if he urged a course of action upon his fellow citizens following proper consultation and procedural requirements, they had a patriotic duty to follow.

Tocqueville's discerning eye perceived changing public and private relationships in liberal, democratic America. Although great care was taken "to trace two clearly distinct lines of action for the two sexes," women, in their domestic sphere "nowhere occupied a loftier position of honor and importance,"[14] Tocqueville claimed. The mother's familial role was enhanced given her essential civic vocation as the chief inculcator of democratic values in her offspring. "No free communities ever existed without morals and, as I observed . . ., morals are the work of women."[15]

Although the father was the family's "natural head," his authority was neither absolute nor arbitrary. In contrast to the patriarchal authoritarian family where the parent not only has a "natural right" but acquired a "political right" to command his children, in a democratic family the right and authority of parents is a *natural right* alone.[16] This natural authority presents no problem for democratic practices as Tocqueville construes democracy, in contrast to Mill. Indeed, the fact that the "right to command" is natural, not political, signifies its special and temporary nature: once the child is self-governing, the right dissolves. In this way natural, legitimate paternal authority and maternal moral education reinforce a political order that values flexibility, freedom, and the absence of absolute rule but requires, as well, order and stability.

Popular columnists and "child experts" in Tocqueville's America emphasized kindness and love as the preferred technique of child nature. Obedience was still seen as necessary—to parents, elders, God, "just government and one's conscience." But the child was no longer constructed as a depraved, sin-ridden, stiff-necked creature who needed harsh, unyielding instruction and reproof. A more benign view of the child's nature emerged as notions of infant depravity faded together with Puritan patriarchalism. The problem of discipline grew more, rather than less, complex. Parents were enjoined to get obedience without corporal punishment and rigid methods, using affection, issuing their commands in gentle but firm voices, insisting quietly on their authority lest contempt and chaos reign in the domestic sphere.

Tocqueville's image of the "democratic family" sees children both as ends in themselves and as means to the end of a well-ordered family and polity. A widespread moral consensus reigned in the America of that era, a kind of Protestant civic religion. When this consensus began to corrode under the force of rapid social change (and there are analogues to the American story in all modern democracies), certainties surrounding familial life and authority as a secure locus for the creation of democratic citizens were shaken as well.

If no form of social authority can any longer be taken for granted in light of continuing challenges to the norms that govern both familial and civil sphere, a case *for* the family as a good in itself and as one background feature that makes possible democratic society becomes more difficult to mount unless one opts for restorationism or celebrates high rationalist hopes that the time is finally ripe to bring the entire social order under the sway of wholly voluntarist norms. If restorationists long to return traditional norms to their once unambiguous status, the voluntarist option is problematic given its implied intent to nullify the moral and social significance of all "unchosen" purposes and obligations. If one finds both these alternatives unrealistic or undesirable, the task of articulating a defense of familial life and authority within, and for, a social world whose members no longer share one overriding conception of the good life, or repose deep faith in the future of human institutions, becomes ever more exigent.

I move in two directions. First, I launch a strong case by taking note of objections to it that yield, in turn, a more ambiguous set of reflections and affirmations. Complicating my argument in this way offers an opportunity to evaluate whether or not the strong case remains compelling, or alternatively, whether a softened defense of the family better serves the social goods at stake in the long run.[17]

DEMOCRATIC AUTHORITY AND THE FAMILY: THE STRONG CASE

Familial authority, though apparently at odds with the governing presumptions of democratic authority, is nonetheless part of the constitutive background required for the survival and flourishing of democracy. Family relations could not exist without family authority, and these relations remain the best way we know anything about to create human beings with a developed capacity to give ethical allegiance to the background presumptions and principles of democratic society. Family authority structures the relationship between adult providers, nurturers, educators, and disciplinarians and dependent children, who slowly acquire capacities for independence. Modern parental authority is shared by mother and father. (Some readers may take strong exception to this claim, arguing that the family is patriarchal, even today; or that the authority of the mother is *less* decisive than that of the father; or that Mill was right. Children, however, exhibit little doubt that their mothers are powerful and authoritative, though perhaps not in ways identical to fathers.) This ideal of parental equality in relation to children does *not* presuppose an identity between mother and father. Each can be more or less a private or a public person yet be equal in relation to children in the way here described.

What makes family authority distinctive in the sense of stewardship internal to it, the recognition that parents undertake continuing solemn obligations and responsibilities. The authority of the parent is special, limited, and particular. Parental authority, like any form of authority, may be abused, but unless it exists the activity of parenting itself is impossible. The authority of parents in relation to children is implicated in that moral education required for democratic citizenship, the creation of a democratic political morality. The *Herzenbildung*—education of the heart—that takes place in families should not, however, be seen as but one item in a larger political agenda. To construe it as such is to treat the family merely instrumentally, affirming it only insofar as it can be shown to serve some externally defined set of purposes. That the family underscores the authoritative rules and norms that govern the wider order may be true. But it also offers alternatives to the actual policies and programs a public order may throw up at any given point in time.

The intense loyalties, obligations, and moral imperatives nurtured in families may clash with the requirements of public authority, for example, when young men refuse to serve in an unjust war because this runs counter to the religious beliefs instilled in their families. This, too, is vital for democracy. Democracy emerged as a form of revolt. Keeping alive a potential locus for revolt, for particularity, for difference, sustains democracy in the long run. It is no coincidence that all twentieth-century totalitarian orders labored to destroy the family as a locus of identity and meaning apart from the state. Totalitarian politics strives to consume all of life, to allow for a single *public* identity, to destroy private life, to require that individuals identify only with the state rather than with specific others—family, friends, comrades.

Family authority within a democratic, pluralistic order does not exist in a direct homologous relation to the principles of civil society. To establish an identity between public and private lives and purposes would weaken, not strengthen, democratic life overall. For children need particular, intense relations with specific adult others in order to learn to make distinctions and choices as adults. The child confronted prematurely with the "right to choose," should parents abnegate their authority, or situated too soon inside anonymous, institutional contexts that minimize points of special, unique contact and trust with specific adult others, is likely to be less capable of choosing later on. To become a being capable of posing alternatives, one requires a sure and certain place from which to start. In Mary Midgley's words: "Children . . . have to live *now* in a particular culture; they must take some attitude to the nearest things right away."[18] The social form best suited to provide children with a trusting, determinate sense of place and ultimately a "self" is the family. Indeed, it is only through identification with concrete others that the child can later identify with nonfamilial human beings and come to see herself as a member of a wider community.

Family authority is inseparable from parental care, protection, and concern. In the absence of such ties, familial feelings would not be displaced throughout a wider social network—they would, instead, be vitiated, perhaps lost altogether. And without the human ties and bonds that the activity of parenting makes possible, a more general sense of "brotherhood" and "sisterhood" cannot emerge.

The nature and scope of parental authority alters over time. Children learn that being a child is not a permanent condition. One of the lessons the family teaches is that no authority on this earth is omnipotent, unchanging, and absolute. Working through familial authority, as the child struggles for identity, requires that she question authority more generally. Examples of authoritarian parents do not disconfirm this ideal case; they do, however, point to the fact that family authority, like any constitutive principle, is subject to deformation and abuse in particular cases. Granting the possibility for abuse, sustaining familial authority, meaning that of both parents in their relations to children, as well as families in their relation to the wider social order, keeps alive that combination of obligation and duty, freedom and dissent, characteristic of democratic life.

The stance of the democrat towards family authority resists easy characterization. It involves a rejection of any ideal of political and familial life that absorbs all social relations under a single authority principle. Families are not democratic polities. With its concreteness, its insistence on the unique and the noninstrumental, the family helps us to hold intact the respective goods and ends of exclusive relations and arrangements. Any further erosion of that ethical life embodied in the family bodes ill for democracy. For example, we can experience the plight of *homelessness* as a human tragedy *only* because we cherish an ideal of what it means to make and to have a home. Thus, a defense of the family, rather than ushering into rigid traditionalism, can help to sustain a commitment to "do something" about a whole range of social problems.

Abusive families are a particular tragedy. The loss of the family and its characteristic forms of authority and relations would be a general debacle from which we would not soon recover. The replacement for parents and families would not be a happy, consensual world of children coequal with adults but one in which children became clients of institutionally powerful social bureaucrats and engineers of all sorts for whom they would serve as so much grist for the mill of extrafamilial schemes and ambitions.

The ideal democratic family here sketched is a feature of a democratic *Sittlichkeit*, one vital and necessary arena of concrete social life and ethical existence. But it may serve as well as a "launching pad" into more universal commitments, a civic *Moralität*. The child who emerges from such a family is more likely to be capable of acting in the world as a complex moral being, one part of, yet somewhat detached from, the immediacy of his or her own concerns and desires given the complex negotiations she has internalized as part of growing up.

DEMOCRATIC AUTHORITY AND THE FAMILY: AMBIGUOUS RECOGNITIONS

The strong case presumes a family that is secure, or can be made secure, in its authoritative role, a family that serves as the bearer of a clear telos. This is spine-stiffening stuff. But it presupposes a wider social surround that no longer exists in its paradigmatic form, American society having ceased long ago to endorse unambiguously the shouldering of family obligations and to locate honor in long-term moral responsibilities. The authoritative norms that sustain the strong case have fallen under relentless pressures that promote individualistic, mobile, and tentative relations between self and others. Modern subjects are enjoined to remain as untrammeled as possible in order to attain individual goals and to enjoy their "freedom." Constraints grow more onerous than they were when it was anticipated that everyone would share them—all women, almost without exception, would become mothers; all men, almost without exception, would become supportive fathers. Located inside a wider ethos that no longer affords clear-cut moral and social support for familial relations and responsibilities, young people, unsurprisingly, choose in growing numbers to postpone or evade these responsibilities.

In acknowledging these transformations, the case for familial authority is softened but not abandoned. Taking account of shifts in the social ethos does not mean that one succumbs to them as if they comprised a new authoritative norm simply by virtue of their existence. But some alterations are warranted, including articulation of less dauntingly rigorous normative requirements for being a "parent" than those implied by the strong argument. The changes I have in mind here are *not* facile reassurances that modern human beings can be unfettered individualists and encumbered parents in some happy, perfect, harmonious configuration. For parental authority both *constrains* and *makes possible,* locating mothers and fathers in the world in a way that *must* be different from that of nonparenting adults. This need not lock parents into a dour notion of their duty that encourages them to overstate their power to shape their children and their responsibility for doing so. The modern family is a porous institution, one open to a variety of external images and influences. Parents are no longer the sole moral guardians, and one's defense of familial authority must take this into account, assessing its meaning in the structure of domestic life.

Critics of family authority might continue the challenge by insisting that even this softened case is "arbitrary" in several ways: because it privileges procreative heterosexual unions, thereby excluding a variety of other intimate arrangements, whether "nonexclusive," "open" marriages and families or homosexual unions, from its purview; because it maintains a notion of the child as a dependent who requires discipline and restriction, thus shoring up paternalism ostensibly in behalf of children but really to deny then their rights; because it limits parental social choices by stressing dependability, trust, and loyalty to the exclusion of adventure, unpredictability, and openness; because it constructs a case for ethical development that is self-confirming in assuming that a set of authoritative norms is essential to personal life.

Perhaps, this critic might go on, behavior modification is a less strenuous and more effective shaper of a child's action. Perhaps children thrown early out of the home and into a group context emerge less burdened by individual conscience and moral autonomy, hence they are freer to act creatively without incessant, guilt-ridden ruminations about responsibility and consequence than those children reared in the family idealized in the strong case. Perhaps children who learn, at an early age, to be cynical and *not* trust adults will be better skeptics, better prepared to accept the rapid changes of modernity, than the trusting, emotionally bonded, slowly maturing children in the family sketched previously.

I will concede that a reflective brief in behalf of family authority should recognize explicitly that every set of authoritative norms will contain some contingent features, contingent "in the sense that, while they are indispensable to this way of life, there are other forms of living . . . in which this special set would not be necessary."[19] But conventional or contingent need not mean arbitrary. In the absence of any authoritative rules and relations, the social world would be more rather than less dominated by violence, coercion, or crass manipulation.

Take, for example, the incest taboo. The incest taboo can be construed as wholly arbitrary, as several radical social critics have claimed, translating that to mean both "illegitimate" and "indefensible," contrary to individual freedom of expression and action. Exposing its arbitrariness, they would liberate children from paternalistic despotism and parents from an ancient superstition. Chafing at restrictions of sexual exploration that construct strong normalizing limits, and establish sharp boundaries between familial and extrafamilial sexuality, as well as between adults and children inside families, these antiauthoritarians celebrate total freedom of sexual exploration as an alternative.

The mistake on the part of the antiincest taboo protagonists is not their insistence that we recognize the conventional features of our social arrangements, but their conviction that such exposure requires elimination of the rules or practices in question. In assuming that a viable mode of social existence might come into being and flourish in the absence of authoritative restrictions, the "antis" emerge as naive and dangerous. They would open up social life to more rather than less brutalization, including targeting children (in the example under purview) as acceptable resources for adult sexual manipulation and coercion. Continued authoritative acceptance of the incest taboo implicates one in a powerful, normative standard true. But that standard is necessary to sustain a social good—protecting children from systematic abuse by the more powerful. Parental power is limited and constrained. That is why we condemn and punish abusive parents. Adult power, shorn of the internal moral limits of the incest taboo, would become more generalized, less accountable, and dangerously unlimited.

A second radical criticism holds, as I have suggested, that in defending the family and intergenerational ties, one privileges a restrictive ideal of sexual and intimate relations. There are within contemporary American life those who believe that a society can and should stay equally open to all alternative arrangements, treating "life-styles" as so many identical peas in a pod. To be sure, families in modernity coexist with those who live another way, whether heterosexual and homosexual unions that are by choice or by definition childless; communalists who diminish individual parental authority in favor of the preeminence of the group; and so on.

But the recognition and acceptance of plural possibilities does not mean each alternative is equal to every other with reference to specific social goods. No social order has ever existed that did not endorse certain activities and practices as preferable to others. Every social order forges terms of inclusion and exclusion. Ethically responsible challenges to our terms of exclusion and inclusion push towards a loosening but not a wholesale negation in our normative endorsement of intergenerational family life. In defining family authority, then, one acknowledges that one is *privileging* relations of a particular kind when and where certain social goods are at stake.

Those excluded by, or who exclude themselves from, this authoritative norm should not be denied social space and tolerance for their own practices. And it is possible that if what were at stake were, say, seeking out and identifying those creations of self that enhance an aesthetic construction of life and sensibility, the romantic bohemian or rebel would get higher marks than the Smith Family of Fremont, Nebraska. Nevertheless, we should be cautious about going too far in the direction of a wholly untrammeled pluralism with reference to authoritative evaluations lest we become so vapid that we are no longer capable of distinguishing between the moral weightiness of, say, polishing one's Porsche and sitting up all night with an ill child. The intergenerational family remains central and critical in nurturing recognitions of human frailty, mortality, and finitude and in inculcating moral limits and constraints. A revamped defense of family authority, then, takes account of challenges to its normalizing features and opens it to ambiguities and paradox.

As I conclude, it seems that the worries of historic liberal thinkers about the family's anomalous position within a civic world governed by contractarian and voluntarist norms were misplaced. Ironically, what such analysts *feared* is what I here *endorse:* a form of family life and authority that does *not* mesh perfectly with democratic political principles yet remains vital to the sustaining of a diverse and morally decent culture. This is an example of one of many paradoxes that social life throws up and that civic philosophers would be well advised to recognize and to nourish. The discordance embodied in the uneasy coexistence of familial and democratic authority sustains those struggles over identity, purpose, and meaning that are the very stuff of democratic life.

To resolve the untidiness of our public and private relations by either reaffirming unambiguously a set of unitary, authoritative norms or eliminating all such norms as arbitrary is to jeopardize the social goods that democratic and familial authority, paradoxical in relation to one another, promise—to men and women as parents and citizens and to their children.

5

The Family Crisis, the Family Wage, and Feminism: Historical and Theoretical Considerations

FEMINISM AND THE FAMILY WAGE IN HISTORIC PERSPECTIVE

Several years ago I found myself at the receiving end of sharp words from an important democratic socialist feminist, in part because I had endorsed, off-handedly, the notion of a family wage in an essay on "Feminism, Family and Community" for *Dissent*.[1] My offensive comments, in a brief I was offering in behalf of "social" as compared to "equal rights" feminism, went like this: "It [social feminism] indicts an economic system that denies families a living, family wage and that forces both parents into the labor force, often against the will of the woman who would prefer to be with her children but must, instead, work at a low-pay, dead-end job to make ends meet."[2] To my surprise, this became the "right-wing denouement" of my argument. In a heated attack (to which I, in turn, heatedly replied), she offered up her objections, insisting that to give men a family wage would require "massive downward redistribution of income"—once a stock-in-trade of conservative objections to progressive endorsements of the family wage (how ideological worms turn!)—and moreover, that the family "that is based on the family wage has always been very much a capitalist, market-bound institution itself." Men, she continued, were paid a family wage "so that wives can stay home . . . [and] children not be sent out to day care, and the family will not fall apart."

61

The male wage "link to capital" doesn't necessarily mean he will share it. Indeed, men are likely to default "short of some plan to conscript them into marriage and compel them to hand over their earnings to their dependents."[3] Not a pretty picture, from her perspective. Taken aback by this onslaught from a *socialist* feminist, I began to wonder just when and how the family wage had earned such a bleak reputation. I also wondered if my endorsement was politically and economically naive, the repetition of a heartfelt but ill-thought-out nostrum.

To return, then, to the not-so-golden days of yesteryear, I will take up discussions by progressives and feminists on the subject in the 1920s and 1930s. Pioneering criticism of the family wage and the matter of family allowances was undertaken by Eleanor Rathbone, whose ideas played a vital role in political discussions both in Great Britain, where she pressed for extension and deepening of the welfare state, and in the United States, where her work was influential in the thinking of such progressive analysts and activists as Paul H. Douglas, a University of Chicago professor of economics and industrial relations and, later, United States Senator (D., Illinois). Rathbone attacked the family wage, or "living wage," from a feminist-oriented, reformist direction. To her the family was "an aggregate of individual human beings, each with an actual or potential value to the community"—this was the family as it "really is"—in contrast to the vision of proponents of the family wage who viewed some members of the family as dependents of a wage earner, hence as "parasitic, accessory, non-essential."[4]

Dating the family wage—and corollary notion of the "dependent family"—from the early nineteenth century, Rathbone set out to debunk the belief that the "arrangement by which wives and children up to the period of adolescence, are normally dependent on the earnings of the male head of the family" was one of "immemorial antiquity, almost inseparable from existence of the family as a social unit."[5] An earlier generation of reformers, anticipating "an immense increase in national productivity," had encouraged mothers to give themselves over entirely to "the care of their homes" but had made "no provisions for this vast army of non-producers except through wages"; hence the requirement that "fathers should earn as much as the whole labouring unit of the family had earned before", and, as well, that "men without wives or without dependent children should earn enough for the needs of an imaginary family."[6] These reformers declared that a family or living wage had its base in "Nature" but must be established by statute in order to maintain families, hence sustain populations.

But there are intractable problems with these assumptions, Rathbone insists. First, what is a family of normal size—what is the baseline for the family wage? Numbers of dependents vary widely and a single family passes through many stages as children grow up. Over the years the customary norm that emerged in sociological writing, economic calculation, and working-class demand was the five-member family of husband, wife, and three dependent children. And this assumption continues to prevail in "a shadowy form in recent wage-negotiations as reinforcing the demand of the working class for 'a living wage' adequate to the needs of 'our wives and families'."[7] Rathbone sets out to undermine this assumption, an easy task that drew upon statistics showing the wide variation in family size from zero to ten dependents or more. Deploying a standard of efficiency, showing the extent of redistribution required if the five-member family wage were to be the overarching standard in practice in paying male wages, Rathbone takes organized labor and public opinion to task. What is at work, she suggests, is a subconscious "prejudice of sex" when leaders of working men "cling persistently to the ideal of a uniform adequate family wage." She asks: "Are they not influenced by a secret reluctance to see their wives and children recognized as separate personalities, 'each to count for one and none for more than one' in the economic structure of society, instead of being fused in the multiple personality of the family with its male head?"[8]

The trade unionist thinks of the family as "his." The "sentimentalist" is "shocked at the bare suggestion that anything so sordid as remuneration . . . should be introduced into the sacred institution of the family and applied to the profession of motherhood."[9] Not so Rathbone. Chiding these hoary notions, showing that they represent impulses by now well out of date and out of harmony with progress, she advocates bringing women's wages up to par with that of men's, plus a system of "direct provision" to mothers in the form of child allowances to assist them in providing for children.

This is much to be preferred, she continues, to plans advocated by some English feminists that would give the wife a legal right to a share of her husband's income. Enforcement of such a provision is impossible. Far better, in Rathbone's view, to recognize that men and women cannot be counted on to share their incomes with their families; that there are more single men without families than women in similar circumstances; hence that the old notion of what is "normal," dependent women and children, does not hold. The family wage is a "sloppy and ill-thought-out theory"; it "fits the facts" badly; and it is impossible to achieve in practice. Equal pay plus a system of family allowances is the true progressive route. Rathbone fought tirelessly for this perspective against the strict laissez-faire school as well as against what she considered a worn-out, tacitly antifeminist devotion to the family wage on the Left.

Picked up by theorists and reformers in the United States, Rathbone's work geared many proponents of welfare-state reform against the living wage or family wage idea. A case in point is Paul Douglas in his influential book, *Wages and the Family*. Endorsing the family wage under the standard family-of-five norm means, in practice, that industry will be saddled "with the maintenance of over forty-five million fictitious wives and children," Douglas writes. The "way out . . . lies in the fixation of a minimum wage sufficient to support single men with added allowances for dependent wives, children, and other adults."[10] The right to a "living wage" can no longer be construed as the old family wage ideal embraced by "workers, budgetary students, and social workers" alike. Why shouldn't the mother be expected to work outside the home? Why are three children considered necessary if the race is to perpetuate itself? None of this holds up under scrutiny, in Douglas's view; moreover, it has the effect of holding down women's wages on the assumption that they are being "provided for" by a male wage earner.

Following Rathbone's strategy for the United Kingdom, Douglas comes up with a figure designed to startle: *if* the family wage norm were to be implemented *fully*, industry would pay seventy-two million nonexistent people. Clearly, his argument continues, the five-member family norm is a fallacious measuring stick and should be abandoned. Unfortunately, there is none that works any better. It follows that the whole idea must be jettisoned in favor of a more efficient and progressive set of policies: a single wage standard for men and women with the cost of dependents being met through family allowances. Douglas calls this, following the work of his wife, Dorothy R. Douglas, the "permanent independence theory, or the theory that her [the woman's] wage must be sufficient to maintain her independence through periods of enforced unemployment, through illness and through old age."[11]

Family allowances should come out of state funds, not from assessments levied upon employers: this is the united view of socialists, labor leaders, and feminists in Europe and Australia, according to Douglas, and it is one he partially endorses. But he also favors bringing employers into the picture with regard to how they classify positions and assign salaries. Allowances should be paid directly to the mother, as only in this way will they "more likely be expended for the benefit of the child" and, at the same time, "constitute a form of wage for motherhood," thus dignifying "her position" and making her "more independent economically of her husband." Breaking the traditional power of the husband is "conducive to a more truly happy and self-respecting family life."[12] Side benefits would include managing the birthrate of the "submerged poor," which Douglas traces to their desperate economic straits. As an additional exigency to improve the race overall, "the feeble-minded and other defectives" should be sterilized.

Because ideas for maintaining population and enhancing its quality were a standard feature of progressive reform in this era, Douglas's suggestion was probably not all that shocking. He writes: "The sterilization of these [feeble-minded] is in no way dependent upon the present system of wage payment, and should be carried out. The adoption of the family-allowance system would indeed probably hasten such a program of sterilization, since it would cause industry and society to realize that they ought not to maintain those who were so patently unable to maintain themselves."[13] In other words, it will be much easier for industry and the state to get control over their populations directly with a system of equal wages plus family allowances than it has been given the "individualistic" notion of the family wage, which presumes that "it is a man's own business what children he brings into the world." Social control will be enhanced by eliminating the social wage.

Where does American feminism fit into this debate? Historic feminism's roots lie in the liberal tradition and the language of rights, a potent weapon against traditional obligations, particularly those of family duty or any social status declared natural. To be free and equal to men was the central aim of nineteenth-century women's reform efforts. Yet, at the same time, and to various ends and purposes, some feminist reformers stressed a notion of women's virtue, particularly as it flowed from their devotion to motherhood. Thus advocates of women's suffrage often embraced two arguments—a declaration that women were the same as men, hence suffrage was just and right on a universal standard, *and*, in contrast, the conviction that women's skills and virtues were required in order to improve, even purify, politics itself.

Strategies for economic and social reform broke along a line separating those who attacked gender categories in favor of a single standard of wages (and everything else) for the sexes and those who, in the interests of "ordinary" and working-class women, insisted on gender-based protection and policy initiatives. For example: women trade unionists and important progressive reformers attacked the Equal Rights Amendment when it was first proposed in 1921 as class-biased and suited only to the experience of professionals or exceptional skilled workers. In 1930, as Nancy Cott points out in a recent work, "still less than 12 percent of the married women in the United States worked for pay outside the home, according to the United States Census. Even a smaller proportion were pursuing 'careers,' which received the lion's share of attention."[14] Female labor reformers and this earlier generation of social feminists of the sort I noted in my *Dissent* debate found themselves caught on the horns of a dilemma. On the one hand, they recognized that many women went to work and kept working and that they required training and equal pay. On the other hand, they were committed ideologically to the concept of the family wage, a staple in the reformist diet. Cott insists that this dual commitment led reformers awry, undercutting efforts to sustain women in the labor market given their tacit endorsement of the family wage concept. She continues:

Widely supported by male trade unionists, the concept of the family wage embraced the common-law meaning of marriage: the husband's duty to support and the wife's duty to render services. As much as the claim for the family wage had arisen as a working-class demand to wrest a decent standard of living from employers, it was also an invidious form of gender distinction in the labor market, making women's economic dependence, and the devaluation of their labor, conditions for the privileging of male workers as providers.[15]

Feminists never sorted out the clash between the interests of working-class, poor, and middle-class and privileged women—not in the nineteenth and early twentieth centuries and not at the present moment. But those clashes are evident in the first great debate over ERA just as they were in the more recent ERA struggle. Although never a *central issue*, the family wage notion figured tacitly in much feminist and reformist strategizing—either as something to defeat and overcome or something to achieve—but in ways that no longer tied it to traditional presumptions of patriarchal privilege.

CONTEMPORARY FEMINISM AND THE FAMILY WAGE

Although most leading female theoreticians, polemicists, and activists in the 1960s and 1970s did not take up the question explicitly, their animus towards traditional family relations disallowed endorsing any policy or strategy aimed at promoting and protecting anything that smacked of the older norm.[16] The question remains a divisive one, although it is rarely couched as a discussion of the family wage and more often taken up under the rubric of equal pay or destroying male dominance.

In her landmark work, *The Feminine Mystique*, Betty Friedan offered a vision absorbed in the quest for identity posed primarily as a psycho-social question. She conjured up an image of happy, ambitious women rather than traumatized housewives, taking upper-middle-class women as her norm, but only if women threw off the shackles of an enforced domesticity. For Friedan, reeducation for victims of the feminine mystique, and education of the next generation of women away from that mystique, were the keys to change. When she extolled work for women it was in the form of architecture, medicine, law, and science like the "boys at Harvard or Yale or Columbia or Chicago."[17] From such an elite-oriented stance, it is easy to see why Friedan did not trouble with specific concerns that bore down most heavily on working-class women, poor women, and women without college educations. For her, equal rights and education would prove a universal panacea.

Feminist thinkers who did take up the family wage explicitly were most often located within the socialist tradition. Not surprisingly, the debate surfaced in stronger theoretical and historical detail in the United Kingdom (with its powerful labor movement) than in the United States. Two socialist feminist theoreticians, Michelle Barrett and Mary McIntosh, in a discussion of the history of the idea and the practice of the family wage framed from a Marxist perspective, conclude that feminists cannot combine a commitment to equal pay with a commitment to the family wage. The former presumes men and women as equal wage earners in a competitive marketplace; the latter locates women in the home. Although working-class interests at one point may have been well served by struggling for a family wage, thereby seeking to improve women's conditions in the family and to assist children, the family wage is not "consonant with the feminism of the women's liberation movement of today."[18] Feminist scholarship, the authors conclude, exposes the family wage as a "myth" in any case, one that never served as an "accurate description of the means by which the working class has been supported and reproduced."[19]

Turning to the case against the family wage, Barrett and McIntosh insist that any such system *by definition* must: "(i) enforce the dependency and oppression of women and subject unsupported women, especially mothers, to severe poverty; (ii) have no necessary effect on the value of labour power; (iii) divide and weaken the working class by reducing militancy, creating the conditions for conflict between individual women and men generally in the labor market and by perpetuating the view that the support of non-labourers should be met by the wage rather than via the state."[20] The family wage, they declare, has never worked, and it is time that politically aware men as well as women "became disenchanted with the fantasy world of the family wage."[21]

In contrast, the work of another socialist feminist, Jane Humphries, urges that, at least historically, the family wage brought real benefits to working-class men, women, and children by providing a nonde-grading form of support for nonlaboring family members and by serving as a locus for creation of working-class solidarity and inter-generational continuity.[22] An American feminist historian, Martha May, also offers a somewhat more benign view of the family wage when she claims that there is more to the matter than a "nasty example of patriarchy, a simplistic argument for women's subordina-tion. Careful examination by feminist scholars has revealed it may be something more complex."[23]

Offering up a useful summary of the historic developments of the ideology of the family wage, May tracks its persistence in the rhetoric of trade unionists and other working-class advocates as one way they found to provide adequate wages and subsistence. "The family wage challenged the ideology of working-class poverty, invoking social wages in the name of the family . . . . Early demands for the family wage suggested that only women, and not children, be withdrawn from its labor force."[24] *The Ten Hours Advocate* (a working-class newspaper) supported a family wage in 1864 in the hope that wives and children might be spared the horrible drudgery of cotton mills. What was an adequate family wage? Sufficient to support an entire family, meet emergency expenses, and allow children access to education.

By the turn of the century, according to May, the idea of the family wage had become a "central feature of analysis in the assessment of poverty and standards of living by progressive reformers, and part of the work of sociologists, economists, and charity workers of the developing social survey movement."[25] But the family wage began to lose this honorific status, even among reformers, as my discussion of Rathbone and Douglas indicates. And among feminists the question was always fraught, with some among the early ranks as well as now finding in the family wage little more than a conspiracy between and among patriarchs, from the working-class family man to the corporate president, to keep women down, and others seeing in the family wage a form of resistance to the worst vagaries of capitalism, on the part of men *and* women of the working classes.

I opt, on balance, for the latter view, recognizing in political struggles over the family wage genuine efforts to gain protection for families, to resist exploitation of the labor of women and children, and to recognize women's domestic contributions as real and important, even though gender distinctions in work roles were no doubt being reinforced as well. It *is* a much more complicated story than a sustained tale of the subordination of women. Recognizing this complex history, we are left with a question for the present; Is there any way to endorse the ideal of a family wage without, simultaneously, endorsing rigid economic and social roles and identities for men and women? If not a family wage, how might we deal with the real and growing poverty of women and children?

IS THERE A FAMILY WAGE IN A (FEMINIST) FUTURE?

Consider the following: an item in the *New York Times* entitled "Former Wives: A Legion of the Needy."[26] We are told that there are 11.5 million displaced homemakers in the United States, with the 1980 census showing a "marked increase" over the 4.1 million identified in a 1976 study conducted by the Women's Bureau of the Department of Labor. Part of what is going on, the article suggests, is the growing economic hardship of women and children in part as a result of changes in divorce laws, namely, the rapid shift to no-fault divorce. Contemporary divorce laws, under the no-fault rubric, are devoted to the notion of equality. But, in practice, this winds up burdening women unequally as they are less well positioned to provide for their own support and to sustain a household than are men of their comparable background and class.

This is but one snippet of a much larger picture. The aggregate wage gap between men and women remained fixed throughout the

1970s in contrast to what was happening throughout Western Europe, whether Catholic societies or Scandinavian welfare states.[27] Fully 45 percent of working women in the United States in 1987 were single, divorced, separated, or widowed and thus have "no option but to take prime economic responsibility for themselves (and often their children). The low earning power of women helps explain why 35 percent of single mothers fall below the poverty line."[28]

Continued wage discrimination against women, a high divorce rate, the perpetuation of staggering numbers of women and children in welfare-client dependency situations that are barely subsistent are the harsh realities hardly balanced off by glowing articles about single career women or supermoms. Child-care subsidies have been cut since 1980 and nothing like a family allowance system—not to mention a family wage—exists in any robust sense. The battle lines between equal rights feminists and social feminists continue to form around these questions, with social feminists putting the issue of mothering center-stage on the grounds that most women, after all, do become mothers.[29]

It is clear, however, that a strong normative brief in behalf of the family wage cannot be sustained and will not be endorsed in contemporary American society. I have in mind here not only the rather loosely developed ideal that emerged in the course of economic and political struggles in the nineteenth and early twentieth centuries but that finely honed and theoretically elegant formulation embedded in traditional Catholic thought. Arguing against contractual freedom and the prevalence of a "current wage" (whatever the market will bear), Catholic thinkers, tracing the lineage of their ideas to St. Thomas Aquinas, insisted upon a strict right to a familial wage as rooted in natural law and right and "measured by the social needs of the workers."[30] Pope Leo XIII's *Rerum Novarum* is the key document, but the notion can be tracked all the way through to Pope John Paul II's encyclical *Laborem Excercens*, with echoes in the United States Bishop's Pastoral Message and Letter "Economic Justice for All: Catholic Social Teaching and the U.S. Economy." The natural, strict right to a family wage as the unassailable right of every adult male working man flows, in their view, from a "teleological appreciation of human labor and of the economic order" and, of course, human biology.[31] The notion that "nature dictates," however, carries little weight with many contemporary Americans, and I am interested in looking at the real possibilities of our situation in and through the political culture we inhabit.

The Bishops recognize that strict articulation of the family wage idea requires moderation in light of the realities of the present moment. Thus, they call for policies and programs that support "the strength and stability of families," and they require that we examine all employment practices, health insurance policies, income-security programs, tax policy, and service programs with an eye to whether they "support or undermine the abilities of families to fulfill their roles in nurturing children and caring for infirm and dependent family members." In line with *Laborem Exercens*, they endorse the structuring of institutions and policies in such a way that "mothers of young children are not forced by economic necessity to leave their children for jobs outside the home," but those that do should not be discriminated against.[32] The bishops also assail the lack of "affordable, quality day care" and call for welfare programs to be "available to two-parent as well as single-parent families."

Should a feminist take umbrage at this? The social feminist would find in the bishops' discussions recognition of the varying needs and desires of women from different social groups and classes. But equal rights feminists would dissent because the bishops here tacitly endorse a view of the family such feminists find constraining or suffocating. While debating normative visions of family life is not the explicit purpose of this essay, such questions cannot be excised from any discussion of the family wage. For we sustain or undermine human social relations, including our most intimate ones, through policy initiatives that require two wage earners or make it possible for people to make a home on one income, not necessarily that of the male. I find nothing inherent in a revised variant on the family wage idea that precludes a father-at-home, mother-at-work situation, or both parents working half-time, if we extend the idea to cover full-time employees with major family responsibilities.[33]

Currently we find ourselves in a system that pays lip service to honoring mothers and penalizes women, whether single or in intact families. We often shore up a normative ideal of the mother but do not provide the means for women to attain that ideal. Writes one contemporary feminist analyst of the welfare state:

By failing to offer them [women raising children without a male breadwinner] day care, job training, a job that pays a "family wage" or some combination of these, it constructs them exclusively as mothers . . . . Now, according to the ideology of separate spheres, this should be an honorific social identity. Yet the system does not honor these women. On the contrary, instead of providing them a guaranteed income equivalent to a "family wage" as a matter of right, it stigmatizes, humiliates, and harasses them. In effect, it decrees that these women must be, yet cannot be, normative mothers.[34]

If the situation faced by welfare women in clientage-dependency relations is the most difficult, that confronted by all women save the most privileged is trying, and that faced by men and women who are attempting to make a home while each holds down a job is a picture of "stress city." Those feminists who persist in picturing a world of coequal individualist male and female careerists avidly exercising their untrammeled choices as their children are tended to in modern and spacious day-care centers, endorse a social myth that is more fantastic by far than any ever embodied in the family wage.

6

The Family Crisis and State Intervention: The Construction of Child Abuse as Social Problem and Popular Rhetoric

Written at a moment when child abuse, not drugs, grabbed the most sensational headlines, this essay offers general arguments about how public issues are constructed.

INTRODUCTION: THE CRISIS IN THE AMERICAN FAMILY

Every political culture has a point at which it threatens to come unglued. Most of the time these lines of fault lie beneath the surface. But social dislocation, economic distress, public fears, or political hopes may bring latent tensions to the surface, compelling us to take a look. Liberal society—our own—quickly reaches the end of its tether where several related issues cluster. At the moment there are at least four: abortion, "the family debate," the proper place of religion in public life, and pornography. What these highly charged issues share in common is the fact that they involve substantive moral imperatives and implicate us in larger, competing visions of social life and possibility. No matter how we resolve the question, or fail to, we only deepen our discontents by making more visible our social cleavages.

Over the past several years the family debate has become more and more acrimonious. Whether the family is falling apart and is doomed unless we engage in a dramatic act of restoration or is simply reconfiguring itself, with the initial dislocation such changes involve, depends upon the reading one gives the situation. For example: as more and more mothers go back to work, often when their babies are a few months old, are we witnessing a salutary act of individual

73

choice and change or a sad commentary on the relentless individualism and materialism of American life? Stark opposites get posed. It
is often difficult to carve out critical and political space between such
warring parties as fundamentalists who urge a return to the good—or
at least better—old days of traditional family roles and, say, those
radical feminists for whom the old days are a bleak picture of female
slavery in the phony guise of marital interdependence.

The debate really heats up in the matter of social and state policy
towards the family. Those dubious about the family and its social
relationships celebrate more intervention in order to shape the family
in line with some abstract vision of what they believe it ought to be.
Their worry is not family autonomy but a vision of social justice and
control. Others, and they are a very mixed group, find nothing new
and certainly nothing wholly benign about advocating policies that
bring more and more people under the wing of client-provider
relationships, hardly models of democratic equality. Family imagery
figures importantly in our social and political symbols and slogans,
permeates our most deeply rooted aspirations, fears, resentments,
and hopes, and runs like a rich current in and through American
fiction. But we seem to have made it almost impossible for families to
flourish. The crisis of the family has become a constant feature of
contemporary social reality.

The terms of this crisis are ongoingly redefined, but that there is a
crisis few seem to doubt; indeed, the crisis has become an endemic
feature of our social order. This raises some fascinating questions
about who gets to decide what constitutes a crisis in a fundamental
social institution, how that crisis gets placed on the political agenda,
and what sorts of remedies are proposed to end the crisis or, at least,
to ameliorate a situation fraught, as a crisis by definition must be,
with portentous implications for who we are as people, how we live,
and how we choose to see ourselves.

At one time in America families were more likely to be imbedded
within a network of kin ties and communal links than are families at
present. Communities and families were thought of as intergenerational groupings. The family was located in the community, yet
extended itself out into the wider social network. This wider network,
itself in part an extension of the family, also permeated each family's
inner workings by helping, at least ideally, to engender self-reliance
and self-respect and serving the emotional as well as the physical
needs of a family's children. At least that was the normative ideal.

Family members, for the most part, were born in or near homes and neighborhoods, though even before World War II demographic shifts were beginning to break up this somewhat idealized pattern.[1]

Whatever remained of the old way was shattered by the war and its aftermath. War industries called millions into the cities. Men, women, and whole families moved into urban centers for jobs in munitions plants, shipyards, and airplane factories. More than fourteen million men and women were incorporated into the armed forces. With men away, more and more women entered industry. After the war, people neither returned to old patterns nor to their traditional communities. The war sped a process of economic and government centralization. Old neighborhood businesses lost out; small farmers were squeezed out. Whole industries sprang up around new postwar technologies and consumer "needs."

The United States has no official family policy, despite the urgings of some welfare-state liberals, heirs of the progressive tradition, that we require one—the sooner the better. Jimmy Carter made the absence of such a policy a major theme of his 1976 presidential campaign. Carter pointed to various indices of family breakdown, including the high divorce rate. (In 1976, two out of five marriages ended in divorce. The figures now indicate that fully one-half of all marriages will culminate in divorce court, making the United States divorce rate by far the world's highest.) Carter also noted the rise in single-parent families—these figures too have continued to grow over the past decade. Given these and other matters suggesting that the two-parent family is under enormous social strain, Carter promised that, if elected, he would call a White House Conference on the American Family to propose a national family policy.

Before Carter could convene such a conference, the Carnegie Council on Children, as the culminating act of a five-year study of how public programs affect the family, proposed a "national family policy" on September 12, 1977. Specifically, the council called for (1) a full-employment program that would guarantee a job for every family's breadwinner, (2) a minimum income level for all families of at least one-half the nation's median family income, (3) a vastly re-vamped tax structure that would tax all income at 50 percent, offset only by a refundable tax credit, set at six thousand dollars for a family of four, and (4) a policy of looking to institutions for child care only as a last resort. The council's report, according to the *New York Times*,

"precedes from the premise that the American family is not disinte-
grating but in the midst of bewildering change."[2]

Tacitly, the council recognized that, in the absence of an explicit
national family policy, the pressure of the United States political
economy had shifted away from what might be seen as an *informal*
family wage structure. This is a complex change, not easy to explain,
that involves the transfer of the income tax burden onto families with
children, forms of federal subsidization, the massive entry of women
into the labor force given inflationary and other pressures, and so on.
The concatenated result of interventions and alterations was the construction of mothers and fathers more and more as wage earners.
Welfare policies often penalized the welfare mother who did not work
and in many states the "no man in the house rule" explicitly precluded
stable family relationships as a precondition for assistance, a contrib-
uting factor in the rise of black babies born out of wedlock. My intent
in this general and brief recitation of very complex social facts is not
to "judge" but to situate the family debate inside a rapidly changing
socio-economic matrix. The Carnegie report concluded that, "The
greatest single harm to children is poverty." The aim was to intervene
in a dramatic and systematic way to alleviate the stresses that helped
to account for the dimensions of the family crisis as the council understood them, including the restoration of a viable family wage.

It is also important to remember that the late 1970s and early 1980s
were times of terrific economic stress on middle-class families given
inflationary pressures. Articles on the "crush of family tensions,"
given the economic squeeze, proliferated in the newspapers. Again,
according to the *New York Times,* fear and insecurity invite psychological stress, and family members reported feeling anxious, desperate, angry, frustrated, and exhausted with husbands and wives "rub-
bing each other raw" in struggles over economic issues.

Working with this scenario, demands for explicit, comprehensive
governmental intervention in the creation of a family policy grew. But
nationwide regional hearings, preliminary to the 1980 White House
Conference on Families, fell into terminal bickering between and
among a variety of groups, including feminists, homosexuals, fundamentalists, welfare-state liberals, racial minorities, radical and conservative antiinventionists—the list goes on. Those in favor of a
national family policy saw it, in Diane Ravitch's words, as "the key to
unemployment, inflation, crime, juvenile delinquency, divorce, inadequate health and housing, poor education, alcoholism and drug
abuse, racial discrimination and media stereotyping, abortion and

family planning, adolescent pregnancy, tax reform, welfare reform, day care, foster care, flexible working schedules for working women."[3]

Both those in favor of and those opposed to a United States National Family Policy could point to family policies in fourteen Western and Eastern European nations, studied in Sheila Kamerman's and Alfred Kahn's *Family Policy*, to buttress robust hopes and to stoke gloomy fears. It is clear that such policies *do* affect intimate human relationships; indeed, such policies try to *guarantee* that such relationships mesh with wider national aims. These might include income redistribution, sex role changes, promoting the well-being of children, and lowering or raising the birth rate. In Sweden, for example, the government worked purposely to undermine what it called the "traditional" family in favor of a "transitional" family—one on the road to, but not yet fully exemplifying, total sex equality (as the Swedes understood it) and children's rights. The result of such intervention was a drop in the marriage rate, an increase in the illegitimacy rate, and a rise in single-parent households. To discourage stay-at-home mothering, the Swedish government disallowed child-care allowances for homemaking mothers. Norway pursued a similar policy, leading to a decline in the birth rate, a doubling of the divorce rate (from 1965–1980), and an increase in out-of-wedlock births. In France, however, children's allowances were available to mothers after the birth of a second child as a way to value at-home mothering. Again, my purpose in this snapshot glance at family policy is not to file a brief for or against such interventions but to indicate that they can have profound effects on private life. The relationship between policy and outcome is complex, but no serious observer doubts that policies as strong as Sweden's do alter social relationships.

Such recognitions, in a society as diversely contentious and at odds as this one, create a nearly hopeless situation if one's aim is to generate a systematic, uniform national family policy. Too many interests and identities clash. Thus, the Carter dream ran ashoal on the shores of acrimony with the National Gay Task Fore submitting a definition of the family as any two or more persons who take responsibility for each other (hence any support to the family in general must go to gay families under this loose definition) to "pro-family" lobbies who insisted that a family is "two or more persons related by blood, marriage, or adoption." Because every national family policy contains, in Ravitch's words, "a model, a point of view, a set of values about what kind of families and what kind of social behavior should be encouraged by government policy," and because no such agreed-upon values or point of view emerged from the Carter conferences, the effort further politicized the family crisis question without resolving anything.

There are no easy measurements for emotional impoverishment and spiritual decay, for the human despair amidst all the tree-lined deserted streets in affluent neighborhoods, for the mothers of young children isolated from parents, grandparents, aunts, uncles, sisters, brothers, and neighbors and with husbands off to work in cities thirty or forty miles away. The family, stripped of its prior centrality in community life, becomes an embattled enclave. For America's working classes, the dream of a better life stays mostly out of reach and sometimes their lives sour on that account. For the more mobile classes the reality of affluence has a dark underside: the stress of unending pressure to perform better, to move up, to move from one's "good" neighborhood to a "better" one in which the houses are bigger and even further apart and success seems to be measured by the capacity of the family to live in splendid isolation from other families and outside any wider community, in any meaningful sense, at all.

American families have borne the brunt of social change. We have passed some genuine watersheds. For the first time in our history the *typical* school-age child has a mother who works outside the home. Since the turn of the century the number of children affected by divorce has increased by over 700 percent. Those women who go to work out of economic exigency often find inadequate day care, or none, for their children. Social services, celebrated by some as a way either to rescue the family or to guarantee that women are rescued from it, penalize the least well-placed women, including the welfare mother who does not work and who would, in most instances, do a much better job of caring for her children, if she had minimal help in doing so, than those alternatives now available to her as she is forced into low-paying, dead-end jobs and prevented from setting up a viable family environment. In 1950, 15 percent of black children were born out of wedlock; by 1970 the figure had risen to 38 percent, in 1980 it stood at 55 percent, and the numbers continue to rise as we enter the 1990s.

These alarming figures, and others, convinced a group of leaders of more than one hundred national black organizations, who held a three-day "Black Family Summit" several years ago, that the black community must return to basic institutions and rely less upon the state. When those who ostensibly benefit the most from current welfare policies begin to criticize its effects the rest of us, especially middle-class liberals who sometimes support uncritically the idea that "more social services" automatically widen people's options and improve the quality of their lives, would do well to pay attention. Substituting state authority for family authority seems, all too often, to result in a situation in which there is no authority at all—no baseline for protecting our most intimate, vital social relations.

Thus, although the United States lacks a comprehensive national family policy, the family is daily affected by government policies in ways direct and indirect. At the moment we are bombarded with evidence that points either to a crisis or to change. In the absence of a family policy directed to "such currently unfashionable issues as child welfare and maternal health, or to children's allowances and a guaranteed minimum income," we respond with *problem-specific crisis intervention* that evades the deeper social issues, most important: Does a democracy have a stake in promoting a particular vision of the family?[4]

Some radical democrats, for example Christopher Lasch, and many middle-ground traditionalists, for example, Brigette and Peter Berger, say yes, that the family is the "necessary social context for the emergence of autonomous individuals who are the empirical foundation of political democracy."[5] Others, many of whom see themselves as progressives or social democrats, seem prepared to have the state take over and the family wither away or transform itself to mesh more precisely with a consumerist and welfarist culture. They dismiss as reactionary atavistic holdovers from some happily bygone era, analyses concerned about the family and about the unavoidable element of paternalism in our present problem-oriented welfare state approach. For example, John Scanzoni celebrates developments others take as signs of distress, reassuring us that the high divorce rate, the rise in single-parent households, and so on, are merely indicators of reorientation as the family jerks into greater harmony with the wider social surround—a market-oriented, mobile society.[6]

In light of our present discontents and drift, it is helpful to climb down from the height of general, broad-sweeping matters and to home in on one particular socially constructed problem that might shed light on present family-state conundrums. The question of child abuse will serve as my exemplar.

THE CONSTRUCTION OF CHILD ABUSE AS DISCOURSE
AND POLICY

Social problems are not like a first snow—immediately apparent to
the naked eye. Social realities can linger in a twilight of nonrecogni-
tion for years before they get designated as official, legitimate
problems, producing discourse and experts authorized to intervene:
battered wives and abused children are two recent examples. Both
phenomena have long existed but neither got lifted up to national
consciousness, media hyperattention, public policy initiative, and
alert police intervention until recently.[7] Every step of this process is
problematic: How does a social problem get "named"? Who gets to
define what is a problem in the first instance? What interests and
power relations are at stake? What interventions are invited and who
is empowered given the nature of the interventions sought?

Because the construction of a problem such as child abuse is closely
linked to the crisis of the family, a look at this specific issue as one
slice of current policy–popular debates helps to illumine the play of
social forces as these revolve around families, privacy, and state
intervention. The rationale for such an approach is this: a crisis
signifies a departure from some desired norm. Urgent cries to restore
the norm, or equally insistent celebration of breakdown as a break-
through to some desirable alternative, define the *range* of discourse by
setting a frame of preferred options at opposite ends of a presumed
continuum. How interlocutors to the debate *read* various social signs;
indeed, how those signs become visible in the first instance, helps the
political analyst get her own bearings as she explores the normative
implications of social problem definition.

Child abuse as a social construction did not exist until 1968. By that
I mean child abuse, which, according to Barbara J. Nelson, "did not
even warrant an entry in the *Reader's Guide to Periodical Literature*"
though 1967, emerged slowly as a matter for legislation and beefed-
up modes of government intervention.[8] By 1973, hearings were held
on a Child Abuse Prevention Act, with the usual parade of witnesses,
the most effective being reformed child abusers. Under the guidance
of Senator Walter Mondale (D., Minn.), the hearings ushered in the
Child Abuse Prevention and Treatment Act, signed into law by
President Richard M. Nixon on January 31, 1974, with a legislative
appropriation of eighty-six million dollars. Child abuse got constituted as a part of public discourse but in and through depoliticized
language.

This legislative initiative arose primarily as a response to *expert* discourse, most important that of doctors and psychologists. The way had been paved with the publication of "The Battered-Child Syndrome," by Dr. C. Henry Kempe and Associates in *The Journal of the American Medical Association* in 1962.[9] As in the maneuvering and testimony that played the determining role in the Supreme Court's abortion decision in 1973, *Roe vs. Wade*, what doctors had to say— medicalized language—was weighted more heavily than other modes of social discourse. Medicalizing the problem, construing it as a matter of individual deformation (a syndrome, a psychic malaise, a maladaption), the issue caught on in way it likely would not have if it had emerged as a question of structural marginalization, and the suborning of whole communities through unemployment, welfare clientage, drug use, and crime.

We—I mean we Americans here—are more open to the possibilities of government action if extant power arrangements remain undisturbed, as our seemingly desultory flailing about in the matter of family policy demonstrates. By medicalizing the question, removing it, in a sense, from political discourse, sponsors of the 1974 legislation garnered widespread support. In Nelson's words: "Strenuous efforts were made to popularize abuse as a problem knowing no barriers of class, race, or culture."[10] Child abuse became an "all-American affliction," one subject to therapeutic intervention with the police powers of the state as backup and backdrop.

Despite the fact that, in the words of Richard Gelles, a researcher in the field, "We don't know a *damn* thing about whether child abuse is increasing, decreasing, or staying the same," the belief that it is on the rise and spreading into ever more pervasive and pernicious forms seems to be one spin-off of concentrated attention on the question as a private psychodrama in which the state must take an interest. Monies appropriated in 1974 helped to fund individual state initiatives to improve reporting of abuse even as what was to count as abuse got murkier. Evading poverty and neglect, matters tied to deeply rooted power arrangements, the enthusiasts in the rapidly emerging child-abuse establishment worked energetically to *define the problem as a social illness endemic to families across the board*. Government intervention, therefore, took a case-by-case form and the pervasive stress on less privileged families created by their socio-economic marginalization got redirected yet again into established, and relatively safe, channels: as a matter for welfare.

That is one part of the story. Another is the way child abuse has been constructed as popular culture, a complex discourse that combines the official medicalized version of events with a hysteria that speaks to deeply rooted middle-class anxiety about what is happening with "the children." Visions of beaten, abducted, and sexually traumatized children exert a terrifying and even morbid fascination. Milk cartons carry somewhat indistinct photos of children under the banner, "MISSING", with an 800 number (The National Center for Missing and Exploited Children) to call if one makes a sighting. Missing children pop up on local and national news and in docudramas. They appear on the screen of movie theaters just before previews of coming attractions.

Glancing through a local publication consisting of advertisements placed by individuals to hawk no longer wanted household items, to sell cars, or to publicize tag sales, I came across a full page ad placed by "Child Seekers." The logo above the headline is a drawing of a human eye. A single teardrop tumbles down, partially covering the letter "d" in the word "child" below. Six children, with data, are pictured. In addition to the 800 call number, I am informed of the scope of the problem in bold capitals:

1.5 MILLION CHILDREN ARE REPORTED MISSING EACH YEAR.

SOME 20,000 TO 50,000 CHILDREN DISAPPEAR EACH YEAR AND THEIR CASES REMAIN UNSOLVED, SOME FOREVER.

3,000 UNIDENTIFIED BODIES ARE FOUND IN THE UNITED STATES EACH YEAR AND HUNDREDS OF THOSE ARE CHILDREN.

This is the stuff of nightmares. In addition to the promised terror of child abduction and molestation outside the home, we are bombarded with statistics and stories of abuse by parents, ranging from neglect, to incest, to repeated beatings, to murder. The May 1984 issue of *Newsweek*, headlined "The Hidden Epidemic," deployed a medical metaphor that signifies an out-of-control disease. The article included a "Letter from a Pedophile," which concluded with the words: "Have you hugged your kids today? If not, a child molester will!"

We are in the midst of a socially constructed crisis concerning this society's treatment of its children. The way this issue, or any highly charged matter, gains public attention is a complex coming together of political, economic, and cultural forces. As in the case of rape and battering, the problem of child abuse has been long with us. The particular ways in which the issues have been constructed as rhetoric and policy help us to understand a complex play of social forces. I shall parse out a bit of it to illumine the matter of just how problematic public policy problem definition really is.

First, who should be believed? Who we listen to tells us something about the climate in which we live. For example: several years ago I researched the "violence against women" question. I learned that the rate of forcible rapes, according to the most reliable statistics, showed little overall change as compared with the crime rate in general. Appalling as rape is, it accounts for a small percentage (about 6 percent) of violent crimes. Yet, as a result of public awareness inspired by the women's movement, and the insistence that the social cleavage that should be given most weight in looking at any issue is male versus female, we are not only *rightly* concerned about the crime of rape, we *wrongly* believe that rape is skyrocketing and that women are special targets of violent crime. But the figures on this score have been remarkably consistent for years: most perpetrators and victims of violent crimes are young males (ages sixteen to twenty-four).[11]

Or, take the highly charged matter of battering. The strongest, recent evidence is that "when all violence is considered, women in a family are as violent as men."[12] "All violence" refers to attacks on spouses with weapons as well as fists *and* assaults on children. This corroborates the findings of Evan Stark, Anne Flitcraft, and associates at Yale University that women attack and kill men "almost as frequently as they are attacked and killed" by men. As well, "as many as half the American women battered each year have no blood or legal ties to the men who assault them."[13] This suggests violence may be a symptom of familial tensions, or relational stress, in a time of widespread social dislocation rather than a *constant* feature of secure relationships in stable settings. It further suggests that we would do well to examine poverty and economic dislocation, especially the vulnerability of men to a stripping away of their social identity in periods of unemployment. For battering appears, again according to Stark and Flitcraft, when persons have been "isolated from potentially supportive kin and peer relations."[14] This implies that we are not looking at an intrinsic feature of family life in general but at a possible outcome of familial privatization given the breakdown of social constraints and supports for families.

But this latter, more radical construction calls into question the structure of our political economy in a way we seem unprepared to deal with; thus, battering has been constructed through a double-pronged medicalized and feminist discourse that stresses pathology, on the one hand, and patriarchy, on the other. Those with a stake in the "patriarchy is violent" hypothesis resist a more historically concrete approach because they divide the world up into male/female oppositions: what must be done is to denude the male of his violent power. They must ongoingly up the ante by insisting that males are violent across the board. Unsurprisingly, much media focus, especially the docudramas on this question, picture a beautiful suburban family, happy outside, corrupt on the inside. The offender is a handsome, high-achieving, professional white male. The distortions involved in getting across this image as a prototypical one are purposeful representations aimed at shoring up discourses that invite moral censure, ideological attacks on "the family," and interventions via the police and juridical apparatus of the state including its therapeutic arm. The more intractable questions of poverty and social marginalization, once again, can be bypassed.

Child abuse taps even deeper fears and rouses even stronger visceral reactions. But when I began to gather data I found it was very difficult to get a sense of the scope of the question—other than the repeated insistence that it was an "all-American problem." The purpose behind such slogans is to disassociate interventions against abuse from considerations of the effects of systematic deprivation. Although "a number of scholars severely criticized this approach and maintained that the larger number of cases found among the poor was not only a function of reporting biases, but was present because poor people actually abused or neglected their children more," not because they were "bad people" but because "the deprivations of poverty were real and encouraged abuse," they lost the discursive war. The "myth of classlessness" discourse of welfare liberals, therapeutic interventionists, and child-saving professionals, as Nelson shows, won the day.

The upshot is that we have entered a shadowy realm in which some form of child abuse is presumed as the norm rather than as a deviation from one. Those with a stake in upping the ante have garnered the media imprimatur. For example, under the headline, "Reports of Child Molestation Increase by 35%, Study Finds," the *Times* cites Anne H. Cohn, executive director of the National Committee for the Prevention of Child Abuse, that the soaring figures represent only "the tip of the iceberg." Her Chicago-based committee's report estimates instances of sexual molestation at 123,000 per year and overall abuse at 1,273,000 per year—again with the proviso that we can let those numbers rise as high as our Hobbesian imaginations take us. The committee report goes on to say that "the more we work to uncover the problem of child abuse, the more we are able to find."

True, no doubt, but what are "we" finding? It is impossible to get any clear definition of what constitutes "abuse" in the first place. Dr. Joyce Brothers, television's favorite pop psychologist, insists she was abused because society told her there were some things little boys were better at than little girls. This is a perfect example of spreading abuse around so that *all* are layered with a patina of guilt and more serious instances get trivialized. Trying to come up with empirical evidence on this question is like trying to eat jello with a table knife. But the most interesting question is not "how much" but "how come": why are we inclined at the moment to believe the most overblown figures? We have lurched to a stance in which those accused are presumed guilty until proven innocent. We have moved from doubting the veracity of children to constructing out of the often wrenching stories of children a scenario that puts all parents under suspicion and adds nursery school workers and child-care providers to the growing list of probable offenders.

Despite the fact that the vast majority of missing children are runaways, not abductees, and despite the fact that the figure of fifty thousand missing children, still used by Child Fund and other centers, is now declared to be "erroneous," we are told to believe the worst, indeed, we are urged to by those promoting various forms of state intervention.[15] Overall, the thrust of current school awareness programs (good touch/bad touch, role playing, etc.) aims to instill in children mistrust of family members and the placing of confidence in helping professionals. The results are not in on what this sort of "awareness training" does to children. It seems plausible that one result is to prematurely sexualize their relations with adults and to implant in the child's mind notions that were not previously there or present only in the form of vague apprehensions and sensations.

Professional child savers insist that we cannot protect children unless we make them fearful and suspicious so that they know when some wrong is being done. Maybe. But stories are also accumulating from divorced or separated fathers who say they are afraid to hold or hug their children, or even change soiled clothing, for fear a suspicious ex-spouse may conjure a tale of sexual abuse out of it. A spin-off of all of this is the fact that families, or the idea of the family, are further delegitimized given a particular configuration of volatile social question.

If families can't be trusted, and fall under suspicion, is day care any better? Not according to child-abuse professionals for whom nearly any situation is preferable to the child's own family.[16] A case of bad nerves about day care is the latest wrinkle. Current fears about day care speak to parental guilt, especially that of mothers, at leaving their children in less than optimal situations—the best many can afford. Anxieties about day care have come into focus at a time when more and more women, driven either by economic need, personal desire, or the growing insistence that women should get out of the home and into the "real world" of market society, are in the labor force. Although the vast majority of working mothers are not employed full-time, those with children under school age require day care. The high divorce rate further promotes a need for day care.

But we have made of day care an economic function, best performed by specialized providers. And the situation, at present, is pretty awful. We don't really respect those who care for children very much, so day-care workers receive lousy salaries, have few long-term prospects, and work under difficult conditions. Child care is severed altogether from the home. Shunting children off to their own places, we often feel something is wrong. But our political discourse doesn't seem to offer a language to grasp that queasiness. A medicalized and criminalized discourse offers answers: the problem is not day care but pathological day-care providers. What is wrong must be with particular individuals, not with the overreaching ordering of a political economy that pushes nearly everyone into a structure in which those who cannot work do not fit, including the very old and the very young.

The debate on day care Deborah Fallows calls for in her controversial book, A Mother's Work—controversial precisely because it calls for such a debate—gets deflected in favor of concentration on horror stories and scandals that tap guilt and promote a climate of fear and suspicion.[17] The overall poor quality of day care falls out of the debate, despite the fact that for-profit centers account for one-half of the country's day-care facilities and spend 45 percent less per child than federally funded centers—and they are not ideal. Eileen W. Linder, director of the Child Advocacy Office of the National Council of Churches, reports that the hysteria accompanying highly publicized reports of abuse in child-care centers prompted one hundred staff members in nine church-housed child-care centers in the Midwest to issue an ultimatum to their director: "Fearing they would be falsely accused of sexual abuse," Linder writes in the *Christian Century*, May 13, 1985, "they [child-care staffers] refused to return to work until the board of directors issued precise guidelines for physical contact with their young charges."

If day-care workers are frightened, and parents are paranoid, politicians and child-intervention professionals are prepared to do various things. One garden variety proposal is to beef up staffs in extant bureaucracies. In the Northeast, for example, budget increases in six New England states would "add a total of 221 child protective workers," according to the *Boston Globe*, June 12, 1985. The Department of Health and Human Services "Model Child Care Standards Act," 1985, proposed screening all potential employees by doing background checks for criminal records or past abuses, requiring probationary periods for all employees "until background checks are completed," and "training staff members" to detect and report abuse. In order to implement such proposals, a whole new level of bureaucracy must be set up. There is no evidence whatever that criminal records checks will prevent child abuse. Diana R. Gordon reported in the *New York Times*, March 2, 1984, that "among the more than six thousand day care workers fingerprinted and reviewed in the wake" of the Bronx day-care scandal of that year, "not a single one" had a record of sexual or any other abuse of a child.

Given our construction of child abuse as a social problem requiring therapeutic and police intervention, we have leapt into the arms of what one critic calls a "Big Daddy" approach. For the "Model Child Care Standards Act" as well as the proposed National Child Protection Act offers as a solution coercion and policing: withdrawing federal day-care funds from states that do not adhere to tight child-abuse monitoring programs and creating a national hotline for reporting allegations of child sexual abuse by day-care workers as well as requiring criminal records checks of all employees of day-care facilities. The likely result is a tightening up of the order and frightening many decent people away from day-care work entirely.

We should not be surprised at where the terms of our construction of child abuse have left us. Because, as a society, we can no longer agree on whether out-of-home or in-home child care is most helpful to human development—and we can't agree, first, because the data aren't clear and, second, because we have a stake in muddling the issue given the powerful forces arrayed on both sides of the question—it is not surprising that we have not determined the type and amount, or even whether, day care is desirable. The day-care centers that work well and do right by children who are happy, talkative, and playful rather than despondent, withdrawn, sullen are those integrated into the home and work life and parentally controlled. To endorse that as a model for day care nationally requires important political initiatives to soften many of the most harsh features of our political economy, including our relentless demands for productivity that constitute people as wage earners, leaving them precious little time to be family and community men and women, parents, friends, activists, and sharers in a way of life. Were we to alter the surround in which child care, both familial and institutional, takes place, this problem would take on more appropriate proportions and colorations. For what is at stake in the family debate is our sense of self, responsibility, and place.

7

The New Eugenics and Feminist Quandaries: Philosophical and Political Reflections

It is especially the female body, with its unique capacity to create human life, which is being expropriated and dissected as raw material for the industrial production of humans. For us women, for nature and for the exploited people of this world this development is paramount to a declaration of war. For us women it means a further step towards the end of self-determination over our bodies, our ability to procreate and consequently our ultimate dependence on medical experts. We declare that we do not need or want this technology and that we fight it for what it is: a declaration of war on women and nature.

> Bonn Conference: Women Against Gene Technology and Reproductive Technologies, April, 1985

Normative heterosexuality must be replaced by a situation in which the sex of one's lovers is a matter of social indifference, so that the dualist categories of heterosexual, homosexual and bisexual may be abandoned . . . . We must remember that the ultimate transformation of human nature at which socialist feminists aim goes beyond the liberal conception of psychological androgyny to a possible transformation of "physical" human capacities, some of which, until now, have been seen as biologically limited to one sex. This transformation might even include the capacities for insemination, for lactation and for gestation so that, for instance, one woman could inseminate another, so that men and nonparturitive women could lactate and so that fertilized ova could be transplanted into women's or even men's bodies. These developments may seem farfetched, but in fact they are already on the technological horizon; however, what is needed much more immediately than technological development is a substantial reduction in the social domination of women by men. Only such a reduction can ensure that these or alternative technological possibilities are used to increase women's control over their bodies and thus over their lives, rather being used as an additional means for women's subjugation. Gayle Rubin writes: "We are not only oppressed *as* women, we are oppressed by having to *be* women or men as the case may be."

> Alison M. Jagger, *Feminist Politics and Human Nature*

I dedicate these reflections to my daughter, Sheri, who has triumphed over such tags as minimal brain dysfunction, cerebral deficit, behaviorally disadvantaged, mentally challenged, and mildly retarded by describing herself, simply, as someone who "thinks different." Also, thanks to Tobi Elkin, who undertook bibliographical searches, photocopied materials, checked out books, and discussed with me the questions I explore in the pages to follow.

This essay is *not* about in vitro fertilization, AID (artificial insemination by donor), embryo flushing, surrogate embryo transfer, surrogate motherhood, sex preselection, cloning—the entire panoply of real or potentially realizable techniques for manipulating, redirecting, controlling, and altering human reproduction—so much as it is a consideration of assumptions that underscore and undermine alternative feminist positions towards these frightening (on one view) or potentially hopeful and helpful (on another) developments. The two preceding quotations offer some inkling of just how vexed the entire matter of radical intrusion into human biology and our ideas, and ideals, of embodiment, childbirth, human intimacy, and intergenerational ties have become to feminists. The Bonn Conference represents a radical *noninterventionist* stance; the position spelled out by Jagger, a feminist philosopher, is radically *prointerventionist*, so much so that it foresees technological elimination of males and females themselves. There are, of course, feminists ranged in between these two polar stances.[1]

But the perplexities deepen as one explores various feminist positions for one discovers that there are often ways in which an *explicit* stance—say, opposition to surrogacy—is undermined by a tacit commitment to a framework embedded in ontological presumptions that erode one's political refusals. Needless to say all this needs parsing out, and I will attempt to do so in a way that does not bog down in analytical finery but remains on ground accessible to all thoughtful and reasonably well-informed readers.

It is necessary to set the stage for current debates, including the way in which such highly visible controversies as the "Baby M." case stirred up so much turmoil inside feminist circles, by locating modern feminist positions within particular discursive and historic traditions. The dominant forms of contemporary American feminism are heavily indebted to a stance I shall tag *ultraliberalism*. One need not espouse all the features of ultraliberalism in order to be held captive to it—it is in the air we breathe, it is, as Wittgenstein might put it, a *picture* that holds us captive "and we cannot get outside it, for it lay in our language and language seemed to repeat it to us inexorably."[2]

No one among us can shed altogether her cultural skin. But each of us can become more reflective about what makes our social and political order what it is. One can reconceive relations and practices, perhaps to reveal a richness and ambiguity received formulae conceal. One aim of the social theory I embrace—an interpretive, desimplifying enterprise—is to work toward a more complete description of what is really going on, of how things are with us. This may be done, or attempted, in a number of ways. One might expose certain practices and doctrines as self-defeating or, alternatively, rescue other practices and ideals as vital to a cherished vision of the human community. No doubt one cannot require of political activists that they be self-critical and reflective about their enterprise from its inception—given the heat of battle, the demand for solidarity, the urgency to get results. So they proceed: "We hold these truths to be self-evident." Self-evident truths are often bulwarks, common rallying points, and powerful symbolic markers. But they may rapidly become a liability, locking social participants into usages that point them down dubious paths to either liberation or wisdom. Such seems to me the story of feminism and the doctrine of ultraliberalism.

The reigning ultraliberal frame cannot be stretched to cover every form of feminist association and identity. My hunch is that many grass-roots feminists, absorbed in immediate and practical concerns like health care, sanctuary for battered women, school curriculum questions, and so on, have not troubled themselves overmuch concerning their underlying philosophy. And that philosophy—again a hunch—would probably emerge as a pastiche, a combination of maternal and community imperatives, including care and sharing, plus evoking "rights" and "choice" as absolutes, or nearly so. The new eugenics puts terrific pressure on feminists who are not ultraliberals in particular ways, just as it compels those in the ultraliberal camp to push the envelope about as far as it can go, to come out explicitly for total human control over "nature"—but only if women control that control. Of this more follows, but first, further unpacking of the dominant philosophic presumptions of ultraliberalism and the stance towards our embodiment they tend to yield—after I lodge the usual cowardly caveat.

I do not share the view of some critics who proclaim our liberal inheritance a rotten deal through and through. Liberalism is not of a piece. By distinguishing ultraliberalism from liberalism as such, I hope to avoid painting a monochrome picture. Although I believe sources for political renewal are present within liberalism, I find these options under pressure to succumb to the force of those beliefs, practices, and commitments I shall criticize. This is a worry. If I am even partially correct, it means that the dominant liberalism, its priorities and doctrines deployed increasingly as vehicles and rationalizations for newer modes of social control, has become self-defeating. Inside this picture, one is stuck with more of what has helped to sicken us in the first place: final rationalization and disenchantment of all aspects of social life; deeper dependency of the self on antidemocratic bureaucracies and social engineering—and now genetic engineering—elites; a more complete stripping away of the last vestiges of personal authority (construed as domination), traditional identities (construed as irrational and backward), and so on. The entanglement of contemporary feminism with *this* liberal project is a feature of the social order that often goes unmarked, perhaps even unthought.

THE ATOMIST TURN IN POLITICAL DISCOURSE: BACKGROUND CONUNDRUMS

What makes ultraliberalism run? The foundational motor that moves the system is a particular notion of the self. That self helps to make ultraliberalism what it complicatedly is, including its characteristic construal of social reality. There is no single, shared understanding of the self that grounds all forms of liberal theorizing. The transcendental subject of Kant's deontological liberalism, for example, is a being at odds with the prudential calculator of Bentham's utilitarianism. Ultraliberalism's vision of the self flows from seventeenth-century atomist discourse, a doctrine linked to the names of Hobbes and, much less securely, Locke. Atomism posits a self as given, prior to any social order—ahistorical, unsituated, a bearer of abstract rights, an untrammeled chooser in whose choices lies his (and initially this character was a "he") freedom and autonomy.

One uneliminable feature of atomism, then, "is an affirmation of what we could call the primacy of rights."[3] Although atomism ascribes primacy to rights, it denies the same status to any principle of belonging or obligation. Primacy of rights has been one of the important formative influences on the political consciousness of the West. We remain so deeply immersed in this universe of discourse that most of us most of the time unthinkingly grant individual rights automatic force: in our political debates rights are trumps. Atomism makes this doctrine of primacy plausible by insisting on the "self-sufficiency of man alone or, if you prefer, of the individual."[4] Closely linked to the primacy of rights is the central importance atomists attach to freedom understood as "freedom to choose one's own mode of life," to constitute and choose values for oneself.[5] In making freedom of choice an absolute, atomism "exalts choice as a human capacity. It carries with it the demand that we become beings capable of choice, that we rise to the level of self-consciousness and autonomy where we can exercise choice, that we not remain mired through fear, sloth, ignorance, or superstition in some code imposed by tradition, society, or fate which tells us how we should dispose of what belongs to us."[6] Solidified by market images of the sovereign consumer, this atomist self was pitted with great success against the self of older, "unchosen" constraints.

Thus we find gender preselection presented as a choice, a consumer preference, or an "option."[7] Surrogacy is lodged in the language of contractual rights, rights so sacrosanct they override the right of the surrogate mother to change her mind and keep the baby after birth: or so 61.8 percent of respondents in a Gannent News Service–*USA Today* poll claimed in the aftermath of the "Baby-M." trial. The rights of Mr. Stern to enforce a contract were favored three to one, indicating that when I write of a society entangled with the atomist project I speak not just of elites but of a wider population.[8]

This atomist picture of freedom remains so deeply entrenched that we tend to see the natural condition or end of human beings as one of self-sufficiency. Atomism's vision of self, its absolutizing of choice, and its celebration of radical autonomy all cast suspicion on ties of reciprocal obligation or mutual interdependence and help to erode the traditional bases of personal authority in family and polity alike. Feminists make their indebtedness to atomist construals powerfully manifest when they proclaim choice an absolute, granting the "right to choose" *prima facie* force. The likely result is that any perceived constraint or chastening of individual choice is suspect and will be assessed from the standpoint of the atomist standard. There is another outcome. Once choice is made absolute, important and troubling questions that arise as one evaluates the writ over which individual right and social obligation, respectively, should run are blanked out of existence. One simply gives everything, or nearly so, over to the individualist pole in advance. Embracing free choice and primacy of rights as self-evident truths makes sense, of course, for, as the daughters of liberal society, women *have* been deprived of freedom understood in the ways I have just described.

Moving from the plane of abstract discussion to a particular question, feminist images of *the body*, deepens our awareness of the background to dilemmas for feminism presented by the new eugenics. The female body has been constituted as the locus of a struggle for control. To appreciate descriptions and evaluations of the body, whether in early radical feminism, liberal feminism, or much Marxist feminism, one must first look back at liberalism's historic suspicion of the body and its desires. Classical liberalism valorized a public world in which adult (male) persons, stripped of particular passion, shared an identical commitment to prudential reason. The arbitrariness of desire was consigned to the nonpublic sphere; it lay outside the official writ of the liberal *episteme*.[9] Yet this potentially chaotic and uncontrollable desire was required to hold liberal rationalism intact, serving as its mirror opposite. Keeping the beasts in their place milling about inside the private corral, liberals aimed to liberate men from a double subjection: to the rule of the traditional patriarch and to privatized passion.[10]

John Stuart Mill accepted this bifurcation, contrasting Reason with the abyss of Instinct, "the worse rather than the better parts of human nature."[11] The rational man, striving for an "apotheosis of Reason," must reject utterly the "idolatry" of "Instinct," an idolatry "infinitely more degrading than any others."[12] When relations between men and women are lifted up to the realm of reason, Mill declares, then and only then will they be free from the taint of unscrupulous desire. The body itself must come under the sway of the wider social force of rationalization and its ethos, one that dictates setting to one side, or stripping away, all distinctions and specific identities that situate us and define us as particular beings rather than universal, abstract agents. And it is true that to make good on Mill's version of the liberal promise, men and women must abstract *from* their sexual identities, eschew "arbitrary passions," and only then usher in the halcyon world of sex equality.[13]

Occlusion and denial of the body became a dominant thread in modern feminist discourse. Mill's insouciance gave way to Simone de Beauvoir's disdain. Her animus, though extreme, makes discursive sense within the framework of Sartrian existentialism. Beauvoir's excoriation of the female body as "inessential," a prefixed abyss that condemned women to a nether world of unfreedom (Immanence), bearing the stigma, "victim of the species," is by now familiar to social theorists. Beauvoir constituted the body as an alien Other, the enemy of the free project of Transcendence. The woman, by definition, was an alienated being given her biological capacity to bear a child. Menstruation, childbirth, nursing—all were portrayed by Beauvoir as a chamber of bodily horrors.[14] Sharing a central marker of atomism, Beauvoir split the rational self from its unfree—if one was female—embodiment.

Beauvoir helped to set the terms for a feminist repudiation of embodiment that reached its apogee with Shulamith Firestone's 1972 tract, *The Dialectic of Sex*. Her indebtedness to Beauvoir made explicit, Firestone located the oppression of women *in nature:* we are oppressed *because* we are embodied. Swallowing whole a depiction of nature as the unfree, unthought—lacking sentience and meaning—Firestone embraced atomism, technocratic hubris, genetic engineering, and a rather muddled notion of aesthetics as her feminist utopia. The question for us now is not whether these are extreme voices but whether, in perhaps extreme form, they point to broader forces at work in, and on, feminism. As the scrambling for position over the new eugenics in its many manifestations shows, our embodiment remains for feminists a serious predicament.

DAMAGE CONTROL: HOW FEMINISTS ARE CONFRONTING THE EUGENICS CHALLENGE

Although feminist discourse from the mid-1960s on was lodged securely in the notion of reproductive freedom, few feminist thinkers paid much attention to newer technologies for controlling human reproduction other than to issue briefs in behalf of a 100 percent safe and effective contraception and in behalf of no limits to abortion on demand. The voices from within the feminist camp that questioned arguments for abortion couched *exclusively* in the language of absolute freedom of choice, or rights, did not prevail in the debates. These voices now seem prescient given the runaway developments in reproductive technology and genetic engineering of the past decade. How, then, are feminists responding?

For one group, the *radical prointerventionists*, the new eugenics presents no problem so long as it can be wrested from male control. Early radical interventionists construed technology instrumentally—it will help to usher in a wholly new social order, a feminist utopia, so long as feminists struggle towards this end. (Though their historic teleology dictated that this end was well nigh irresistible.) Thus

Firestone offered us the cybernetician as the modern saviour. Her scenario for salvation went like this: (1) free women from biological tyranny; (2) this freeing will undermine all of society and culture, which is erected upon biological tyranny and the family; (3) all systems of oppression, including the economy, state, religion, and law erected upon the family will erode and collapse. The woman who absorbed Firestone's position could work to attain this promised future by *seizing control* of reproduction and *owning* her own body. Ultimately, Firestone continued, test-tube babies would replace biological reproduction as the chief means of reproduction, pregnancy having been declared "barbaric" with the "fat lady" peered at by strangers, laughed at by children, and deserted by feckless husbands. Full victory would be achieved when every aspect of human life rested in the beneficent hands of a "new elite of engineers, cyberneticians."[15] The child, with no need to be "hung up" by authoritarian parents (parents having pretty much melted away), is free to bargain for the best deal in contracted households.

Interestingly, although some feminist theorists criticized Firestone from the moment her book appeared, it is only with the advent of the new eugenics that her work is being treated with widespread skepticism—if it is mentioned at all. Thus Anne Donchin writes:

Though Firestone's advocacy of technological reproduction aims to serve feminist interests, it rests on conceptual foundations that have much in common with the presuppositions of researchers and policymakers who would . . . support technological interventionists for the sake of the monopoly of power it would make possible. Both sorts of interests view technology as "a victory over nature." . . . Both see human biology as a limitation to be overcome—for Firestone, because she takes the relations of procreation to be . . . the source of women's oppression; for those who would support "a brave new world," because the diffusion of power among women and families threatens their own power hegemony.[16]

At the heart of the radical interventionist position is an insistence that biological "tyranny" must end with its corollary demand that biological sex and social gender can, and must, be sharply severed— at least until such time as these categories have altogether disappeared. The only possible opposition to the new eugenics that might emerge from the prointerventionist camp takes the form of warning that evil forces—masculinists, antifeminists—are controlling the means of control. Therefore an ongoing political struggle is required to be sure patriarchalists do not succeed in this effort. But prointerventionist caveats have been compromised by the fact that they *share* rather than *oppose* all the ontological assumptions of their opponents: that "nature" must be overcome; that where human beings find the will to indulge such acts of transcendence they must find a way; that only the fearful and the backward will cavil at these inexorable developments—again, with the interventionists insisting that if women are in charge the outcomes will be beneficent.

I find nothing in the prointerventionist literature that offers up a strong, principled objection to a claim such as the following—from Peter Singer and Deane Wells: "If the creation of new forms seems a godlike power, what more noble goal can humanity have than to aspire to it? Like Prometheus, the mythical Greek hero who defied the gods and stole from them the secret of fire, should we not challenge the gods and make their powers our own? Or to put it in more scientific terms, should we allow ourselves to remain at the mercy of genetic accident and blind evolution when we have before us the prospect of acquiring supremacy over the very forces that have created us?"[17] Seeing in women's links to biology, birth, and nurturance only the vestiges of our animal origins and patriarchal control, anything that breaks those links is by definition to be applauded. Firestone's celebration of a technological resolution to woman's "control deficit" portrays absolute control over reproduction as the "final freedom"—a position she shares with nonfeminist prointerventionists. But they are now on the defensive, as feminist apprehensions have risen.

RISING CONCERN AND THE GREENING OF FEMINISM

In June 1979, a workshop on "Ethical Issues in Human Reproduction Technology: Analysis by Women" was held at Hampshire College, Amherst, Massachusetts. The workshop was structured around important issues: contraception; sterilization abuse; prenatal diagnosis; neonatology; sex preselection; and such "manipulative reproductive technologies" as in vitro fertilization, egg fusion, and cell manipulation. The organizers aimed for a "women-centered analysis," defined as "total: physical, mental, emotional" in contrast to "male-centered" principles of domination, objectification, exploitation, hierarchism, and profit. Foreseeing the final resolution of *all* value conflicts once women's values came to prevail, one of the conference organizers optimistically looked forward to "real solutions" to the many dilemmas of the new technology.

Divided between the bad "them" and the good "us," the conference paper givers—with few exceptions—presaged more recent developments pitting patriarchalists against women/nature. Tellingly, only one participant raised the question of eugenics—claiming that women shouldn't really be talking about "amniocentesis and similar techniques without putting it in the context of the search for the 'bad gene'." Ruth Hubbard went on to remind participants that the eugenics that had its heyday in the latter part of the nineteenth and early part of the twentieth centuries (and that was supported by such birth-control advocates as Margaret Sanger) died because its techniques were imperfect. But our techniques have improved—so must our vigilance, she insisted. One participant challenged feminist use of gender preselection as a way to eliminate male fetuses—following artificial insemination—as "stupendously sexist." But for the most part participants celebrated women centering and the need for women to control reproductive technology.[18]

The ten years since that conference have witnessed an efflorescence of feminist antitechnological efforts concentrating on nuclearism and war, on the one hand, and biology, on the other. The powerful voices to emerge are more "green" than "red," more separatist than integrationist, that is, they believe women must stand apart from the principles of patriarchal society rather than seek equality on a par with men. The *radical noninterventionists* now dominate the debate and other feminists are compelled to elaborate their own positions in relation to those of the radicals. Seeking to salvage the principle of women's right to choose and wrest it from men's attempts to control, the noninterventionists have fashioned a potent rhetoric and conjured with terrifying scenarios inviting, or catalyzing, moral panic on the part of readers who are, as I am, sympathetic to many of their concerns.

Continuing to "demand the right to choose," the noninterventioists are pondering the nature of the many coercive choices the new reproductive technology seems to throw up. Is amniocentesis really a free choice or is it a manipulative and coercive procedure with only one *correct* outcome, to abort if the fetus is "defective"? What about the "right" to a child—is it absolute or is this, too, yet another imposition of patriarchal society upon women who see themselves as failures if they cannot get pregnant? As well, the values identified with mothering (even under patriarchal controls) are now being reassessed as feminists are encouraged to experience maternity in a "nonexploitative way."

The antiinterventionist argument, as articulated by its most radical proponents, shares with prointerventionists the assumption that all of human social life and all of history is patriarchal. The difference is that the antiinterventionists hold that all modern technology is designed explicitly to deepen and extend patriarchal control and masculinist patterns of thought. They are deeply skeptical that *this* technology can be turned to good purposes. Thus nuclear arms cannot be controlled; they must be eliminated. Thus nearly all new forms of reproductive engineering cannot be reconfigured to meet feminist and women's needs; they, too, must be deconstructed. Working from the analogy of prostitution, radical noninterventionists insist that just as males moved successfully to control female "sex parts" through various forms of prostitution (including marriage), so they seek a new reality: the reproductive brothel. Writes Andres Dworkin: "Women can sell reproductive capacities the same way old-time prostitutes sold sexual ones . . . . While sexual prostitutes sell vagina, rectum, and mouth, reproductive-prostitutes will sell other body parts: Wombs. Ovaries. Eggs."[19] (Needless to say, this position is condemnatory of all men and contemptuous of many women.)

Gena Corea, perhaps the most visible North American feminist antiinterventionist and founder of FINRRAGE (Feminist International Network of Resistance to Reproductive and Genetic Engineering), insists that the patriarchal state reduces "women to Matter." She portrays men as having such total control that they compel the choices "women learn to want to make." Her book, *The Mother Machine,* is a scary portrait of present and future horrors as she moves from the farmyard to the bedroom, showing the ways in which methods first developed as part of animal husbandry are making their way—all part of patriarchal plots, on her view—into human lives.[20] It would be all too easy to dismiss the arguments being made by noninterventionists because their underlying philosophic assumptions are so dubious: women = nature = good; men = antinature = bad. But it is hard to figure out how to pick and choose.

Here are a few suggestions. The hard-line feminist antiinterventionist can be questioned, not so much because of what its proponents *oppose* but because of the reasons proffered for this opposition. Their arguments turn on no developed moral position concerning the nature of the human community and moral responsibility, preferring to focus instead on dubious equations of women and nature, hence as the only true source of creativity. As well, by continuing to assert an absolute right to choose but *only so long* as the choices are *true* choices, not *false* ones, the antiinterventionists promote a world in which good girls (women-identified women) must fight not only patriarchs but bad girls (male-identified women). Thus the lesbian who wants to assert her right to "independent motherhood" has every right to artificial insemination. But the woman in a heterosexual relationship who, with her husband, opts for in vitro fertilization is a hapless dupe of patriarchal wiles. This won't do.[21]

One can share the apprehension of antiinterventionists concerning eugenics but deepen and expand their worries as part of an alternative philosophy. I read document after document condemning the new reproductive engineering *because* it meant patriarchal society would seek to eliminate women through genetic manipulation—a rather wild idea. Screening out and eliminating imperfect fetuses also got targeted by many antiinterventionists as a patriarchal perversion. Most do not want to interdict the possibility, but the decision to abort a "defective" fetus must be solely that of the mother and made in a noncoercive setting. Yet this early detection and selective elimination of the imperfect unborn relies on the very technology the antiinterventionists condemn as patriarchal. To be genuinely compelling, the antiinterventionists would have to extend their opposition to eugenics to include gender preselection on the part of feminists going through AID (artificial insemination by donor). Either one does or does not have moral permission to eliminate the unborn on the basis of gender. But this they will not argue because a preferential option for the female fetus is part of the arsenal of weapons to fight patriarchal society.

The radical antiinterventionists are right to insist that "technical progress is not neutral." But to counterpose good women's values to bad male values gets us nowhere. There are women as well as men who support these technologies—some in the name of feminism. To insist, as does one antiinterventionist, that "we can no longer subscribe to the technocratic utopia of Bebel and all the other scientific socialists who think that the liberation of women will come with the electrification of the kitchen (Bebel) or with microprocessors or even through technical 'liberation' from the biological process of childbirth (Firestone), in short, by the further 'development' of productive forces plus socialism . . . . The so-called new technology does not bring us and our children any kind of qualitative or quantitative improvement in our lives, it solves none of our basic problems, it will advance even more the exploitation and humiliation of women; therefore we do not need it," strikes a very sympathetic chord with

many who do not share the full panoply of antiinterventionist
assumptions.[22] And warning flags are going up in unexpected places,
including the *Village Voice,* which featured a piece on "the selling of in
vitro fertilization" in which the author indicates that "tears of
gratitude" sprang to her eyes when a priest on an ethics panel
mentioned "conjugal intimacy"—the only person to do so in a
week-long discussion of reproduction that was otherwise "desexed,
disembodied, dehumanized."[23]

MODERATE INTERVENTIONISTS AND QUEASY FEMINISTS

We have traversed enough territory for the reader to appreciate the
python-like grip of the atomistic world view, of ultraliberalism, on the
thinking of interventionists and antiinterventionists alike. The more
consistent—though deadlier—position of the interventionists, whether
of the feminists I have discussed or the many more plentiful technocrats,
"pharmacrats," scientists, and profit makers is thoroughly saturated with
the ontological presumptions of this potent *Weltanschauung.* The radical
antiinterventionists feature a farrago of ultraliberal and preliberal,
romantic-expressivist presumptions linking women and nature: I have in
mind the hard-core greens. But most feminists, and most people generally (or so I would guess), belong fitfully in between, hopeful that real
help might come to infertile couples but in ways that seem human and
humane; concerned to "do something" about human suffering but worried about eliminating human beings who seem, to many eyes, to *be*
suffering by definition. (I refer to children born with spina bifida, or
Down syndrome, or any number of other congenital conditions.) Most
folks support contraception and do not want abortion made illegal—but
neither are they "proabortion."

Take, for example, a report issued by the National Council of
Churches of Christ (USA), who offered a "cautious but positive
stance" toward the emerging technology. Casting human beings as
cocreators, the report builds on a particular interpretation of dominion from Genesis and Psalm 8, going on to a claim that the Scripture
"exalts the idea that men and women are coming into the full exercise
of their given powers of co-creation" with genetic engineering as the
case in point.[24] Or the position of Ruth Hubbard, cited earlier, who
opposes eugenic and fiscal arguments for abortion but supports
particular women who may want to "avoid bearing a child with a
disability"—in light of an often unsupportive wider social
surround.[25] One finds a shaky combination of *sic et non.*

The Baby M. case crystallized this queasiness and prompted further refining of what might be called the moderate position. (Just how
moderate is, of course, a matter for debate.) Here was a case in which
everyone "freely" agreed to a contract. Unsurprisingly, the upsurge
in feminist opposition to commercial surrogacy and Judge Sorkow's
decision flummoxed several well-meaning sorts, including one David
Lipset, who wrote a letter to the *Times* in favor of "orthodox western
feminism," which, he claimed, *must* support surrogacy as a way to lay
"to rest the old Freudian saw that women were biologically destined
to little more than mother."[26] Why were feminists perversely reaffirming the importance of biological motherhood, he opined, or,
rather, pined?

A good question. Betty Friedan claimed that the initial decision
denying Mary Beth Whitehead *any* claim—she was no mother of any
kind in any way—had "frightening implications for women." Warm-
ing to the subject, Friedan continued: "It is a terrifying denial of the
personhood of women—the complete dehumanization of women. It
is an important human rights case. To put it at the level of contract law
is to dehumanize women and the human bond between mother and
child."[27] Feminists homed in on Judge Sorkow's attack on Mary Beth
Whitehead's competency to mother and on the degradations of the
commercialization of surrogacy, with intermediaries receiving fees of
ten thousand dollars or more for arranging contracts: "pimps" Friedan
and others called them. (Of course this makes surrogate mothers
prostitutes but perhaps it is best not to spell this out.)

Some feminists pointed to the fine points in the contract that
required that Mary Beth Whitehead abort on William Stern's demand
should the fetus show any signs of "physiological abnormality"
following amniocentesis: many found this repugnant and, yes,
immoral—*because* the male got to order it, not because such abortion
is repugnant on principle. All feminists aroused by this question
circled around a vital point—that, in Friedan's words, "the claim of
the woman who has carried the baby for nine months should take
precedence over the claim of the man who has donated one of his fifty
million sperm." The most eloquent statement of feminist outrage
came from Katha Pollitt who wrote, in *The Nation*: "What William
Stern wanted, however, was not just a perfect baby; the Sterns did
not, in fact, seriously investigate adoption. He wanted a perfect baby
with his genes and a medically vetted mother who would get out of
his life forever immediately after giving birth."[28]

In the several years since the initial shock of Baby M., feminist queasiness *concerning* feminist queasiness has begun to appear. Ellen Willis put it this way in the *Village Voice:* "To permit surrogacy for pay encourages the exploitation of women; to ban its limits women's autonomy. To let the biological mother abrogate a surrogacy contract if she changes her mind—and not give the father the same right— violates the concept of equal rights and responsibilities for both sexes; to force a woman to give up a child she has borne—or let a man decide not to take the child—denies the difference between pregnancy and sperm donation, between men's power and women's vulnerability." Willis finds a way out—feminists just haven't been radical enough, hence this quandary (posed within the framework of ultraliberal assumptions, of course, as she parses the matter), namely, "Since it's only in a system in which children belong, literally, to their parents that the concept of surrogacy makes sense, the starting point for sorting out its contradictions should be questioning the nature of the family."[29]

We are back full circle, to concerns with the nature of human intimacy and the family. That is as it should be. The new eugenics cannot be disarticulated from a wider cultural and social surround. All eugenics world views with which I am familiar aim to eliminate, undermine, or leapfrog over the family in order to achieve their ends. The same holds for modern eugenicists: the family is a drag on radical forms of social and genetic engineering. Women's attachment to their own children is a problem. The fact that people continue to sort themselves out into families is a problem. It would be far easier if natural pregnancy could somehow be phased out. But, in the meantime, newer and better ways to convince people to participate in eugenics efforts (under other names, of course) must be devised.

What makes this so complicated a concern for so many feminists is the fact that many spokesmen and women committed to a strong normative vision of the two-parent family, particularly those who sustain this vision with religious commitment, oppose the new eugenics. But feminists indebted to ultraliberalism, having located the family as the root of oppression, find it difficult to make common cause with those who see the family as the preferred social site where vulnerable humanity should be nurtured and sustained. Thus one finds feminist attacks on the Warnock Report (the report requested by the government of Great Britain) because it states: "We believe that as a general rule it is better for children to be born into a two-parent family, with both father and mother." This gets construed as elitist and denying to women the possibility for "independent motherhood."[30]

My conclusion to these reflections, then, is a recognition: feminist quandaries concerning the new eugenics inexorably pitch feminists back into discussions of men, women, children, families, and the wider community. To insist with all radical and many equal rights and Marxist feminists that we must *have* done with evoking any norm of the family that consists of men, women, and offspring and must, instead, remain neutral as to how people organize their private lives may, paradoxically, have opened up those lives, especially the lives of women, to more extensive forms of control. The evocations of "independent motherhood" that I keep running across are really rather sad. For the minuscule number who opt for such robust independence—whether as part of a lesbian relationship or on the part of an economically well-off career woman who can afford full-time child care after she has given birth to her out-of-wedlock baby—there are tens of thousands who are displaced homemakers or client-dependents of a welfare-state bureaucracy. These women would *prefer* to be part of an intact family. Outside of that network they are more, not less, vulnerable.

But simply reaffirming a family norm will not do either. Somehow we must find a compelling way to think about the entanglement of the lives of all Americans, but especially upper-middle-class educated sort of Americans, male and female, with the atomist project, including the notion that one can and should achieve as much control over one's life as possible. The search for intrusive intervention in human reproduction comes from those able to command the resources of the genetic engineers and medical reproduction experts. They are prepared to accept a remarkable degree of surveillance and manipulation of their intimate lives given the fetish of control fused with the strange *demand* that babies can and must be made whenever the *want* is there. In this way human procreation is transformed into a technical operation and that, in the long run, promotes a project of what Oliver O'Donovan calls "scientific self-transcendence." O'Donovan claims that in our own culture *curiositas* has become a "sin of the masses . . . . The liberal revolution arose, and will continue to evolve, in answer to a mass desire of western civilization, in which we all participate and not at the behest of a few scientists."[31] It is important to locate feminism within this wider project and to recognize that many feminists are troubled by the Frankenstein monster we seem to be unleashing.

Section Three

Going Public

Reformers, martyrs, revolutionists, are never fighting against evil only; they are also placing themselves in opposition to a good—to a valid principle which cannot be infringed upon without harm.

George Eliot

8

Relying on Nature: Are You Eligible for Membership in Allan Bloom's Fraternity?

Everybody got into the act on this one. Debates about Bloom's book raged for months. The furor has died down, but the issues remain salient.

THROWING DOWN THE GAUNTLET

Confronted with a phenomenal best-seller that has nothing to do with our waistlines, our pocketbooks, our orgasms, our neuroses, or our titillation at others' waistlines, pocketbooks, orgasms, and neuroses, reviewers and critics tend to fall into ponderous prose that signifies their *own* seriousness at taking a book seriously. This may help to explain the initial solemn reception of Allan Bloom's self-important tome. As well, *The Closing of the American Mind* is the latest entry in a long line of books that have done well by telling us to be good and chiding us on the ways we are not.[1]

Sinclair Lewis savaged the American middle class who gobbled up his satires with alacrity and now advertise his birthplace with pride. H. L. Mencken made a decent living by dubbing nearly everybody else mentally or morally deficient, including that collective American subject, the "boobi Americani." More recently, Christopher Lasch catalogued our culture of narcissism and, with an irony Lasch appreciates, many of those immersed in the phenomena he depicted ingested his critique along with the latest consumer items. Now it is Allan Bloom's turn. Unlike Lewis and Mencken, he lacks serious wit although he shares Mencken's aesthetic mistrust of democracy. Unlike Lasch, his political motivations do not tend towards a revivification of America's dream of democracy. Instead, Bloom recreates a now-gone American academic world in which a few men became gentlemen at elite institutions, those who by *nature* were capable of making the transition from "natural savages" to "knowers." Such students were a charming lot just on the brink of "the first flush of maturity," ripe to be inducted into the great secrets of the great books by *bona fide* knowers like Bloom himself.

This world is nearly lost, or we are in danger of losing it, argues Bloom. Higher mental life in the United States is at stake. No, more: the judgment of America "in world history" everafter is up for grabs. The "fate of philosophy" is, for Bloom, the fate of America: "The crisis of the West . . . is identical with a crisis of philosophy." Never has so much weight been placed on so few books. For those of us who might have supposed that America's future course was more likely to be determined by how we handle foreign relations and negotiations, or the vagaries of our economy, or racial and regional conflicts and pressures, or the future of families and neighborhoods, or the tension between our celebration of individualism and our ideals of community, Bloom offers the startling news that the pervasive influence of Nietzsche and Heidegger has brought us to near ruin. It has done so by eroding, first, the great European universities and, second, the great American universities modeled after the great European ones.

Critics—most notably Martha Nussbaum and Alexander Nehamas—have challenged Bloom's reading of the classical texts he reveres as well as the Nietzschean texts he lambastes. Robert Paul Wolff impishly suggests that Bloom is really a character created by Saul Bellow, who contributes a forward, and *The Closing of the American Mind* a work of parodic fiction. My own tack will be somewhat different. I am troubled by much in Bloom. Although he addresses issues of great importance to the university, and although he is right that some modes of combating racism, sexism, and all the rest may be suspect, his own responses are sadly deficient. For all his incessant celebration of the elite of knowers, Bloom is unlearned in the ways of the wider world, untutored in subjects on which he makes definitive pronouncements, untouched by generosity in his response to those who, unlike Bloom himself, whether through necessity or choice, do not date the beginning of their "real lives" from the moment they glimpsed the University of Chicago (or Harvard Yard or, like Thomas Hardy's doomed Jude, the spires of Oxford).

Most offensive is Bloom's patronizing attitude towards American youth. His prototypical youth is the figment of a human mind feeding on lofty notions as the rest of us go about our grubby lives. Bloom gets to dictate who among us is a "serious candidate for culture," an honor denied one "naive and good-natured" student who once posed a question to Bloom about sublimation that charmed Bloom by its candor but indicated "the lad" was already so far gone in the ways of American culture he could never glimpse "the sublime." Bloom assumes that "young Americans," at a happy earlier point in time, arrived at the university as "clean slates unaware of their deeper selves and the world beyond their superficial experience." Their lives were "spiritually empty," whether they came from the city or the country, from devout Christian or Jewish families, whether they had dedicated high school teachers, wise pastors or priests, devoted mothers or fathers—it mattered not to Bloom. They were ciphers. Arriving at university, the best of them found their slates being written upon by the best of them: male professors who communed with the distant and the deep and were not afraid, as Plato insists his Guardians must not cavil, from treating human material as blank slates. Their very blankness was, for Bloom, "a large part of the charm of American students."

Alas, the charm is gone, replaced by demented beings immersed in the "gutter phenomenon" of rock and roll and having succumbed to hostility to reason, to barbaric appeals to sexual desire. Thankfully, a few "good students" remain to whom Bloom can introduce Mozart. But the vast majority, having been inducted into barbarism by Mick Jagger, offer a sorry spectacle indeed compared, say, to "the role . . . Napoleon played in the lives of ordinary young Frenchmen throughout the nineteenth century." Softened up by Jagger, they are easy prey for the pervasive Nietzschean undertow, defenseless against the Heideggerian hit, pummeled unawares by the "influence of Thomas Mann's *Death in Venice* on American consciousness."

The pop culture Bloom despises is one of America's great original contributions, a robust coming together of black gospel and white folk and hillbilly, music that springs from the lives and souls of ordinary people celebrating joys and lamenting tragedies, expressing hopes and confronting fears. To be sure, there's a lot of schlock in pop and imagery that troubles. But the point is to learn to distinguish between the good and the bad. That is difficult to do if you despise your subject matter, as Bloom despises America's young and the wider culture that helps to sustain them—for better or worse.

Bruce Springsteen, for example, has helped to make hunger and homelessness and the complexities of adult commitments popular, political, and moral questions. Springsteen understands that music alone cannot change the world (a real contrast to Bloom's arrogance about philosophy) but that it does hold forth a promise to make the world "a less lonely place . . . more than just a place." Springsteen extends our sympathy in unsentimental ways. What a contrast to Bloom, who sees nihilism lurking in each dissent, barbarism in any popular song. *The Closing of the American Mind* is an example of what Albert Camus urged us to try to avoid with these words: "We all carry within us our places of exile, our sorrows and our savages. But our task is not to unleash them on the world: it is to fight them in ourselves and others."

The mechanism Bloom devises for unleashing his own particular ravages upon the reader and the public is *nature,* a fraught term he deploys with apparent insouciance as if the matters he calls upon nature to settle were transparent, obvious to anyone capable of right reason.

RELYING ON NATURE, OR HERE COMES THE JUDGE

Nature is a central term of political discourse. This is but one of our legacies from the Greeks. The story goes like this: With the emergence of settled human existence, and the articulation of what life in the *polis* was, or should be, the Greeks evolved the distinction between nature *(physis)* and culture *(nomos).* Ideas about authority, sexuality, the gods, death, males, and females were imbedded complicatedly in representations of both "nature" and "culture." Debates ensued over what existed "by nature" and what did not: over what social forms might be dubbed "natural" in the sense that they fulfilled some given human potentiality and what, instead, thwarted or even contravened nature. My point is that from the very beginning of discussions about and divisions between nature/culture there was by no means an ultimate knockdown argument for preferring one understanding against another. Rather, nature *and* culture constituted what later political analysts were to tag "essentially contested concepts."

An essentially contested concept is internally complex or makes reference to several dimensions in turn, which are linked to other concepts; open textured, in that the rules of its application are relatively flexible; and appraisive in that the state of affairs it describes is a cherished accomplishment.[2] One can account for the ferocity of historic battles fought over the application of such ideas as nature or culture precisely because these are concepts that are imbedded in the language of social life and hence constitutive of that life in important, not trivial, ways. Use of the term "nature" or "natural," for example, may serve either as a weapon to put pressure upon social practices and institutions in order to reform or reconstruct them or as part of the arsenal of defense against such pressures. The framework one adopts in thinking about dimensions of nature or the natural implicates one in the manner in which these terms are linked to some notion of human needs and may become a rallying point for political action or criticism.

Jean Jacques Rousseau in his key political texts (including *The First and Second Discourses, The Social Contract,* and *The Emile*) deploys the terms "nature" and "natural" to a number of diverse ends and purposes.[3] He uses "nature" in one sense to present a vision of the natural state of human beings, to paint a picture of a preferred reality. Rousseau insists that his state of nature is no abstract postulate; rather, he proffers a plausible reconstruction of actual past epochs. That is, Rousseau presumes a "truly natural," prepolitical, presocial existence, a historic condition from which the human species evolved slowly. Rousseau uses nature in a second sense to describe those traits that have emerged in evolutionary history and have become humankind's "second nature." He also uses "natural" to convey desired outcomes or preferred relations, social forms, and ways of life. This use enables Rousseau to indicate notions of what is appropriate and proper for human beings once social forms are created and human nature becomes, in some sense, social even as it remains, in some sense, natural.

Much turns on the debate over the natural, for what theorists locate in a state of nature, or presume to exist *a priori*, and what they see as creations in history through human activity will help to determine their stance towards social change. It is, of course, the case that traditions that emerge at one point in history begin to take on the appearance of having always existed "by nature," and individuals may come to believe things have "always been this way." The humanly constituted origin of the practice, rule, belief, or tradition lies shrouded behind a veil of historic myth and the accretion of time. Rousseau knew this and recognized it as one of the most tormenting of dilemmas: How is one to tell what really existed by nature and what emerged historically? Furthermore, what difference does the locating of an institution, practice, or tradition in nature, or as natural, make?

These, at least, are the sorts of questions that are exigent to any political theorist who traffics in what might be called "nature discourse." They are dilemmas of the most vexing kind. (Of course, one could opt out of this language entirely, or nearly so, by eschewing all arguments from, or references to, nature or the natural. But that is not an option for my discussion given the thorough entanglement of Bloom's project with its repeated references to nature.) If Rousseau presents us, and himself, with dilemmas, Bloom issues a series of judgments and recommends solutions that rely on nature. The contrast between Rousseau's discursive struggles and Bloom's cavalier assessments is instructive. What, for Rousseau, is a pathway into and through a series of loaded and contested ideas serves for Bloom both as a stick with which to beat his opponents and a magic wand to sprinkle the stardust of classicism, intelligence, right reason, decency—high culture at its very highest—over the pages of his book. Nature works as a charm, or so Bloom seems to believe, because he does not find it necessary to defend his incessant recourse to the concept—its evocation alone is enough to settle matters.

Figuring out how nature à la Bloom works its many wonders is a frustrating task because Bloom does not offer the reader any guidelines as to why and how the rhetorical shifts in his own argument occur. He proclaims nature transparent—to him and to any serious candidate for culture. If his nature discourse seems muddy or murky, the fault lies not in the penumbra of stardust that surrounds his pages but in the abysmal shortcomings of the reader himself or, more likely, herself. This *is*, I know, a point that needs defending. I will begin by assaying the many conflicting and incompatible ways that Bloom uses nature discourse.

Parsing out Bloom's indulgences, insights, and indictments into a series of arguments is tricky. Here's why. Bloom deploys the term "nature" in at least three major ways without making any distinctions between these diverse uses. There are at least two key forms in which "natural" occurs and recurs. Enmeshed with this veritable outburst of "natures" and "naturals" are assumptions about convention or prejudice; "the good"; and philosophy itself. Reader, prepare yourself for a bumpy ride!

Nature 1: The argument goes like this. Human nature is a single entity, which can be fulfilled against the deforming forces of "convention and prejudice." This human nature needs the intellectual midwifery of a latter-day Socrates like Bloom in order to be made manifest. All human needs must be analyzed in relation to nature.

Human nature is unchanging. Yet the man who fulfills his nature must separate himself from nature. He can't just be a piece of nature or he will disappear. (Here Bloom appears to make tacit reference to the early Greek distinctions between *physis* and *nomos*, but it is all rather murky.)

Nature 2: Here nature becomes Nature, a proper noun, an actual entity with foundational or ontological status. We require Nature in order to have a standard by which to assess our own lives; indeed, by which to *judge* our lives. Serving as judges are the true philosophers whose own code and gifts permit them to *know* Nature, to penetrate her secrets, hence to be in full attunement with Nature. Nature is a *she*, a feminine representation, that requires male interpreters, as philosophic midwives. On this score Bloom is voluble. The rhetoric gushes. Nature needs proper nourishment. Nature is the only thing that counts. Nature herself, in all her "lush profusion," might appear to be a prejudice, but no! She simply requires the cooperation of convention in order to manifest herself.

To give some indication of how central Nature 2 is to Bloom's case, I counted the term no less than *six* times on one page (p. 105), *four* times on another (p. 114). Nature 2 routinely peppers the pages when Bloom desires either to praise or to excoriate. Thus the women's movement is *not* founded on Nature; indeed, feminism forgets Nature. This makes it bad by definition.[4] Nature 2 thus far is benign, the Good, the Standard by which to judge. But, it turns out, Nature 2 has a dark underside, a strange mirror image, a miscreant sister. This darker Nature remains a "she" and continues to require male intermediaries, not so much to fulfill her requirements as to curb her excesses.

Bad Nature 2, if you will, is "indifferent to good and evil." She leads men to war or her imperfections "cause war." She is a miserly stepmother. The stepmother metaphor occurs when Bloom characterizes Nature 2 as an ontologized feminized representation who has left us as poor orphans, unprovided for; thus we had no choice but to master her. When we "revered" her we were poor so we—mankind—*had* to conquer Nature, to wrest her secrets from her. We are forgiven, however, for the reasons we had to master Nature came from "nature itself." (The appropriate response at this point is a dizzy sensation.) But Nature got her revenge. We began to experience her negatively through fear of death—hence the political thought of Hobbes for whom Nature is near and unattractive. We began to experience her as an absence—hence the political thought of Rousseau for whom

Nature is distant and attractive. Rousseau, or Bloom's Rousseau at any rate, wants to restore a lost wholeness and to rediscover primitive feelings. It is Rousseau who set in motion the modern "nostalgia for nature," a yearning Bloom deems suspect because it seems to pitch us into a foolhardy rediscovery of nature as sacred.

It is once again judgment time as Bloom brings Nature 2, in the several strong ways he has deployed it, to closure. He makes no attempt to clarify the benign mother/miserly stepmother imagery. Instead, he opts out of that discussion entirely with Socrates as his *deus ex machina*. For it was Socrates who showed us (we philosophic few) how we can truly conform to Nature, meaning Nature 1. (I will capitalize this "nature" as it is given agentic force.) Either Nature 1 has a lawful order or it does not. Bloom insists it most assuredly does and this order is discernible in and through—Culture! Culture 1 now joins Nature 1 as the standard of judgment over men and their deeds. It is Culture 1 (Culture 2 will make its appearance shortly) that restores our lost wholeness. Culture 1 denotes the capacity of a few to be attuned in such a way that no contradiction between the desires of nature and the imperatives of social life exists for them. Socrates taught us how man's reason can grasp the "whole of nature" and it is in and through this grasping that nature/culture get sealed. We arrive at this nature through midwifed reason. The culture we thereby attain is the only alternative to various dehumanizing notions of "rights based on our animal nature" and to sinking into the sloth and rank subjectivism of Culture 2 or bad convention.

Bloom sees current convention—he means contemporary life in the United States—as deformed, a tissue of prejudicial and impoverished pseudo-standards and debased relativisms, as I observed earlier. Modern America is a world of artificial souls in which there is a shocking poverty of "living examples" of what Bloom calls the "highest human types." In and through our gray network of cultural concepts, we have become incapable of moving into attunement with nature through right reason. We are doomed to MTV.

One further rhetorical replay of nature appears in *The Closing of the American Mind*, Nature 3 or the "state of nature." The move Bloom makes with Nature 3 is rather interesting. Noting dutifully, as any political theorist must, that Locke, Rousseau, and others evoked the state of nature and insisted that by nature all men are free and equal and that our own constitutional forebears relied upon nature and nature's God, Bloom chides us moderns once again: "It is now fashionable to deny that there ever was a state of nature," he claims, though he doesn't make the case for why in fact we should insist on the actual preexistence of such a state. Repeating the phrase "state of nature" four times on a single page (p. 162) is his substitute for argument.

At any rate, Locke, Rousseau, and company are quickly forgotten, for Bloom has other fish to fry. His state of nature is more or less synonymous, it turns out, with bad convention or Culture 2. We are, even as I write, back in a state of nature. Bloom makes this claim four times on page 109—perhaps it must be true. He insists that his insistence is *not* a rhetorical ploy but the characterization of a dire reality. We are so many solitary savages in the modern state of nature. Nature, real nature or Nature 1, is "distant from us now." (Doesn't this sound suspiciously like that Rousseauian nostalgia he finds dubious, an inspiration to hippies and other undesirables?) Yet *that* real nature (here emanations of Nature 2 are evident) was a condition of absolute desire without virtue; that, finally, is what is found "in the state of nature," and that, precisely that, is what Allan Bloom has found in the state of America. We are back in a bad state of nature, a world of unleashed desire in the absence of virtue. We are living psychically in such a world. That is why we are so culturally impoverished. Bad nature/bad convention—a double whammy.

To the rescue comes "the Natural" (again in several senses), the good, and the philosopher. Natural, on one construal, is natural rights as fundamental principles that help us to preserve the sentiments of nature in the civil order. They set limits. So we have a natural rights–based politics of some sort. Natural, in a second construction, refers to "human goods," including a "natural hierarchy" of the soul's inclinations that enable us to distinguish bad desires from lofty virtues. Of course, Bloom acknowledges, all peoples prefer to see their own way of life as "natural." One problem with the modern West is that it demurs. We are so far gone in the ways of relativism that we don't assert our way of life as "natural" or in line with "the good." But this is soggy ground for Bloom and a position he cannot really sustain or it would invite rival claims to "the natural" that could not ultimately be adjudicated.

Be that as it may, "the natural" weds "the good" such that the fulfillment of "natural human potential" in its entirety constitutes the nature of the good. Bloom locates "the good" as a standard by which to judge—"the good as such" no less. The mechanism for Bloom, one that enables him to slide past any tricky discussion of what on earth "the good" is anyhow, is philosophy and philosophers—the real ones, not the many fake prophets scurrying about preaching bad relativism and mushy tolerance.[5]

Behold Philosophy! The only true science. America was founded by philosophers. Philosophy offers a treasury of great men and great thoughts and of such men and thoughts there will always only be a few. "Philosophy is the rational account of the whole nature": no underlaboring for Bloom. Socrates embodies the nature of the know-ers. Socrates applied nature to his own life. He lived the hierarchy of true value, eschewing the baser appetites, despising such animal acts as intercourse and eating. His nature was noble. The writings of such later nobles as Kant and Goethe give us unadorned "mirrors of nature." Modern Knowers, living in these unfortunate days, are a tiny band of men who will always be the soul of the university, men who are truly alive when they are reading Plato and Shakespeare. It is difficult for this fraternity. Bloom acknowledges that some genuine candidates for culture, real Knowers, become morose. Having found out "what happened to Glaucon during his wonderful night with Socrates"—and the image of a sexual excitement is not at all subtle here—they despair of recreating the magical Athenian atmosphere. Here's how, in Bloom's own prose:

After a reading of the *Symposium* a serious student came with deep melan-choly and said it was impossible to imagine that magic Athenian atmosphere reproduced, in which friendly men, educated, lively, on a footing of equality, civilized but natural, came together and told wonderful stories about the meaning of their longing. But such experiences are always accessible. Actually, this playful discussion took place in the midst of a terrible war that Athens was destined to lose. . . . But they were not given to culture despair, and in these terrible political circumstances, their abandon to the *joy of nature* [emphasis mine] proved the viability of what is best in man, independent of accidents, of circumstance.

A remarkable passage, filled with eroticized (albeit sublimated) layerings—magical, longing, abandon—and requiring, for its fulfill-ment, a few men, men who are capable of enacting what Hamlet vexedly could not—shuffling off this mortal coil. Men for whom circumstance, the contingencies of existence, count for nothing. This brings me to my conclusion. Most of us are not eligible for member-ship in Allan Bloom's fraternity. And that, I am convinced, is not a bad thing at all. For Bloom's ideal of what the Greeks called *eudaimonia*, or human flourishings, is a cramped thing indeed. I would not abandon any such ideal but I would enlarge and enrich it, democratize it, if you will, by opening it up to the vagaries of our complex human existences.

We are not, *pace* Bloom, confronted with a stark choice between an abstract, disembodied Platonic truth or a messy, all too embodied relativism. There are alternatives and to sketch mine, very briefly, I shall call upon Martha Nussbaum's discussion of Greek tragedy, Plato and Aristotle.[6]

Nussbaum insists upon the ethical value of the so-called irrational parts of the soul—our appetites, feelings, and emotions. For our bodily and sensuous natures link us to a world of risk and mutability. The severe goal of self-sufficiency, which aims to master the appetites totally, is an attempt, which seems more and more desperate the more one thinks of it, to immunize human beings from life's vulnerabilities and conflicts. Nussbaum finds in Aristotle's more modest aims, and his greater attunement to the discourse of tragedy, an alternative to Plato's radical philosophical oversimplification of life and thought. It is not my purpose to make a brief in behalf of an Aristotelian-based ethic but to insist, with Nussbaum, that the project of Socrates, endorsed uncritically by Bloom, imbeds in its heart the Athenian "mythology of autochthony that persistently, and paradoxically, suppressed the biological role of the female and therefore the family in the continuity of the city."[7]

As I noted in *Public Man, Private Woman*, the only solution Plato can find to individual malaise and social sickness is a thoroughly rationalized order in which all motives and occasions for discord and disunion have been eradicated. Private homes and sexual attachments, devotion to friends, and dedication to individual aims and purposes notoriously militate against single-minded devotion to a quest for Truth. "Our ordinary humanity," in Nussbaum's words, "is a source of confusion rather than of insight, and our lives stand in need of transcendence through the dialectical activity of the intellect."[8] So it is the philosopher alone who has the correct standpoint and the proper criteria. That he *is* a he is no doubt the case but that is less interesting than what is required of him. He, this paragon, is required to characterize our everyday activities in a way that evokes images of besmirchment and defilement. Our bodies are not ourselves—or are so only for the lowly sorts. The body is that which the philosopher must rise above. And the pity is that this sort of "hard work," this struggle for a vantage point totally outside the realm of "appearances" is—Nussbaum is right on target—"futile and destructive." It is destructive because the glory of the promised abstract goal makes the "humanly possible work look boring and cheap."[9]

So, with the vast majority of others, I am not eligible for membership in Bloom's fraternity. I do not hanker after the magical Athenian atmosphere and a "wonderful night" with Socrates. Instead I call for a recognition of the joys and vexations, values and purposes, of everyday life. In *Public Man, Private Woman* I wrote—and I can do no better so I will simply repeat the words:

Within an ethical polity the individual would, or could, have many irons in the fire. The prevailing image of the person would be that of a human being with a capacity for self-reflection as to the ends and means of public and private action. Such persons would tolerate the ineradicable tension between public and private imperatives, thought and action, aesthetic standards and ethical principles. He or she could distinguish between those conditions, events, or states of affairs which are part of a shared human condition—grief, loss through death, natural disasters, and decay of the flesh—and those man-made injustices which can be remedied, or which one can work to remedy. Above all the human being within the ethical polity never presumes that ambivalence and conflict is the wellspring of a life lived reflectively and that we are all enriched by the messy reality which is our lot.[10]

9

Pornography Politics

Another matter that won't go away, pornography battles have abated somewhat as a feminist project over the past few years, but the issue is always
simmering just beneath the legal, political, and moral surface. This is a much
expanded version of my piece, "The New Porn Wars," *The New Republic,*
June 28, 1984.

Why is pornography so hard for us to deal with? Why does it create
such divisiveness? Why does the debate get framed as it does—
unlimited freedom of expression versus enhanced modes of social
control and constraint? The answer lies in part in the incomplexities
of our social history and the founding principles of our polity.

Liberalism, as such, is indifferent to the ways of life individuals
choose to pursue, that is, our constitutive political morality is agnostic
as between alternative conceptions of the "good life." Holding as
self-evident a view of the person as a bearer of inalienable rights who
must be free to choose his or her own ends, liberal society promul-
gates and protects negative freedom. The citizen is free *from* imposition upon him or her of a substantive public morality he or she may
not share and free as well from the intrusions of neighbors into
private affairs. Jefferson's classic pronouncement that it mattered not
to him whether his neighbor believed in twenty gods or no god—it
neither picked his pocket nor broke his leg—captures the governing
ethos well. Religious belief is private; the morality or amorality of
others is their business *unless* it impinges on my person or my pelf. If
I am threatened, I may call upon civil society to guarantee my
protection just as I may, if necessary, challenge that society should it
threaten the rights its procedures are duty bound to protect. This
bracing ideal requires that politics touch *only* externals. Behavior
alone can be regulated or punished and only if it can be demonstrated
that this behavior touches directly and negatively upon another.

Our political morality, then, sets a particular context. Presuming a sharp cleavage between public and private, the political language of liberalism celebrates individual choice and rights but grants no similar status to principles of belonging or obligation. Aspects of our moral experience located in ties of friendship, family, and community life fall through the grid of liberalism's regulative principles. In practice, the sharp wedge liberalism drives between the public citizen and private person breaks down. American life was stitched together historically by a dense web of communities whose glue was religion, ethnicity, shared associative purposes, and immersion in substantive civic moralities to which the broader framework was officially agnostic. The important point—as background to the pornography debate—is just this: in the absence of a language of public morality, reformers are compelled to make their case in and through a language of individual rights, choice, and "freedom from." They must, in a sense, "prove damages" to get the machinery of civil society moving in a punitive or positive direction. They must also attempt to break down the liberal public-private divide, either by politicizing "the private" or by claiming that privacy is being eroded and must be restored.

The present phase of this old debate highlights the tensions inherent in our political morality and illustrates limits to the vocabulary of individual rights where matters of substantive morality are concerned. This may account for the rhetorical overinflation pornography invites. Given the disintegration of the wider social surround, with traditional constraints of community corroded under the pressure of decades of relentless change, the language of rights and freedom from discrimination is pressed into service to bear an impossibly heavy burden. One example of this phenomenon in our recent past can be found in the rhetorics of various sexual liberationist texts that proclaim gratification a *political* right. (I refer here not to protection from discrimination on the basis of sexual identity but to acts of sexual pleasure themselves.) Thus one writer, in a call for the unrepressed (hence free) society termed masturbation a "right," going on to argue that once that right was either seized or granted an individual's development of new and better "masturbatory techniques" might well be his or her way of making a "political contribution." Clearly, "rights" cannot bear all the heavy weight—and panting in this instance—being placed upon them. But the fact that we move this direction and can find no other effective way to press a case for political change or cultural revolution highlights the paradox in which we find ourselves. Having been officially indifferent to the inner worlds of persons and to the moral visions that animate them and hold them together (or drive them apart), we find ourselves in a situation in which the collapse of any distinction at all between public and private seems increasingly attractive, hence more likely. Rhetoricians and political combatants can find no other way to get at various problems. And our political actions and reactions endlessly repeat an all too familiar scenario: freedom versus community; rights versus constraints.

That is part of the background to the present story. Another is the explosion of pornography that got underway, in its new forms, in the loosened up sexual climate of the 1960s and showed little or no sign of abating until the impact of AIDS began to be felt. (So much for the satiation hypothesis—the widely held view that people would grow rapidly filled after they had sampled all the pornographic consumables available—and pornography would fall back into some unspecified but limited proper place.) In 1976 *Time* magazine ran a cover story on the "Porn Plague," the metaphor suggesting that pornography had become a natural force, akin to an epidemic, and that we were unable to inoculate ourselves against it. Pornography's progress from the twilight zone of major cities to the main street of middle-sized towns is a story of an aesthetics of mechanistic and sometimes cruel sexuality, and of profit. Its proliferation tells how ineffective any longer are the old unwritten rules of internalized constraint—taboos, shame, and scandal. In tossing off those constraints in the name of freedom—in ways that were genuinely liberating for many—we seem to have opened the floodgates to a new coarseness and brutalization in our representations of human sexuality.

The usual move at this juncture is to pose Lenin's instrumental question—what is to be done—but I propose instead to move towards Hannah Arendt's insistence that we find some way to "think what we are doing." For thinking what we are doing, considering how it is we think when the subject at hand is pornography, is a form of politics. Such discussions create political space. To insist that we know all there is to know and what we must do at the moment is close ranks and fight—as the radical feminist antipornographers demand—is *unworthy* as a model for a feminist politics that looks to *democratic renewal*. Not only are the arguments posed by radical feminist antipornographers crude as an analysis of the problem, they require and invite specific *antidemocratic* responses, or responses and strategies having antidemocratic implications.

These are controversial points requiring detailed defense, and I intend to develop them as I go along. The ideas animating the antipornography struggle in its most publicized and absolutist forms are not new—they turn on a theory about male sexuality, indeed male nature, which sees that sexuality and that nature as depending for its pleasure and identity on the wholesale, remorseless victimization of women. A patronizing view of women's passivity, one in which women have neither agency nor complicity in any complex social or sexual outcome, is a direct implication of the arguments I shall touch upon briefly. All social evil, in this scheme of things, comes from the Other in its collective guise, Man, as if men formed a coherent category, dominated by evil intent, and arrayed permanently and relentlessly against the collective category, Woman. It is disturbing that the best *publicized* feminist critiques are based on such simple-mindedness, for pornography is an important topic. (As well, there is a body of feminist argumentation that does not see male sexuality as *necessarily* violent.)

One of the most disturbing features of current antipornography efforts is the move to close out politics. If you accept the view of pornography espoused by radical feminist antipornography activists, to dissent from their view is to betray women by definition. If you look closely at the argument that underlies antiporn politics you find the contention that pornography *causes* violence, whether it is implicated in direct physical harm or not. The mere existence of pornography, in this view, is a form of violence. At work in their understanding is an insistence that pornography is what heterosexuality *is*—behind closed doors. Pornographic representations *mirror* ordinary sexual relations between men and women: "it is what women are in theory and practice."

One author in the collection *Take Back the Night*, for example, calls that vapid trio of sexual liberationists—Hugh Hefner, Bob Guiccionne, and Larry Flynt—"every bit as dangerous as Hitler, Mussolini and Hirohito." She then goes on to trash liberals, for "the very same liberals" who spoke out against Hitler are silent about his analogue, Hefner, thereby promoting a "holocaust" against women. The utopian vision of the pornographer, who presents us with a world without limits, is here counterposed to a similarly utopian vision of a purified sexuality possible after demons equal in horror to totalitarian genocidists of the twentieth century are eliminated. These extreme representations are not truly in opposition but, instead, require one another and help to hold one another intact.

Embracing the argument that "pornography is the theory; rape is the practice," protestors in Minneapolis, led by Catherine MacKinnon and Andrea Dworkin, a radical feminist legal scholar and polemicist, respectively, proposed an amendment to the city's civil rights ordinance that would classify pornography as "a form of discrimination on the basis of sex," hence a violation of the civil rights of women and a denial of equal protection under the law. Specifically, the ordinance—passed by a seven to six vote of the Minneapolis City Council on December 30, 1983, and vetoed January 5, 1984, by Minneapolis' troubled liberal Mayor Don Fraser—defines pornography in the broadest, most wide-ranging terms.[1] The ordinance defines pornography as follows:

The sexually explicit subordination of women, graphically depicted, whether in *pictures* or *words*, that also includes one or more of the following: (a) women are presented as sexual objects, things or commodities; or (b) women are presented as sexual objects who enjoy pain or humiliation; or (c) women are presented as sexual objects who experience pleasure being raped; or (d) women are presented as sexual objects tied up or cut up or mutilated or bruised or physically hurt; or (e) women are presented in postures of sexual submission; or (f) women's body parts—including but not limited to vaginas, breasts and buttocks—are exhibited such that women are reduced to those parts; or (g) women are presented as whores by nature; or (h) women are presented being penetrated by objects or animals; or (i) women are presented in scenarios of degradation, injury, abasement, torture, shown as filthy or inferior, bleeding, bruised or hurt in a context that makes these conditions sexual.

Attempting to leave no stone unturned, the statute extends the notion of *harm* to encompass *any situation* in which a "woman . . . could claim that she had been injured, or coerced," including, for example, a chance encounter with an "offensive" magazine cover in the supermarket.

The ordinance dramatically extends the notion of harm with the proclamation that pornography constitutes a form of sex discrimination; hence compromises by definition a violation to a woman's civil rights. Dworkin, a writer who argues that "men love death. . . . Men especially love murder," as a generic truth about the gender, claimed in an interview: "What it amounts to in the supermarket, is that you or I go into the supermarket to buy a dozen eggs. My rights as a citizen are violated because those magazines that show me as an *abject degraded* victim in fact subordinate me when I am in the supermarket. They change my *civil status* and make it different from yours, because you're a man and I'm a woman." As the injured party, the woman could bring suit under civil law against "a particular person, place, distributor, exhibitor."

Statute proponents insist that pornography by definition sets up a clash between First Amendment guarantees, on the one hand, and equal protection under the law, the Fourteenth Amendment, on the other. Author Dworkin shows scant interest in First Amendment concerns: "I find the civil liberties stance to be bourgeois hypocrisy a lot of the time." The ordinance offered a wide-ranging answer: Anytime a woman determined her civil rights had been violated she could sue. The First Amendment is seen primarily as an impediment to the achievement of desired ends and the question, in that case, is the instrumental one: How can we get around it?

Predictably, the scope and language of the ordinance aroused civil libertarians. The Minnesota American Civil Liberties Union entered the fray in opposition to the proposal, vowing to fight it all the way to the Supreme Court if necessary. To First Amendment absolutists (or nearly so), this latest antiporn crusade confirms a world view that no doubt comes to them too easily: the belief that *any* attempt to curb or regulate the new, more pervasive pornography invites censorship and threatens liberty. By promulgating a definition of pornography so broad it might indict an Updike novel along with a snuff film, feminist protesters confirmed the civil libertarian's worst fears. But the battle lines were drawn long before Minneapolis. Alan Dershowitz, a Harvard constitutional law professor, is quoted in a *Time* magazine article, August 27, 1979, as proclaiming, "Women who would have the government ban sexist material are the new McCarthyites. It's the same old censorship in radical garb," and Aryeh Neier, in *The Nation*, June 21, 1980, termed the women's campaign against pornography a feature of "the new censorship," citing the denunciation of defenders of the First Amendment by Dworkin, Susan Brownmiller, and others. "Let us make certain the new censors are labeled for what they are," Neier concluded, "that is the best way of impairing their ability to attract adherents to their cause." In addition to the ACLU, outspoken opposition to the Minneapolis ordinance was voiced by such liberal newspapers as the *Minneapolis Tribune* (in the name of "free expression, constitutionalism, and common sense") and the *Washington Post*, which termed the ordinance "absolutely batty" and in its own odd way "repressive." Interestingly, the porn industry itself was an invisible interested party to the Minneapolis dispute. But the Minnesota Newspaper Association, the Association of American Publishers, and the American Booksellers Association all lobbied energetically for defeat of the ordinance. Although the pornographers did not enter the Minneapolis dispute openly, they are nonetheless the somewhat unsavory silent partners of the civil libertarians.

Similarly, feminist antipornographers often find themselves in a tacit alliance with right-wing crusaders against pornography as our worst form of modern vice. For example: Joseph Sobran, a syndicated voice of new conservatism, launched a broadside against films and magazines that degrade women and objectify their bodies, insisting that "the nut who hates women" can find legitimacy for his sexism in such visual and written representations. His position is identical to that of a Women Against Pornography broadside that proclaims: "The essence of pornography is the defamation of womanhood." This is a view shared by such conservative groups as Morality in Media, Inc. and Citizens for Decency through Law. Feminist protesters are vehement in denying a mutuality of perspective or interest with conservative campaigners, however. In their view, conservative groups have the heaviest stake of all in maintaining male dominance. MacKinnon, for example, states that "right wing men have been too much staked on their dominance" to be seen as even tacit allies in the struggle against porn.

But if, as radical feminists claim, pornography has as its explicit intent keeping women in a subordinate position by humiliating and degrading them, it is hard to figure out why "right wing men" wouldn't favor pornography, seeing it as a weapon in their own self-interest. Despite disavowals from both sides, an implicit coming together of right-wing and radical feminist efforts has become part of the political landscape on this issue. The arguments differ but the ends sought—the *total elimination* of pornography as defined broadly by each group—are identical. (One major difference is the more explicit attention conservative protestors pay to the portrayal of men and children in pornographic representations, The Minneapolis ordinance framers added men and children somewhat grudgingly to the final version of their proposal.) Overinflated rhetoric and claims of unrelenting victimization, together with a proposed remedy that features single, aggrieved women going to court, shows how difficult it is to get out of a world structured by narrow proceduralisms and bereft of any animating vision of a political community.

This becomes powerfully evident when one bumps up against that paradox, or seeming paradox, I have already noted: the fact that pornographers and their radical feminist opponents share a world view. For Dworkin and many antipornography polemicists, together with leading pornographers, to the man the phallus functions as synecdoche—it stands for the male as a whole and it is, by definition, an instrument of domination and control—as well as pleasure. By presuming pornography is a mirror of "ordinary" heterosexuality, feminist antipornographers confirm the fantastic scenarios that pornographers present. They share a vision of atoms bumping up against one another. Both pornographers and antipornographers extend the image of dominance and subordination from the porn theater to the average heterosexual bedroom. This runaway rhetoric of cruelty insists that violence is everywhere and pornography is telling us the bitter truth of it. But if pornographic representations mirror anything, its scenarios are more and more a playing out of themes of loss of control and efficacy in a world in which human beings in general and males in particular (for they are under a heavier burden of performance and stalwart individualism) see themselves as objects of social forces over which they have no control. Pornography offers for voyeuristic consumption a vision that attracts precisely because it signifies to "public man" what he is not—in either public or private: he increasingly lacks the power to bend others to his will.

What this tells us about complex textures of social life may be this: rather than holding up a lens through which to view "normal" heterosexual intimacy, to see it for what it *is*, pornography instead offers us a magnifying glass that enlarges actual features of our broader landscape: mechanistic work, atomized social relations, disconnections from place, anonymous bureaucratic controls, rapid changes in sexual and social standards, and a background of historic desexualization (or hypersexualization) of the female. To transform our fantasies, we must change the broader context in which they occur. Given that context, strategies that can only set us up as individual victims and litigants, and that extend the atomized vision of human beings into all areas of social life, reinforce those features of our lives that gave rise to the porn plague in the first place.

Civil libertarians cannot treat the complex question of relations between sexual and political moralities and identities, or between public virtue and private ethics, either. Their notion of freedom precludes consideration of substantive morality and disconnects at the base reflections on the way in which pornography may be symptomatic of wider features of American society. For we have reached a point at which the rights of children to have sex with anyone they want, if they can only first be freed from their "brutal, authoritarian family persons and rulers," is promoted as just another extension of the American dream by one recent celebrant of the freedom of pedophilia. The civil libertarian challenges this view with the language of consent—children are not old enough to choose to be sodomized or otherwise gratified—but he or she cannot get beyond a picture of essential isolates, bound up in their rights and their "freedom from," going through the world *en guarde* against possible constraints from aroused and potentially "repressive" communities.

The conservative alternative, as presented by George Will in a column on the Minneapolis case, is in contrast to liberalism's official agnosticism in these matters, attractive in its acknowledging that the inner life matters and that the character of citizens has something to do with the tone and texture of a policy. Will insists on including an explicit moral dimension the Minneapolis ordinance sponsors rejected. According to MacKinnon, protestors were disinterested in coming up with some feminist notion of obscenity or any other "moral" concept. By repudiating altogether a moral dimension, antiporn protestors mirror official agnosticism on matters of public morality and competing visions of "the good life."

Will places the moral question centrally—but in a way that liberals and most feminists must find problematic. He begins by noting the "extravagance" of feminist claims. As well, he locates the need for a rhetoric that insists that pornography as such causes actual acts of violence—as if human beings were so many pots put on to boil at so many pornographic degrees Fahrenheit—in "the logic" of liberal society's jurisprudence, which "requires such unreasonableness before reasonable action can be taken." But he leaps from this point to a blanket condemnation of "libertarian laws that express the doctrine that law should be indifferent to the evolution of the nation's character" and takes the Minneapolis protestors to task for rattling "on and on about individual rights and equality." Certainly Will has a point—an important point—about the difficulty of expressing "collective concerns" in liberal language. But he forgets that traditional communities, for these serve as an implicit contrast model to the excessiveness of the liberal present, historically disallowed women full civic identity. To hope to strip away individualism and immersion in rights, rather than to challenge instances of their overinflation and unwarranted extension to all spheres, is to lose a central feature of our political society and to threaten the real gains made by women and others in and through the prism of rights. The conservative option situates us too deeply *inside* community even as the civil libertarian alternative has no way to speak about communal concerns or freedom at all.

We find, then, a constellation of reactions that keeps the overall structure of the moment intact: distention of the language of rights and the pursuit of political ends through individual litigation rather than broader popular strategies; conservative cries to return to real community and an overreaching and deep-reaching public morality; first amendment absolutists and pornographers in a wary alliance to prevent any inroads at all into constitutional guarantees. Visible is the relationship at work between pornographers, their clients, and their adversaries, as well as their often reluctant defenders. A peculiar symbiosis emerges between those who shock and those who are shocked. For example: the patronizing view of woman as the sexual slave of man presented by many antipornography rhetoricians is precisely the view of women the pornographic imagination demands and feeds on. When modern pornographers and their opponents dance to the same tune—a melody in which the woman is dominated, enthralled, pliable—the possibility of a different theme song recedes into the distance. Nor does the heavenly chorus hummed by Will promise to change the theme song of the present in the long run.

While it may be true, as a columnist for the *Wall Street Journal* proclaimed, that "had the Moral Majority" written the Minneapolis ordinance it would "have been laughed out of this liberal town," that does not discredit all efforts to come to grips with pornography. One of the reasons pornography has been so difficult to deal with historically is not only the obvious fact that few agree on what it is but that pornography itself is a changing social form. Both authoritarian right-wing societies and socialist revolutionary societies have been sexually repressive. Some construe pornography as a liberating force—breaking through the crust of social convention and scoffing at official sanctities—while to others pornography is perversity and always presents a threat to personal and civil morality. Feminist theorist Shelia Rowbotham, in *Women, Resistance and Revolution*, notes that pornography in the eighteenth century expressed unrestrained sexuality or "nature" breaking the bounds of "culture" and despising the constraints of religion, family, and social order. Rowbotham claims that pornography represented a retreat for upper-class men from the burden of a growing self-consciousness, a search for the absolute "feeling self" in the absolute "unfeeling thing"; hence, the denial, in pornographic representations, of human response in the female object of desire. Rowbotham suggests that pornographic images would have been called into question if women were explicitly or independently enjoying themselves. This implies that a brassy, sexually provocative harridan like Mae West, for example, is unsuited for a pornography of submission and domination for West not only admitted her sexuality but vamped it. She is not a pornographic subject; nor is she acceptable to conservative religious crusaders against pornography; nor, it seems, to feminist antipornographers who see robust heterosexuality only in terms of oppressor and oppressed. (Dworkin, for example, has stated that sex with a man is okay so long as his penis is not erect.)

There are multiple explanations for why pornography is, or seems to fill, some need. The compensatory dynamic I mentioned previously is one sketched in debates on the topic. Todd Gitlin, in a discussion of pornography and the Left, argues that the need for pornography in contemporary society is both "authentic and degraded," fulfilling an authentic desire to "see representations of sex" but in a "perverse, dehumanizing way." Steven Marcus in *The Other Victorians* finds a similar dynamic at work in the nineteenth century, seeing an inverse relationship between the rise of dominating and sadistic images of masculine sexuality in pornography and the diminution of these qualities in everyday life. But the bottom line for antipornography advocates is whether current pornographic fantasies have any right at all to exist. Need anything be demonstrated beyond the content of pornography itself for porn to be outlawed or curbed? No, say feminist protestors and the right. Yes, insist civil libertarians. And those liberals, or radical democrats (in whose ranks I would include myself), unable to lurch wholly one way or the other, find themselves increasingly uncomfortable straddling a fence between "rights" and "community protection." Our political language is not up to this task, it seems; we lack a vocabulary to deal with the question in some clearly nonrepressive way. And all those who seek pornography's final elimination in favor of a uniform, approved standard of what constitutes benign sexual representations, holistic and harmless, invite repression.

Yet this seems too easy, finally. Although some feminist antipornographers would have few compunctions at seeing the pornographic productions of "major artists" suppressed, the concerned citizen need not share these views or traverse this route to determine that something should be done to drive porn back underground, at least somewhat. Before I turn to my own sense of a politics that takes up pornography but eschews apocalyptic analyses and solutions, let me share a few additional speculations and put them in the form of questions that require serious reflection.

1. Can and ought we distinguish with John Paul II, in an interesting piece on the "theology of the body," between textual representations and what the Pope calls "porno-vision"? He uses the term to distinguish films and videos from pornography, which refers to literature or writing. His argument is that the very nature of social communications and the mass media is such that human dignity is offended when the body's intimacy is withdrawn from interpersonal relations and exposed to a general or unknown audience. "The human body is a manifestation of the person, and of his or her self-giving to another who can respond in an equally personal way." By turning what belongs to intimacy, to privacy, into public property the "self giving is, as it were suspended in a dimension of unknown reception and unforeseeable response. The truth about human beings, by reason of their bodies and their sex, is especially personal and interior and creates limits which it is not licit to go beyond. The whole problem of porno-vision . . . is not the result of a puritanical mentality or a narrow morality." Rather, "it is a matter of very fundamental values, in the face of which we cannot remain indifferent." What is attractive about this argument is the explicit distinction between forms of representation and the fact that the moral concern can be raised without launching into dubious and inflated insistence on cause, on a correspondence theory between porn X and outcome Y.[2]

2. Michael Ignatieff, in the essay "Homo Sexualis" in the *London Review of Books*, asks the Foucaultian question: Why is sex so important to us anyway? Why has the late twentieth-century culture of narcissism embraced homo sexualis as its definition of human essence? Why have sex and our gendered identities become the central part of being, the privileged site in which the truth of ourselves is to be found? If we pose these questions, we can locate much feminist discourse on the eternal antimony between female desire, constituted as an unspoiled pool of pure human eroticism in opposition to patriarchal evil, as an attempt to push the view that sexuality is a continuous natural object of historical discourse, a position Foucault stoutly rejects.

3. Susan Sontag's illuminating essay, "The Pornographic Imagination," challenges our tendency to locate discourse about pornography inside frames that see it as a malady to be diagnosed and an occasion

for judgment, as something one must be for or against. Her views cannot be readily encapsulated, but she insists that human sexuality is and will always be "a highly questionable phenomenon and belongs, at least potentially, among the extreme rather than the ordinary experiences of humanity." Pornographic literature necessarily drives a wedge between one's existence "as a full human being and one's existence as a sexual being." Most of us most of the time neither seek nor want this. But some do—they want to lose the "self" in obsessive sexual feeling, and porn literature from Sade through surrealism "capitalizes on that mystery and makes the reader more aware of it," inviting us to participate.

The paradox and peril of the present moment is this: by not tending to the relation between inner worlds and outer life, we make more likely moves to "reconstruct" people rather than to change the contexts in which they find themselves. We cannot tend democratically to the porn problem through languages of total community or languages of absolute (or nearly so) freedom of expression and freedom from constraint. But we can move towards reflection on available options by drawing from conservatives the insistence that the character of human beings matters, and that this character is related to the contexts in which people live, and from feminist protest generally the imperative that women are or must be free to become full civic beings.

For feminist and conservative protestors, the strategies now available for communities to tackle pornography are manifestly inadequate; for civil libertarians these same strategies are, or can be, dangerously localist, giving aroused communities too much potential power to censor. Currently, pornography falls under the 1973 Supreme Court decision in *Miller v. California* in which the Court developed a three-part test for obscenity: (1) whether an average person, applying "contemporary community standards," would find the work in question prurient, (2) whether the work is a "patently offensive" depiction of sexual conduct specifically proscribed by state law, and (3) whether the work taken as a whole, "lacks serious literary, artistic, political, or scientific value." These tests are vague, and can be cumbersome, but they are also pluralistic, recognizing no single, uniform standard.

In the *Hamling* case, 1974, the Court reiterated that contemporary community standards were not to be defined on a statewide or nationwide basis but in terms of a particular locality in these words: "It is neither realistic nor constitutionally sound to read the First

Amendment as requiring that the people of Maine or Mississippi accept the public depiction of conduct found tolerable in Las Vegas or New York City." And in the 1973 decision *Paris Adult Theatre v. Slaton* the Court articulated state interests in restricting pornography, including "the interest of the public in the quality of life and total community environment."[3] In expressing their complete dissatisfaction with available efforts, including education and consciousness raising, the feminist antipornography campaign curiously aligns with the civil libertarian in a wholesale dismissal of localism: to the former it is insufficient; to the latter it is too much.

In this repudiation of local initiative—whatever one may think of the particular stipulations of *Miller v. California*—we see the terms of much of our political discontent. Such radical critics and theorists as Sheldon Wolin, John Schaar, and Harry Boyte have pointed out often and eloquently that the eclipse (in Boyte's words) of "localist, voluntary, and historically grounded institutions has all too often been seen as unimportant or even beneficent" by reformers committed to grand overreaching visions or to nonpopular strategies. Hannah Arendt's prescient comments are worth recalling in this regard: "Liberals," she wrote, "fail to understand that the nature of power is such that the power potential of the Union as a whole will suffer if the regional foundations on which this power rests are undermined. The point is that force can, indeed must be centralized to be effective, but power cannot and must not. If the various sources from which it springs are dried up, the whole structure becomes impotent." A project for the political long haul is to work to bring the periphery back to life.

Citizens acting as civic beings, if pornography is the question, can begin in a number of ways. First, because communities are formed from the diverse comings together of men, women, and children, of young and old, of friends and protagonists, a defense of erotic intimacy between men and women that does not patronizingly brush aside the difference between "normal" heterosexuality and pornographic cruelty is central. Radical feminists conflate the two and antisexual moralists deny the former. Second, at odds with libertarian focus on "externals" only, citizens would recognize the extraordinary power of visual images to shape identity and to open up or squeeze out space for moral reflection. The brutalizing potential of manufactured mass porno-vision cannot be dismissed out-of-hand, nor should a causal link to actual behavior be necessary in order for communities to take some action to prevent an aesthetic of cruelty from taking over

Main Street. Communities should have the power to regulate and curb open and visible assaults on human dignity, but they should not seek to eradicate or condemn either sexual fantasies or erotic representations as such. This, invariably, must be a process of open, political give-and-take with all points of view represented in the community taking part in the debate. Remedies at law are available if this, rather than the socialwide elimination of all forms of pornography defined so broadly as to sweep up any sexual representation any woman finds offensive, is endorsed.

To the extent that pornography is symptomatic of, and helps to further, modes of social disintegration, creating contexts in which the least powerful (*especially* children) suffer the most, it becomes an appropriate target for action, regulation, and reproof. But with this proviso: knowing we cannot return to a harmonious way of life in which we share a complete set of moral values, communities must leave space for putting pornography in its place rather than seeking to eradicate it altogether. Here the language and reality of First Amendment freedom chastens overly zealous efforts to create or demand a coerced consensus. If we moved in this direction we might break free from the unacceptable alternatives our civil society seems to throw up fairly consistently: freedom versus community, virtue versus vice, liberty versus constraint. Just perhaps we might arrive at some future point where the remorseless fantasies of pornographers no longer carry the force of the present moment because such fantasies would cease to speak to our fears, our fragmentations, and our resentments.

10

The Power and Powerlessness
of Women

The discussion of power in political science is known to practitioners in the discipline, but it is news to most people. This essay is dedicated to Rene S. de Epelbaum and Maria Adela de Antokaletz, Mothers of the Plaza de Mayo, Linea Fundadora, and it is intended for generalists, not specialists. It first made its appearance as an address at the University of Leiden, Holland, as part of a conference inaugurating a women's studies program.

It is *not* the task of the political theorist to tell people "what is to be done"; rather, our vocation, as Hannah Arendt articulated it, is to *think* what we are doing. And, I would add, to serve as a moral witness to the perils and possibilities of one's time.

What follows is a reflection on power and powerlessness, on the who and the what of it, or at least a bit of it. I begin with a conundrum: women are and have been powerful; women are and have been powerless. There is no contradiction here. Instead we find a resonant paradox, an ambiguity that seeps through all reflective attempts to confront "the powerlessness of women." In recent decades, to be sure, important commentators reflecting various feminist positions often ignored or denied associations of women with images of authority, potency, and power, concentrating instead on women's historic oppression, "second-class citizenship," and, in the view of some, universal victimization.

There are many theoretical and political reasons for this focus in recounting the story of women in culture and history. But in telling only one side of the story the commentators to whom I will offer a counterpoint sometimes wound up portraying women as so uniformly and universally downtrodden, demeaned, infantilized, and coerced that men came to seem invincible, individually and collectively terrifying in their power and their intent to oppress. It was hard to see how women might emerge from the shadows confronted, as they were, by such an implacably hostile external force. The "oppressed group model," as Kathleen Jones has described it, "tended to present a one-dimensional view of women's experiences that denies categorically that there was anything redemptive, or politically valuable about them. Ironically, this view incorporated the devaluation of women's experiences, and accepted the patriarchal reading of the significance of women's lives it claimed to be criticizing."[1]

Yet women themselves really knew—and *know*—better, whatever the reigning ideology might dictate. We know that we are not wholly without resources as we bring our personal and political authority to bear in complex social situations. We know that we have various means to attain at least some of our desired ends. We know that our foremothers deeded to us much more than a sustained tale of woe. We contemporary women are the heirs of centuries of women's stories and strengths, all the many narratives of perseverance and survival, of determination to go on through tragedies and defeats. We know our mothers and grandmothers often had laughter in their hearts, songs on their lips, and pride in their identities. Knowing this, we cannot accept any account that demeans women in the name of taking measure of our powerlessness.

It is difficult for me to think of women as powerless in any total sense. I am a child of the rural American West, the state of Colorado. If one has seen either one's grandmother or mother or aunts drive a tractor, load cattle for market, organize a charity drive, manage the household finances, kill a rattlesnake, start a small business, purchase a truck, make clothing out of flour sacks, preserve fruits and vegetables for the winter, break ice in sub-zero weather so the cattle can drink, stand for election to the governing body of the local school district, get a high school diploma through an extension course, become a citizen at the age of sixty-five, or make determined stands on a number of issues ranging from where the family will live to what job the husband-father should take and what would be too disruptive to the family, one shares with the writer Alice Walker a tradition that assumes women are *capable*. Yet we also know that our foremothers did not—save for a few extraordinary and rare royal leaders—run countries, fight wars, explore and conquer new lands, make the laws and enforce them, or determine the shape of official, bureaucratic arrangements in the modern world. They were neither industrialists nor generals, presidents nor judges, political theorists nor polity founders. Women do not figure in the canon of Hegel's "world historic figures."

Our legacy is riddled with ambiguities. Our thinking about this legacy must grapple with a double edge: power and powerlessness. I will not go over by-now familiar ground, all the data on earning disparities, sexual victimization, lopsided poverty, and institutional invisibility. I presume the reader shares some general recognition of the structural dimensions of women's social and economic power-lessness. But this is the beginning of the story. Facts never speak for themselves. We use them to tell stories. We locate them inside wider webs of meaning and significance. Our conceptual frameworks turn on the way we understand key terms, most important, "power" itself.

DEFINING POWER: WHY POLITICAL SCIENTISTS HAVE MISSED SO MUCH

I teach in a department of political science. But I describe myself as a political theorist. The self-understanding embedded in my effort to distance myself from the label "political scientist" is no mere quirk. For those among my colleagues who assume the authority of "sci-ence" believe that terms of political discourse, including power, can be defined and understood operationally. To this end, such inescap-able concepts as "power" get reduced to stipulative definitions that enable the researcher, or so the story goes, to formulate and test hypotheses on whether, and to what extent, power is operative in a particular instance.

Thus the definition of power developed initially in mainstream American political science got reduced to the formula: X has power over Y if he can get Y to do something Y would not otherwise do. We can observe Y's behavior and assess the force X brought to bear. The locus for such observations is extant decision making or political institutions—national, state, or local governing bodies or organized associations that aim to influence such bodies—corporations, unions, and interest groups. Power is a form of compulsion exerted by the already (relatively) powerful upon one another within official political institutions designed to promote the aims and interests of competing groups. It is of, by, and for elites.

Power as a form of direct pressure on a social actor to take a specific action here becomes a thing in itself, measurable like amps on an electric meter. There is no room in this discourse for moral debate or judgment. As interesting and important as such debates might be, they have no legitimate role to play in scientific politics. Values are one thing; facts and nothing but the facts are another. Within the larger political vision presumed by this one-dimensional view of power, women got construed as apolitical beings by definition. This is the way I "learned" it in graduate school. The argument was really quite simple. Women and men have different social roles. The social role of women promotes a value system based upon women's life experience inside "non-political" areas of social relations—marriage, the family, religious and communal associations. Not occupying decision-making roles and arenas, women are severed from the give-and-take of interest-group politics and its rule-governed power brokerage. Women are neither the Xs, with the power over, nor the Ys, whose behavior is compelled. Women do not figure in the geometry of power relations. Even voting by women is essentially an apolitical activity, a means whereby women, who tend to be moralists, hence conservative, support those political parties that appear to confirm their values rather than promote their interests. Promoting interests is a political activity; preserving values is nonpolitical. (Needless to say, this argument has not aged well.)

Pinioned inside this discourse of tautologically confirmed and confirming meanings, women faced a perpetual double bind. Concerns that arose from their positions in the private sphere, including the health, education, and welfare of children, were construed as mere expressions of personal values and moralistic concern. But hard-nosed realistic talk about power from women meant they had forfeited the right to represent to or within the public sphere the private world they had forsaken by definition when they chose to locate themselves as political beings.[2]

Recognizing the conceptual shortcomings and political complacency of this once prevailing view, a few rebellious analysts worked to broaden the scope of analysis by extending the meaning of power. One important attempt along these lines by two political scientists yielded an alternative formula. Power, they argued, is not limited to X making a decision that compels Y but to X devoting himself to limiting the scope of political decision making to consideration of only those issues he finds nonthreatening. Power may be operative when no specific behavior or action is discernible, for one tacit aim of those who wield official power is to *preclude* action and to forestall debate. Thus it is that some issues are organized into politics and some are not. Those that are not remain "private discontents" outside the purview of public policy. This unacknowledged face of power enables the powerful to deny that politics is involved in many situations and outcomes because no overt public conflict has occurred.

This second, more complex definition of power, although it retained an institutional focus on decision makers, opened up some important questions. It directed the attention of researchers to how and why some questions get defined as "political" while others do not. It helped analysts see that every social order is sustained in ways sometimes hidden from public scrutiny and accountability. It disrupted the complacency with which mainstream political scientists justified nonparticipation in political life by assuring themselves that those who did not participate in politics were those for whom participation was not a value. That is, according to the complacent view, ignorant, indifferent, or satisfied persons or groups preferred the value of nonparticipation by definition. If they reckoned participation highly, they would participate. There are, after all, no legal barriers to running for office, joining a party, becoming a lobbyist, or promoting one's interests. Even among men *Homo politicus* is a relatively rare animal. The majority of working-class men, for example, are not politically active because their values dictate nonparticipation. The same is true of all but a few women—their values locate them outside the realm of politics proper.

All this seems very abstract, very "academic" indeed. But academic debates exert real effects on the lives of real people given the power to "name" and to define we lodge in experts. To insist that women play and have played no political role from a standpoint that offers a full-blown rationalization for their—and others'—nonparticipation is to justify a social order while claiming merely to describe it. Thus it is that congealed political realities get refracted through thought in a mutually reinforcing relationship. Those defined outside the boundaries of concern confront not only institutional barriers but unreflective analyses that name them in ways they themselves have not chosen. Perhaps I have said enough to signal my dissatisfaction with inherited understandings from positivist political science if we would think in supple ways about women's power and powerlessness. Does political theory, that enterprise with which I associate myself, do any better?

THINKING ABOUT POWER THEORETICALLY

Rousseau, it seems, knew something. For it was Rousseau who proclaimed that those who separate politics from morals must fail to understand both. A detour through the past in the form of those texts that comprise the canon of Western political thought yields many riches. This tradition is not of a piece, encompassing Aristotle and Aquinas, Augustine and John Stuart Mill, Machiavelli and Marx. It offers multiple understandings of power, its meaning, its range of application, its legitimate and illegitimate uses, and its relation to authority, justice, and political order. A few Western political theorists took up "the women question" explicitly; most did not. But even those who did not instruct us through their sometimes torturous attempts to explain and to justify the political powerlessness of women or, perhaps better said, women's nonpolitical being and identity.

I cannot recount this centuries-long tale here.[3] Most important for our consideration are the many "power" words in classical languages, a plethora of contrasting, sometimes overlapping, sometimes competing meanings. For power has not yet been shrunk down to meet the requirements of secularized and scientized analysis. Thus we find *imperium, virtù, arete, potestas, potentia, dynamis,* and more.[4] Power is construed variously as creative energy, as ritual, as force, as legality. The dictionary (OED) reflects this kaleidoscopic conceptual inheritance. "Power" occupies a full column divided into three major categories of usage: as "a quality or property," as "the ability to do something or anything, or act upon a person or thing, or to act upon a person or thing," or as "a particular faculty of body or mind," "the ability to act or affect something strongly; physical or mental strength; vigor, energy, force of character."

Within the relational, contextual, and shifting boundaries of power as used and understood in political and social life historically, women can be seen as having the ability to act upon a person or thing, particularly children, hence as powerful. As well, individual women certainly possessed faculties of body or mind that offered them "the ability to affect something strongly." We know this from folklore and social history alike.

Yet neither women as a group nor individual women could leap over embedded constraints on the form and scope of their power. Women could be saints but not popes, queens but not legislators, angels of mercy but not warriors of death. Whether our historic forebears regarded such constraints as unacceptable is not an easy question. Not holding our ideas of power and equality, not being members of modern secular society that celebrates individual choice and downgrades community obligation, what strikes us as intolerable perhaps seemed to the overwhelming majority of our premodern ancestors part of nature's plan and God's design. Women were authoritative in ways men were not; men governed in ways women did not. (It is important to remember that male choices and roles were restricted and constrained too, although, from our vantage point, men in general and men in the ruling stratum in particular appear to have had a good deal more pomp in their circumstances than similarly placed women.)

If one takes an even longer view of the story of power, before Plato, Aristotle, and the self-conscious beginnings of political thought, sacred, mytho-poetic usages predominate. For power is indispensable to various ways of thinking about things—not only politics but God and the sacred. Political meanings in the West got layered upon older understandings, potent images of ritual, taboo, the demonic, the sacred. "Thine," says the Bible, "is the power and the glory." This is reflected in the OED, which shows power as a characteristic of political or national strength, a usage dating from 1701—a "late use," claims the dictionary, and one preceded by "a celestial or spiritual being having control or influence; a divinity."

Whether to what extent women were powerful or powerless, silenced or heard, revered or reviled in past societies, Western and non-Western is an assignment for a lifetime. We do know certain things, however. Every human society differentiates maleness from femaleness, and widely differing societies have located complementary forms of power with the two sexes. Historic and ethnographic evidence suggests that women's economic and political power and authority is most likely to occur where one finds a "magico-religious association between maternity and fertility of the soil," thus associating women "with social continuity and social good."[5] Cultural anthropologists argue that to view male and female authority in societies like the Iroquois, where women wielded as great a power in some areas as men did in others, as sexually unequal by definition reflects a Western, state bias. In dozens of societies, they insist, neither sex was wholly dominant over the other, but each prevailed in demarcated areas of social life.

Recent women's studies scholarship suggests that such societies, whose lives run as subtexts within the dominant narrative order, retain this mode of complementarity. In her introduction to Marla N. Powers, *Oglala Women. Myth, Ritual and Reality,* Catherine Stimpson writes: "Powers argues that Oglala society rebukes the theory that gender is a hierarchy universally demanding female subordination, a theory that women's studies has frequently found plausible. Particularly today, Oglala women may devise a fiction of male superiority. In actuality, relations between female and male tend to be 'complementary,' with female and male roles having equal strength and power. For the Oglalas and for their traditions, sexual difference breeds mutual respect."[6]

One thread that seems to run through the tangle of historic and ethnographic evidence is a picture of *formal* male power being balanced or even undermined by *informal* female power. Myths of male dominance are often maintained when males do not actually dominate in the secure ways the myths proclaim. In peasant societies, for example, beneath the appearance of total male dominance lies a complex reality in which women exercise effective control over many aspects of community life and men are not allowed to interfere.[7]

In societies, past and present, in which the household is the hub of human life, an arena of economic production as well as human procreation, a school, a hospice, a clinic, a symbolically and actually potent place, women are often the repositories of several understandings of power associated with that sphere. Such female power is complementary to the more institutionalized and juridical authority of men. "The roles and power ascribed to women are informal and uninstitutionalized in contrast with the culturally legitimated statuses and authority attributed to men," writes one cultural anthropologist.[8]

What are we to make of all this? We cannot return to presecular, premodern ways of life. But we can see that secular male dominance is most visible in societies in which complementarity of powers has given way to an enhancement and expansion of institutionalized male authority accompanied by a simultaneous diminution of women's domestic, sacral, and informal authority. As the world of female power recedes, the sphere of male power encroaches, absorbing more and more features of social life into the orbit of the juridico-political, the bureaucratized, the legitimately powerful: the state. Women are left with few apparent options: to acquiesce in their historic loss of symbolic-domestic authority; to manipulate their diminished social role as mothers inside increasingly powerless families; or to join forces with the men, assuming masculine roles and identities and competing for power on established, institutionalized terms. If one embraces a strong version of the teleology of historic progress we have inherited from the Enlightenment, with its attendant ontology that locates women on the negative side of the ledger along with nature, emotion, and passion, one has little choice but to leap into the arms of the hegemonic discourse and to embrace the already established vision of the free, rational, wholly independent male self and his powers and power.

If none of these options seems particularly attractive, perhaps we need to rethink the terms of our current situation. I am searching for a language that helps us to see that dependence and independence, powerlessness and power, are deeply related and that not all forms of dependence or human vulnerability can or should be jettisoned or rationalized out of our theories and our ways of being in the world. Knowing that women have been powerful in many times and places; recognizing that women have not been uniformly subjugated and powerless, we are invited to search for new forms of public and private power. As our focus shifts from obsession with images of female victimization, we recognize the often terrible costs of being the institutionally and politically powerful sex. For is it not ironic that in some contexts the dominant sex has also been the most expendable— that, historically, male bodies have been sent into battle to kill and to die in order that female bodies of their own group be protected? Do we not convey a peculiar double message to our eighteen-year-old sons whose social power and social vulnerability is signaled by registration for the draft?

Such recognitions spawn competing responses. To many contemporary feminists being powerful means assuming legitimate authority as well as male political and military responsibility. They proclaim a "right to fight." Other feminists seek to create a society modeled on female principles, one in which all male-constituted social and political forms are destroyed and a wholly new order dominated by women prevails: matriarchy must supplant patriarchy. Many women who do not identify as feminists yearn for a return to traditional complementarities in which they are provided for, looked after, and sheltered from the grim realities of the rat race and the shocks of political combat. (This dream can be realized only by middle- to upper-middle-class women. Poor women, black women, and working-class women were never sheltered in this way.) But Western political theory, that is to say, ideas within the grasp of those of us constituted in part by social absorption and authorization of categories central to that tradition, may harbor the tentative promise of another.

TOWARD A REFLECTIVE UNDERSTANDING OF POWER AND POWERLESSNESS

Potestas is one Latin term for power, especially political power, control, supremacy, or dominion. *Potentia,* another Latin word for power, is understood as might or ability, efficacy, potency, especially "unofficial and sinister." These contrasting usages demarcate roughly the boundaries of male and female forms of power historically.[9] Males have been the official wielders of institutional power and dominion; women the unofficial (hence politically uncontrollable) repositories of nonlegitimate, "nonpolitical" power. *Potentia* conjures up the sinister, threatening, and deviant, occupying a boundary that touches on the polluted, the uncanny, the potentially disordered.

But suppose we put another spin on this matter. Suppose that what we have to fear today is not so much the uncontrolled, because uninstitutionalized, power of the now-powerless but the overcontrolled ministrations of the institutionally powerful. Suppose the institutional forms designed to limit, contain, and curb excesses of power are themselves increasingly powerless. Suppose the powerful are daily disempowered by the very magnitude of the force at their disposal. Suppose what has become of dominion is not so much the power to act but a compulsion to react.

No doubt this supposes too much. But suppose my suppositions are even partly true. What are the implications? The most dire is that highly institutionalized forms of government, increasingly bureaucratized and dominated by technologies that facilitate centralized control, erode space for political action, for beginning something anew, for creating and sustaining social forms that allow human beings to be at home in the world. Conjuring with fantasies of perfect control, we find ourselves dominated by our tools, our instrumentalities of violence, genuflecting at the relentlessly moving altar of consumerist fantasy, obsessively seeking more and better and the best.

Psychiatrists speak of nuclearism. Scientists conjure with the stuff of life itself: genetic engineering it is called. Missiles proliferate. Acid rain falls. Toxic waste stagnates. Species are added to the endangered list. Teenagers in North America commit suicide in growing numbers. Who are we? What have we become? Powerful or powerless: does it matter? Are we not more and more equalized as potential victims of the historic quest for power as control in the West?

The answer is a yes that must be deployed with caution. To give in too fully to the apocalyptic mode tempts us to allow full play to our most deeply rooted apprehensions, thereby blinding us to possibilities that may lie within our reach. Ends—it has become a truism—are also beginnings. I am searching for a vision of power as productive, as an incitement to both discourse and action. An enticing project for feminist theory and women's studies might be to trace historically, or, better, genealogically, paradigms of "the female" and "the mother" that have served as catalysts for action, sources of female authority, on the one hand, and, on the other hand, those paradigms that have constrained, inviting privatization and pettiness of purpose. One must then go on to offer critical reflection on these exemplars. An example would be the strength of the reencoded image of the Spartan mother, which has located women in the social and political world, served as a source of meaning and civic power, but, simultaneously, reinscribed the centrality of war making, what I tag "armed civic virtue" in my book, *Women and War,* in the grand narrative of the West.[10]

A central feature of the engendered power I am urging on is that it have within it the means to put earthly force and dominion on trial and evaluate it with reference to certain moral ends. This means that the realm of necessity, the world of everyday human meaning and life, no longer be either despised or defined as the unworthy mirror to the freedom of politics. In classical antiquity, the exclusionary *polis* and coercively universal empire got supplanted by the ideal of a universalist egalitarianism to be instantiated in particular, redefined communities. Although this heady moral revolution failed to secure earthly peace and justice, its promise of a peaceable kingdom lives on wherever men and women refuse to make peace with making war; wherever love and care are gifts freely given, not revocable allowances that may be stingily recalled; wherever the power to forgive is reckoned at least on a par with the power to punish.

Some interesting historic parallels are called to mind by this historic fragment. If the early Christian man or women was a "fool" to the received "wisdom" of the powerful and worldly, women have been constituted in many ways as: a potential threat to "that which makes the city one" (Plato); a temptation to forsake civic virtue (Rousseau); an "everlasting irony" in the bosom of social life (Hegel): and a brake on the process of civilization given their devotion to the particular (Freud). Perhaps women are the "fools" in Western political thought and practice whose official powerlessness grants them a paradoxical freedom from full assimilation into the dominant public identity whose aims, in our day, are efficiency and control. This freedom invites despair as one's dreams of doing or becoming a surgeon, a president, or an electrical engineer evaporate in the harsh realities of a competitive, male-dominated world. This freedom invites bitterness if one fears daily that one's children may lack food and clothing and even minimal safety. Nevertheless, if at least partial exclusion from wholesale absorption into terms of institutional power is maintained,

space for critical reflection and challenge to that power is more likely
to be sustained.

Power and politics, yes, but what forms of power, what sort of
politics? I put this as a difficulty, another conundrum, borrowed from
the Czech resister, writer, and now, miraculously, president of
Czechoslovakia, Vaclav Havel: the politics of the power of the
powerless, or resistance in the face of the radical absence of choice.
What Havel and the Polish dissident and theorist of *Solidarnösc*, Adam
Michnik, offer to considerations of gender and power is this: they
remind us that to continue to think in the inherited categories of
Right/Left, progressive/regressive is, in Havel's words, to give one a
"sense of emerging from the depth of the last century." He writes: "It
seems to me that these thoroughly ideological and many times
mystified categories have long since been beside the point."[11] Such
binary opposites fail to capture the complexity of feminist reflection
and cannot come close to the content of our actual beliefs and actions.

In language that makes contact with contemporary feminist awareness of, and emphasis on, difference and plurality, Havel insists that
between the aims of what he calls the "post-totalitarian system" or
what I dub, more generally, monological statism, there lies a "yawn-
ing abyss: while life . . . moves toward plurality, diversity, independent self-constitution and self-organization, the post-totalitarian system demands conformity, uniformity, and discipline . . . the post-
totalitarian system . . . is utterly obsessed with the need to bind
everything in a single order."[12] Human identity is surrendered to the
homogenized identity of the system. Havel calls this "social auto-
totality," a system that depends on demoralization and cannot
survive without it.

What the movements in Prague and Gdansk share in common with
some strands of contemporary feminist and postmodernist discourse
is the attempt to eschew old categories and to refuse to privilege the
state, in a sense, to worship it by unambiguously valorizing its
sovereignty. As feminists explore and search for forms of power that
do not replicate business as usual, one powerful reality must be kept
in mind: war is immanent within the form of the modern nation-state.
To hope that one might use the state as a vast instrumentality to be
turned unambiguously to our good ends and purposes is to be naive
and, paradoxically, to find oneself supporting practices that subvert
the democratic-egalitarian core of feminism.

These movements also insist on the centrality of a movement's style
of action, including a refusal to deploy base methods in order to be

effective and to respect the dignity of those they oppose. They make contact with a political vision that acknowledges the vulnerability of, and need to nurture, all new beginnings, including those of a political sort. This may seem a weak and problematic reed, but if one is to protest the breaking of bodies and minds in the politics of our troubled epoch, it is, I believe, the point from which we should begin.

I discovered, or, perhaps, *learned* this lesson anew in the hours I spent with members of the Mothers of the Plaza de Mayo in Buenos Aires, Argentina, in August 1986. By their public presence and courageous action, the Mothers shattered the systematic deceit that had shrouded the disappearances of their children; they transgressed official orders in marching in the Plaza. "Las locas," the madwomen, they were called— beyond the pale, outside the boundaries of legitimate politics. Yes, we are crazy, they said, turning the epithet on its head. They reversed the strategy of the authorities and fashioned it into a political weapon. The language they spoke was double: the language of the anguish of a mother's loss and the language of human rights.

Here are fragments of one of our exchanges:

Author: "Do you expect to go on indefinitely?"

Maria Adela de Antokaletz: "What we want is that the Mothers of the Plaza de Mayo must endure forever, much more than in our own lifetimes. It has to do with having a guardian position on society in order to watch so this will not happen again. Not here, not anywhere."

Rene S. de Epelbaum: "To watch and to denounce. Perhaps it won't be necessary for us to go to the Plaza if the criminals are punished. But we want to witness, to denounce every violation of human rights. Because, you know, at the beginning, we only wanted our children. But, as time passed, we got a different comprehension of what was going on in the world. Today I was listening to the radio and there was somebody who sings very well who was singing about children, about babies starving. This is also a violation of human rights. Perhaps it is not much that we can do, but people for human dignity and human rights must realize justice where they can."

Maria Adela de Antokaletz went on to tell me, to emphasize, that the struggle they had carried out had always had a "clear moral purpose" and had "always been non-violent and carried out with dignity." *Solidarnösc* as a movement shares with the Mothers (and, by implication, with the feminism towards which I am moving) a repudiation of the false transcendence of violence; a rejection of any order built on doubles and mirrors by which one keeps alive that by which one feels threatened. The aim of Las Madres and *Solidarnösc* was to liberate themselves by refusing to sacralize any new victims. "Neither maggots nor angels," Adam Michnik says—no one is utterly repulsive; no one utterly good.[13] There is truth here: not a big, booming, grandly teleological Truth, but a truth that disallows he or she who grasped it to serve as judge and executioner. And there is something of the nature of the Fool as well, one who refuses to conform to the wisdom of the world, whose folly reveals the established lunacy of princes, whose identities are a brake against deadening normalizations.

The last voice to be heard in this overlong meditation will be a woman's, but one who saw herself first and foremost as a citizen and a political philosopher. The categories of citizen and political philosopher essentially defined her, Hannah Arendt insisted; gender did not. Yet Arendt challenges the received notions of political beginnings presented as the actions of male hordes or contractualists, warring or pillaging until compelled by fear or self-interest to seek civic order. Such accounts of political founding deny the realities of human social beginnings from the bodies of women and from the fragile bodies of children. Not so Arendt, who embraces a metaphor of birth. Seeking the ontological root of hope, the human capacity that sustains political being and our capacity to act, Arendt finds it "in the fact of natality." Her metaphor, most fully elaborated in the following passage from *The Human Condition,* is worth quoting in full:

The miracle that saves the world, the realm of human affairs, from its normal, "natural" ruin is ultimately the fact of natality, in which the faculty of action is ontologically rooted. It is, in other words, the birth of new human beings and the new beginning, the action they are capable of by being born. Only the full experience of this capacity can bestow upon human affairs faith and hope, those two essential characteristics of human existence . . . that found perhaps their most glorious and most succinct expression in the new words with which the Gospels announced their "gladtidings": "A child has been born to us."[14]

The infant, like all beginnings, is vulnerable. We nurture that beginning, neither knowing, nor being able to control, the end of the story. Birth is a "miracle" that renews and irreversibly alters the world. Arendt's configuration stirs recognition of our own vulnerabilities and dependence on others. It offers, as well, a form of reason that rejects subduing and mastering others as essential to the attainment of one's own power and status as a human being.

In and through their powerlessness, women understand what it means to be vulnerable. Their openness to beginnings, even under conditions of hardship and privation, terror and torture, daily renew the world, making possible future beginnings. The challenge at this fateful juncture is to keep alive memories of vulnerability as women struggle to overcome structurally sanctioned inefficacy and to reaffirm rather than repudiate interdependencies as they seek a measure of institutional legitimacy. That I here call for a heroism that cannot reasonably be morally binding (for none of us is required to perform acts of supererogation) may be true. That I impose a weighty political burden on women, and that this is in some sense unfair, is undoubtedly the case. But women, from a double vision that straddles powerlessness and power, are in a powerful position to insist with Albert Camus that one must never avert one's eyes from the suffering of children and, seeing that suffering, one is required to act.

11

Realism, Just War, and the Witness of Peace

Consider the following: several years ago I delivered a seminar to the Columbia Women's Studies Seminar in New York City. My topic was "Realism, Just War, and Pacifism" and the implications for feminism of each of these complex political and ethical theories. This was an initial formulation of the considerations that later emerged in my book *Women and War*. I talked about the dominant image of the man in his capacity as war fighter, a character I tagged the Just Warrior, and I discussed as well his female counterpart, the Beautiful Soul, a collective representation embodying the values and virtues of home life once domesticity had been sealed off from concerns with the wider world.

I was careful to lay out the central concerns and premises of just war thinking. I did so because I wanted those who were listening to recognize that justifying war from a narrowly strategic or *Realpolitik* perspective and assessing whether war is just or justly waged are different kinds of activities, structuring the moral and political universe in dissimilar ways. I was not successful in this effort. My audience assumed that the just war position was little more than a patina on crudely fashioned *Realpolitik*; moreover, that hard-line Machiavellianism was preferable to all this moral glossing of violent realities. An eminent feminist philosopher, who was that evening my interlocutor and who discussed my essay in wise and discerning ways, shared my frustration. She, too, tried to convey a sense of what just war had meant historically and what it might mean, or might yet come to mean, for our own times. But we found an unreceptive audience. Our listeners were determined to collapse any distinction between realism and just war. They assumed that just war was and

149

always had been a weapon fashioned by the powerful in order to justify any and all wars the powerful sought to fight, to oppress persons in other societies, and to legitimate continued congealment of male/female identities. It was a frustrating night.

A second moment, this from teaching: for several years, I have taught a course called "Issues of War and Peace in the Nuclear Age." My students are interested, lively, concerned, skeptical, and irreverent, the best sort of students. As part of this course I use films, both Hollywood war films of the classical genre, for example, John Wayne's *Iwo Jima*, and antiwar films that have become classic, for example, Ingmar Bergman's *Shame*. But I also turn to films made by our own War Department, now Department of Defense, in various eras, including World War II. One of these is a striking film directed by John Huston called *The Battle of San Pietro*.

The film conveys the terrible life and death struggle to capture one hillside leading to one small village during the American campaign being waged up the Italian boot towards Rome. In and of itself the village of San Pietro was not terribly important, but it overlooked the Liri Valley; the Germans had dug themselves in and it was deemed important to get them out. Casualties were extremely heavy. The film shows young frightened men trying to slog their way up the hillside against sniper fire and, from time to time, we see one of these men crumple and collapse like a rag doll tossed to the ground by an angry child. The film's conclusion is haunting, for the Italian villagers, to escape the depredations of their German captors, had dug themselves into a mountainside. Many had been living for months in caves. They emerged tentatively from the caves into the light—ragged, filthy, gaunt, ill, barefooted. And they greeted the American GIs with great affection, as liberators. The Americans are then shown delivering supplies to the village and helping to detonate leftover mines and other incendiary or explosive devices before moving on to the next engagement.

In the discussion that followed the film I was shocked that many of my students, from a stance of hardened cynicism, no doubt on the underside of which lies crushed idealism, said that they considered the film a hoax. They didn't think the deaths were faked or the bullets were unreal but that the reaction of the Italian villagers to the presence of American soldiers was fraudulent. How could Americans be greeted as liberators? They simply couldn't believe it. They didn't believe it in part because they could not accept the possibility of just war. War for them was definitively encapsulated in the word 'Vietnam.'

Reading from *that* standpoint back into history, they could see in scenes of GIs helping to clear rubble, to deliver food, and to protect an area so that villagers could sow seeds in their fields and return to peaceful life only media chicanery. For them the image of Americans and villagers in time of war is represented by My Lai, not San Pietro. They had forfeited the notion of just war, at least as a possibility for the United States, past or present, even as many of these same students vociferously proclaimed the justice of "Third World revolutionary struggles."

Finally, one additional sign of the times. In a piece in the *New York Times* by Janusz Glowacki, a Polish playwright and novelist, we find a discussion of the dozens of ways that Shakespeare's *Hamlet* has been played.[1] As "a criminal melodrama, a drama of metaphysics, a lesson in Viennese psychoanalysis, or an internal passion play." Glowacki offers the suggestion that at the end of the twentieth century "Hamlet once again looks beyond the man to the state of the nation and seethes with politics." Reviewing several recent representations of Hamlet with the political theme held foremost, the Oedipal theme downplayed, he notes that in the shocking final moments of a recent production of *Hamlet* by Ingmar Bergman, Fortinbras's army "enters by demolishing the back wall of the stage, carrying machine guns and boom boxes that blast a deafening roar of hard rock. On their heads they're wearing black helmets with protective plexiglass shields. They're a cross between Middle-East terrorists, New York crack dealers, and South American guerillas. Expertly they toss corpses into a common grave followed by the furniture." And Glowacki observes that when he watched the play with a largely student audience at the Brooklyn Academy of Music this entry of Fortinbras's army was received with "carefree laughter" from the audience. Why? Because America "has not had any experience of the loss of independence, foreign armies, or occupations." Glowacki, who has had such experience, didn't laugh. "Not me," he says, "I belong to the nervous generation."

The happy laughter of that student audience is a mirror image of the cynicism of my students. They are secure in the knowledge that our power protects us even as they revile that which is done to sustain this power. So, on the one hand, laughing, safe, protected; on the other, convinced that we live in a world in which the rule of force is dominant and all else pales beside it.

It has been an object of curiosity to me for a long time how a cynical construal of war and war fighting, particularly when Americans engage in it, may go hand in hand with support of armed struggle in other arenas. One frequently hears celebrations of the possibility of a future of peace if only those who now wield power in unjust ways are bested, curbed, and curtailed. The dream is that those who have defensively engaged in armed struggle will no longer find it necessary to do so; that pacifists will have won the day with their insistance that we can solve problems if we just talk *to* rather than past one another; and that an era of peace and nonexploitation will have been ushered in. Current views on the part of the young, then, often seem an amalgam of fragments of *Realpolitik,* just war, and pacifist hopes.

I propose to explore our current discontents with this clash and melding of perspectives in mind, asking whether we can recapture just war thinking for our time, and, if so, what it would look like and what it might do for us that other ways of approaching these dire and solemn matters cannot. What is demanded of us as citizens if we take seriously a just war perspective? Is just war a viable civic philosophy, a robust way to structure the thinking of contemporary American citizens on issues involving war and peace?

First, I will discuss current alternatives to just war, setting these options as ideal types, hence necessarily exaggerated. And then I will go on to show the ways in which modified versions of each of the positions I will reject make contact with and help to enrich a just war framework.

The first alternative to just war is that of pure war. A hard-line, so-called realist posture tracks its genealogy from the Athenian generals telling the representatives of the Island of Melos in Thucydides' *Peloponnesian Wars,* "We're not interested in arbitration. We're not interested in negotiation. We've got the power. We are prepared to use force. You are undone"—the might makes right posture.

Essential to the pure war stance is the following: Between Athenians and all others—foreigners—the rule of force comes into play. Limiting instances of that rule are possible, that is, one might negotiate, one might arbitrate, but one is not required to do so if force is more certain and effective. The only requirement is to look out for one's own strategic concerns and to pursue with the greatest economy what will guarantee the most favorable outcome to oneself. Easier, then, to kill the men of Melos and take the women and children captive than to sit down over time and work out some kind of agreement, not knowing, of course, whether they will keep their end of the bargain; not knowing whether or not they may then strike some deal with Athenian enemies. In pure war, we find a world of war as politics, politics as war, a world that squeezes out persuasion, hence a stance that has fed bellicist imperatives throughout the history of the West.

Within the world of pure war the other, the foreigner, is *always* an enemy *in situ* or actual. The world is, as Colonel Oliver North repeatedly said, a dangerous place. But those dangers are understood in a particular way, in and through the notion that the "other" or *all* others are either enemies or potential enemies. The hard-line realist, as a theorist of pure war, makes of *disorder* an absolutized given, the *natural* condition of humankind. Anarchy is the defining feature both of relations between states and, as well, of domestic or internal affairs until order is imposed. But that order is inherently unstable. One must be constantly on guard. War is the primary way that states have relations with one another. War is as natural as the disorder that requires it. Heraclitus deemed war the father of all things, arguing that it is through strife alone, as a natural law of being, that anything is brought into being.

This concept of pure war helps to make possible the concept of total war or holy war in which the other is fit only to be obliterated or quelled, and all *right* is on one side. To move from pure war to justifications of holy war requires ideologies and doctrines, alas many of them historically religious, that promulgate a universe of Manichean absolutes: the Believer, the Infidel. Engrafted upon notions of we *versus* the barbarians, amalgams of pure war with right, with religious and ideological conviction, invite and have invited total and holy wars. But there is a version of contemporary realism that I will draw into contact with just war discourse. My reference point is a particular text, Michael Howard's *The Causes of War*.[2] Framed within a horizon set by realist assumptions, Howard nevertheless *rejects* a pure war, bellicist stance.

Howard argues that the contemporary realist must look at the political circumstances out of which conflicts arise. He finds two forms of abstract war thinking extremely dangerous. One, contemporary nuclear strategic doctrine, has separated itself from reality in a terribly dangerous way. He expresses his bewilderment as he reads the "flood of scenarios in strategic journals about first strike capabilities, counter-force or countervailing strategies, flexible response, escalation dominance, and the rest of the postulates of nuclear theology." And he indicts this kind of thinking as something Clausewitz, who remains the greatest theorist of war, would oppose because it is divorced from any coherent political context.

As well, Howard insists, the leaders of the European peace movement, and I think he would add the American peace movement, are also living in an abstract dream world. Many believe problems of power would melt away were it not for the vested interests of various rogues—governing classes, arms manufacturers, or other easy to indict, specific forces that block the road to what Kant called perpetual peace. Howard carves out a realist position as an alternative to *abstracted* realism run amuck, pure war, which ceases, therefore, to be realistic *and* to a peace politics untethered as to historic reality and possibility.

Howard insists that state war fighting is not pathological: it is a particular kind of conflict, the way collectivities have dealt with one another for better or for worse. States can and have moderated or eliminated conflict within their borders, but states or peoples will continue to find reasons to fight, either to preserve or to acquire a capacity to function as independent actors in the international system.

War is inherent in the structure of the state; states historically have identified themselves by their relations with one another, asserted their existence, and defined their boundaries by the use of force or the imminent threat of force. So long as the international community consists of sovereign states, war remains a possibility. We can mitigate, we can mute, we can and should negotiate. What is at stake is not just *raison d'état* but also *raison d'system*. This means having a stake in preserving a diverse international community. There is here an imbedded ethic, an ideal of a world of autonomous states that can and should attempt to resolve conflicts. But this is not at all times and in all places possible, and one's commitment to a diverse international community composed of multiple loci of power may require, sadly, and for limited ends and aims only, going to war.

To those who find this an unpalatable argument, Howard asks: What is the alternative? Continuous eruption of murderous local conflicts, whether tribal, familial, ethnic, or religious wars that were enormously destructive and repressive prior to the formation of states? The state is the guarantee of internal order. It has eliminated much of that conflict. The only realistic alternative available to us is the breakdown of the nation state, hence the loss of internal order. Balkanization, a term that always comes up in these discussions, or, perhaps, in our own time better put, Lebanonization, would be the result. He says: Is this what you want? Because that is what you are going to get if we move away from, or seek to defeat, undermine, or erode the power of nation states and the always present possibility of war.

It is important to be clear here. Howard's is neither a pure war nor a holy war perspective. He opposes crusades. Indeed, he would argue that holy wars historically have been made possible not because of the wily maneuverings of realists but because of the stalwart convictions of idealists, those who set the world up in and through highly moralized categories including visions of peace that are parasitic upon a totalized image of war. For if pure war is a story of absolute conflict, we find a vision of peace as a world of perfect harmony, perfect order, as its mirror image.

Just as there is a strong version of pure war there is a similar narrative of pure peace. I will now discuss the paradigmatic case of pure peace, explore why it is problematic, and elaborate a modified version. Within the horizon made possible by these two elaborations, I will argue that just war discourse can function as a compelling and vital civic philosophy.

Visions of perfect peace draw upon Christian dreams of the Kingdom of God. These, in turn, were parasitic upon mythologies of a lost Golden Age of fructifying harmony and full transparency in which none was an enemy to the other. The Christian gospel proclaims peace as the highest good, arguing that peace is not reducible to the terms of any earthly order. This Christian New Jerusalem was balm for the weary but proved over time a vexation for the impatient determined to bring peace to earth, the sooner the better. The high point of utopian peace hopes, prior to our own epoch, were sixteenth- and seventeenth-century utopias, and all contrasted the disorder they found with the *perfect* order, the world without conflict, that they sought. Peace discourse seeks to bring the transcendental down to earth in supreme confidence that human beings might enact eschatological feats. But, as I argued in *Women and War*,[3] this peace is an ontologically suspicious concept. It never appears without its violent *doppelgänger*, pure war, lurking in the shadows. Peace is inside, not outside, a frame with war in its most powerful and absolute expressions. War is threatening disorder, peace is healing order; war is human beastiality, peace is human benevolence; war is discordance, peace is harmony.

The apogee of proclaiming peace as an *absolute* good and an absolute possibility within our own tradition was the political philosopher Immanuel Kant's essay "On Perpetual Peace."[4] Kant absolutizes order. He celebrates republican commonwealths: if we are going to have peace, every society must be ordered internally in identical ways. Peace that is not perpetual is a mere truce; a genuine peace must nullify all existing causes of war. Any and all disorder, for Kant, is a falling away from preternatural wholeness. The peace that follows in his schema is a dream that can exist among like kinds and equals only, making of the mere existence of otherness a flaw in the perfect scheme of things. It is not so much that the lion will lie down with the lamb as that the distinction between the lion and the lamb will no longer even interest us; it will not be an occasion for any kind of concern or reflection. As in pure war, difference itself is a block to the end of peace. It is a source of danger that must be denied or eliminated. Peace is a series of ontological endorsements that project a world of ongoing equilibrium, harmony, and perfect order.

There are feminists historically who have been attracted to this vision of peace. For example, one finds in the World War I era, as well as eras before that and after that, arguments that women are to be the saviors of humanity, with pacific motherhood cast as the harbinger of future order. One finds contemporary spokeswomen contrasting masculinism, patriarchy, violence, and disorder with feminism, matriarchy, nonviolence, and harmonious order.[5] We are told that when feminists seize power it will appear only in its healthy form, as holistic understanding, which leads *naturally* to cooperative and nurturing behavior. Ironically, this feminist variant on pure peace requires its dialectical opposite, *pure war*, to sustain itself; it defines itself with reference to its other. Just as there are visions of realism that back away from pure war, there are visions of peace that eschew pure peace contsruals. There are stories of peace neither as perfect order nor perfect confidence in the human capacity to fashion on this earth a way of life that looks something like the vision we have of heaven. I refer here not to celebrations of harmony and wholeness but to arguments about how one might go about fighting. Rather than assuming absolute disorder and hoping for absolute order, one struggles to fashion a world of relative order and stability that makes room for and accepts the possibility of conflict. The question is how one responds to conflict, what brings conflict about, and what ways of fighting may preserve our human commonalities rather than setting others up as entities either to be obliterated into nonexistence or to be embraced into nonexistence so that no distinctions finally remain.

Pacificism as a way of fighting is associated with Gandhian *satyagraha*, with Martin Luther King's Southern Christian Leadership Conference, and so on. Here we find an insistence that disorder, fighting, and struggle can take a form that doesn't make absolute enemies out of others. In this way people transform themselves through participation in struggle. This alternative to pure peace involves an openness to suffering, including the possibility of drawing upon yourself the violence of others, always in the hope that they might forebear and in the belief that they—one's opponents—are open to moral example.

We are here inside a moral universe of real but limited goods and exigencies. It has none of the grandeur of the universe of pure force, the universe of Kurtz in *The Heart of Darkness,* or the universe of Kant, a world of perfect harmony. It is instead a sphere of partial achievements, of struggle that eschews violence and that accepts the possibility for and even the necessity of disorder. It is this view of peace that makes contact with just war thinking. So, at long last, it is to just war for our time that I will turn. What sort of civic philosophy does just war offer? Is it within our capacities to endorse that civic stance? Is it within the repertoire of our own possibilities? We cannot make just war thinkers of ourselves or others if neither we nor they fail to find within our own histories and identities possibilities that might be called forth in the form of just war considerations and just war purposes.

The Vatican II document on the Church in the modern world, *Gaudiam et Spes,* stated that Christians, even as they strive to resist and prevent every form of warfare, should have no hesitation in recalling that, in the name of an elementary requirement of justice, a people has a right, even a duty, to protect its existence and freedom by *proportionate* means against an unjust aggressor. This is not an obscure or abstract statement: it is a straightforward insistence upon a right to self-defense as an elementary requirement of justice. But that right cannot and must not take the form of total or holy war; it must be proportionate to the nature of the threat.

As a theory of war fighting and resort to war, just war thinking is a cluster of injunctions: what it is permissible to do, what it is not permissible to do. For example, that a war be the last resort, that war be openly and legally declared, that means be proportionate to ends, that a war be waged in such a way as to distinguish between combatants and noncombatants. The just war thinker, whether in his or her capacity as someone evaluating the resort to arms or evaluating the bases and nature of internal order, makes certain presumptions. One is a belief in the existence of universal moral dispositions. Another is an insistence on the need for moral judgments, for being able to figure out who in fact in this situation is more or less just or unjust and more or less victim or victimizer. Another, finally, is an insistence on a particular form of power, the power of moral appeals and arguments.

Just war thinking, as I argued in *Women and War*, requires much of us. It demands deep reflection by all of us on what our governments are up to, which, in turn, presupposes a self of a certain kind, one attuned to moral reasoning and capable of it, one strong enough to resist the lure of violence's seductive enthusiasms, one laced through with a sense of responsibility and accountability—in other words, a morally formed civic character. Alas, much just war thinking in the modern era fails to make contact with such possibilities.

Contemporary just war argumentation is often enormously abstract, featuring cheese-paring, recondite discussions about double effect, collateral damage, and so on. Whatever importance this mode of argumentation may have for moral theologians and formal ethicists, it does not connect with civic discourse. Mostly we do not think in and through abstract, systematizing categories. We think in terms of horror and injury, and, yes, just and unjust. What we bring to bear in terrible circumstances will be shaped by whether what is foremost in our minds at a given moment is the suffering of an individual child, say, or a threat to the autonomy of our state. It will depend as well upon whether an individual has constructed herself as a civic being within a frame of aggressive, outward-looking claims or more defensive civic concerns. Just war thinking becomes utopian if it relishes the hope that statesmen and stateswomen, as well as men and women in their everyday lives when they put their minds to it, will be attuned to and be able to insert themselves within the refined arguments of moral theologians. That is not only unlikely, the weight of historic evidence is against it.

But what just war thinking as a civic philosophy does have to offer is this: what is an expectation requiring little justification for the realist—namely, war, violence, and the resort to force—requires explanation and justification for the just war thinker. An additional strength of just war thinking in our time is that it pictures the individual within a framework of overlapping communities, commitments, and loyalties: families, civil society, state. We each carry a set of legitimate expectations about what these overlapping institutions and social relations mean and the ends they might serve. We also, on a gut level, react to injustice.

This sort of populist moral concern is assumed by just war thinking, required by it, and necessary to it. For just war is also a tacit account of politics that aims to be nonutopian yet to place "the political" within an ethically shaped framework. Once one spells out the implications for a just war position, the possibility of sustaining the moral ethos necessary to support such a position may seem overwhelming, beginning with the fact that people may be enjoined to die rather than to kill.[6] That's only the beginning. In addition, in recent years, Pope John Paul II, the American Catholic bishops, and others have proclaimed peace a value that cannot coexist with injustice. Peace is not the mere absence of conflict, it is a kind of completeness, a *tranquilitas ordinis;* hence, injustice signifies moral disorder. For example, John Paul has called upon various peoples to form transnational orders based on the basic needs of humanity. He emphasizes peoples rather than states, stressing the possibilities for reconciliation and justice such that what is for the common good of a nation can be for the common good of the family of nations.

The stakes in all of this are high. There is an emphasis on the dignity of the human person, an insistence on the primacy of dialogue as a means to change, a commitment to deconstructing a lust for power in order to create space for alternatives, and a stress on sin as a form of moral disorder and division. If one shares these concerns, it is easier to see just war thinking in its full elaboration as a theory of international *and* domestic politics. It gives us leverage that we might otherwise lack to evaluate how the inner determination of state systems may deform the dynamic of the relations between and among states. The broader definition of a violent order is not just the absence of war but a false and unjust peace characterized by "the exploitation of labor, imperialism, and injustices of the field of the spirit." Such formulations place a heavy weight on the possibilities of achievement in the temporal realm, its worth, its value, and its capacity to attain justice.

But is there not a possibility that the persons from whom the just war thinker draws his constituency—religious persons whose dispositions are specifically Christian or, to a certain extent, Christianized—are thus placed under a temptation to sacralize the secular order or our attempts to reform it, thereby losing what was essential to just war in its inception, a vision of a perfect order *beyond* our reach that we can nevertheless use to assess an imperfect earthly order? In this latter scheme, we must never make the mistake of believing that we can bring a vision of pure justice to pass fully and completely on earth. To do so is to lose just war as a potent way to describe, assess, and understand the City of Man. It is, instead, to turn it towards utopian aspiration. But there is, within the just war tradition, a powerful brake to chasten such urges to sacralize—it is called St. Augustine.

Let us return to St. Augustine briefly. Recall Book 19 of *De Civatate Dei*, of *The City of God*.[7] Augustine has already rebuked the *Pax Romana*, that false peace, in which peace and war had a contest in cruelty and peace won the prize. Do not be taken in, he warns, by the empty bombast that blunts the edge of our critical faculties with high-sounding terms like honor and civic glory. What the Romans have done is not unlike what the pirate does with his tiny craft, but because the emperor does it with a mighty navy he is called an emperor rather than a pirate.

Unpacking the lust for domination, Augustine is devastating in his irony. The Romans, he claims, should have worshipped foreign aggression, *iniquitas aliena*, as well as Victoria as a diety, since they claimed all their wars were defensive. Peace, he admits, can be a term used to describe a coercive order. It is called peace, and people acquiesce in this definition because they do not want their repose disturbed. For peace is an instinctive aim of all creatures, even as it is the ultimate purpose of war. There is, then, a peace of justice and a peace of injustice. Yet even the peace of injustice is worthy of the name of peace as a fragile human achievement. It provides some partial order to the universe, some appropriate object of desire. It is dear to the hearts of humankind even when it is not a scheme of perfect justice.

This is the language just war thinkers should recall, at once a denunciatory language and a language of delight, of the longing and the yearning for peace as a real but limited good. Augustine writes that even the savage beasts safeguard their own species by a kind of peace. What tigress does not gently purr over her cubs and subdue her fierceness in order to caress them? How much more strongly is a human being drawn by the laws of his nature to enter upon fellowship with his fellow men and women. Even the wicked, when they go to war, do so to defend the peace of their own people and desire to make all men their own people, if they can, so that all men and things might be subservient to one master. War, paradoxically, may emerge from an overly robust yearning for peace as perfect order or dominion.

Augustine reminds us of our mortal natures, of what gets stirred up in us through civil strife, the temptation to ravish, to murder, and to devour in order to insure peace. This is a language at once evocative, morally evaluative, and rhetorically potent that we need to recover if we are to make just war discourse a real possibility for our own time; if we are to encourage people to think in and through its terms; if we are to seek peace as a worthy longing and then to think about what is worthy of the name of peace.

Augustine enables us to see that a lust for domination is at work in all human affairs as is dutiful concern for others. A pride in taking precedence over others is at work but so is compassion. He elides the distance between grand moral philosophy and ordinary moral reflection. He offers up a theory of civic possibility and of statescraft, reminding us of the problem of dirty hands within the *saeculum*, the realm of worldly affairs. He urges us to recognize with the realists that we live in a world of constraint and of unpredictabilities but that we need not endorse the pure war conviction that we are surrounded on all sides by enemies. What we are surrounded by is autonomous actors, not necessarily hostile enemies, but strangers, sources of independent action that may affect us. Such entities are potential enemies or allies; thus we are urged to forge alliances that preserve our independence yet make commonalities possible.

Just war thinking is a cautionary tale of internal and domestic order, a story of the systemic requirements and purposeful uses of power and order. It is a product of Western ethics, but it is also a proposal concerning the nature of the international system. If we think of just war in this way, we can more readily urge its consideration upon those who do not share our own tradition.

At the conclusion of *Women and War*, I argued that we must break the deadlock of war's mobilized language. I might have said the language of war and peace. I argued that a politics beyond war and peace refuses to see all right and good on one side only. Such a politics offers values for which one might die but not easy justifications for the need to kill. The political embodiment of this attitude is a character I call the chastened patriot, one who has no illusions, who recognizes the limiting conditions internal to international politics, and who does not embrace utopian fantasies of world government or total disarmament.

Chastened patriotism evokes compassion and concern for country, civic involvement in country, always with the recognition of the love and concern others bear for their countries. One's own actions are limited, not in spite of but because of one's loyalty to one's own particular polity. The chastened patriot has learned from the past. The chastened patriot is someone committed and detached, someone who can reflect about civic ties and loyalties. This stance is more likely if we have multiple ties and loyalties, to our families, our friends, our religious communities, and our voluntary associations as well as our polity. Recognition of our multiplicity is, as I have already indicated, one strength of just war thinking. Diversity and commonality are not only tolerated but cherished. A view of ourselves devoid of all utopian and universalistic pretentions, a view that takes account of the element of relativity in all antagonisms and friendships, that sees in others neither angels nor devils, neither heroes nor blackguards, is extolled.[8]

How does one simultaneously animate and chasten civic impulses? If there are any real possibilities open to us at the present moment along these lines, I believe they will come from a reconstructed just war tradition that makes room for patriotism even as it offers a critique of aggressive nationalism and imperialism; that makes room for internationalism even as it offers a principled rejection of an ideal of one world or one state.

The final word shall be Augustine's. From Book 19, chapter 11, *City of God:*

For peace is so great a good that, even in relation to the affairs of earth and of our mortal state, no word ever falls more gratefully upon the ear. Nothing is desired with greater longing, in fact nothing better can be found. So if I decide to discourse upon it at somewhat greater length, I shall not, I think, impose a burden on my readers not only because I will be speaking of the end of the city which is the subject of this work, but also because of the delightfulness of peace which is dear to the heart of all mankind.[9]

12

On Patriotism

What can England of 1940 have in common with the England of 1840? But
then, what have you in common with the child of five whose photograph
your mother keeps on the mantelpiece? Nothing, except that you happen to
be the same person.

And above all, it is *your* civilization, it is *you*. However much you hate it or
laugh at it, you will never be happy away from it for any length of time. The
suet puddings and the red pillar-boxes have entered into your soul. Good or
evil, it is yours, you belong to it, and this side the grave you will never get
away from the marks it has given you.

George Orwell, "England Your England"

*This essay, really an address, first saw light of day—or one version did—during the
1984 presidential campaign when the so-called new patriotism, President
Reagan's—"It's morning again in America"—was much bandied about. By contrast, I
presented a cautionary, yet hopeful, civic tale. I reformulated it four years later, but it
remains what it was in 1984—a tale of civic caution, a tale of civic hope. As an oral
presentation, footnotes were unnecessary, but I have gathered the sources I drew upon
in a long citation, which appears as notes to chapter 12.*

This is a story with patriotism as its ambivalent protagonist.[1]

Once upon a time patriotism was a discourse of high moral purpose
calling men and women to civic duty in behalf of their loyalty to a
particular political space: a country, a people, a homeland. For those
of us who think of ourselves as skeptics or rational, enlightened
liberals, patriotism has become a discourse of cynicism. We indict
patriotism as the first rather than the last refuge of scoundrels. We
link patriotism to political ruthlessness and national chauvinism.
Older ideals of living for, or in service to, one's country bear the tinge
of archaic usage or seem vaguely sinister. In an illuminating essay on
patriotism, published originally in 1973, the political theorist, John

163

Schaar, declared: "Patriotism has a bad name among many thoughtful people, who see it as a horror at *worst,* a vestigial passion largely confined to the thoughtless at *best;* as enlightenment advances, patriotism recedes." He added that "intellectuals are virtually required to repudiate it as a condition of class membership," and he proclaimed: "We have lost patriotism." Yet throughout much of the 1980's we were awash in what some called the "new patriotism." To reclaim patriotism, as I propose to do, and to distinguish it from much that is currently tagged patriotic is an act of remembrance, an act of criticism, and an act of hope: hope that we might retrieve ideals that open up space for political action as a way of being in the world. Walter Benjamin once wrote that the historian—and I would add the political thinker, as civic philosopher—must "seize hold of a memory as it flashes up at a moment of danger. . . . In every era an attempt must be made anew to wrest tradition away from a conformism that is about to overpower it." With a topic that bears such great historic and moral weight, always threatening to sink under the accumulation of centuries of hope and despair, nobility and chicanery, it is difficult to know where and how to begin. *That* one should begin seems to me a matter of some urgency. For patriotism is on the agenda and it is simplistic and arrogant to dismiss the issues involved as an easy matter of reactionary atavism, on the one hand, and rational progressivism, on the other.

Casting about for markers to locate myself within the density of patriotic lore, I turned, as many of us do, to the dictionary and found that *Webster's New World Dictionary* and I disagreed. Using the etymological derivation of the term patriotism from *patria* or *patrie,* from father, makes of the patriot one who, in words of the dictionary, "loves and zealously supports his own country," and that country is a "fatherland." Yet many nations and peoples see their homelands in feminine terms and through feminine iconography and myth. Holy Mother Russia joins the triumphant vision of a feminized republic, Marianne, emergent from the French Revolution. (The French *patrie* is ambiguous as a gendered representation, for it is *la patrie* with the feminine article—the feminine fatherland.) Our own Statue of Liberty, "lady liberty," is the feminized symbol of our Republic. America has been a "she" throughout our history. Recall Walt Whitman's ode "For You O Democracy," which taps both masculine and feminine evocations of country:

Come, I will make the continent indissoluble,
I will make the most splendid race that sun every shore upon,

I will make divine magnetic lands, With the love of comrades, With the
life-long love of comrades.
I will plant companionship thick as trees along all the rivers of America, and
along the shores of the great lakes, and all over the prairies,
I will make inseparable cities with their arms about each other's necks,
By love of comrades, By the manly love of comrades.
For you these from me, O Democracy, to serve you ma femme! For you, for
you I am trilling these songs.

The poem is at one and the same time a song of love by a patriotic
son to a feminine democratic mother and a robust proclamation of a
specifically masculine solidarity. Male and female images intertwine
in the poetry, song, and politics of patriotism.

But where *Webster's* and I really part company is in the dictionary's
insistence that patriotism is "love and loyal or zealous support of
one's own country, in all matters involving other countries" and it
offers as a synonym "nationalism." I dissent, and it is to patriotism
and nationalism, or patriotism *versus* nationalism, that I will now
turn.

It is the case that, for the most part, we no longer distinguish
between patriotism and nationalism. We collapse the one into the
other; we use them as the dictionary does, synonymously; or we are
simply indifferent to nuance. Yet patriotism and nationalism structure the political world and compel individuals in distinctive ways.
The historic triumph of aggressive state-centered nationalism unrav-
els patriotism, understood as the desire to protect and to nurture a
particular way of life.

All this needs parsing out. Our understanding of patriotism
cannot be simply definitional. For patriotism is too thick with life.
One must turn to symbols, examples, stories of lived lives. One's
answer to the riddle of patriotism will, of necessity, be a fragile
construction, subject to further refashioning. Patriotism *does,* as
Aslasdair MacIntyre has argued, name a *virtue.* But it is a far more
problematic virtue than he allows in his defence of *strong patriotism.*
Patriotism and nationalism can and do shade into one another. Each
calls up or calls upon a cluster of typical figurations, a family of
politically resonant notions including duty, honor, citizen, roots,
civic freedom, sovereignty, *raison d' état,* republic. Nevertheless,
because each evokes distinguishable realities, and because the most
interesting writers on the subject differentiate between the two, it
makes sense to tease out an argument that rescues patriotism from
the clutches of nationalism. What follows is the articulation,

overdrawn for expository purposes, between patriotism and nationalism as what Max Weber called ideal types.

Patriotism creates a political space of limits. A specific culturally
and politically defined homeland is a counter-universalist form. For
the patriot, the expansion of his or her political space beyond its
determinate limits may be a self-defeating exercise, for a true patriot
is one respectful of limits, one who acknowledges a pluralist world.
Patriotism is tied historically to traditions of civic humanism and
republicanism and, in American society, to a founding covenant that,
over time, called forth a republic out of a multinational mix of
peoples. The patriot enters the world indebted and bound: he or she
is not a free-floating ahistoric being but is instead a subject responsible to, and for, his or her political community. The patriot shares in
the identity, the purposes, and the virtues that action in common
with others provides. Joseph Mazzini, the great nineteenth-century
theorist of Italian nationhood, wrote: "The Country is the sentiment
of love, the sense of fellowship which binds together all sons of that
territory"—and, he should have added, though he did not, the
daughters, for women were and have been essential to the realization
of patriotic visions.

There are many ways to explain this desire to seek or sustain a
homeland, a country of one's own. John Schaar writes of a form of
"natural patriotism," by which he means that dense web of language,
ritual, song, myth, and legend, tied to a given spot on this earth—and
none other—into which we are born. As well, encultured human
beings are endowed with a powerful drive both to come together and
to distinguish themselves from those who do not share what they
share. The patriot, then, is one who embraces limits in part because
she recognizes that her identity as an encultured being is particular as
to a given historic time and space. This invites, as one possibility,
respect for the construction of identities different from her own, for
others have need of their particular containers for beings as well.

The nationalist, however, is one who challenges limits—limits of
territory and history and limits on despoilation—as possible means to
enhance the power of his own state in relation to all others. The cult
of national power too easily supplants a civic-minded love of country.
Contemporary nationalism frames political space from the top down,
not, as does patriotism, from the ground up. To be sure, modern
nationalism is usually traced from the French Revolution and the
mobilization of an entire nation—men, women and children—for war
in its aftermath based on the principle of popular sovereignty. But the

centralized nation-state, having come into being, drains power from the peripheries to the apex. For the nationalist, state sovereignty—that state as the monopoly of the legitimate means of violence, the state proclaiming loyalty to its sovereignty the highest human good—is key. For the patriot, a sense of "peoplehood," the bringing into being of cultural and civic ideals takes precedence. But there is no necessary constraint built into the nationalist idea save that of force as the final appeal. That is, in principle a nationalist state could extend its sway until it was checkmated by counterforce.

Nationalism more easily corrupts, inviting arrogance through our identification with a state's awesome preserve of force. Over time, nationalism disempowers us as civic beings. A statist society demands acquiescence or encourages passivity. From time to time, it may require the mobilization of workers, soldiers, and women. But to be available as raw material for mobilization or to be constituted through civic participation are qualitatively different experiences.

The enthusiasms of nationalism are sporadic and often occur at the expense of others: we gain the upper hand; we win the war; we triumph. Most of the time we "couldn't care less" because we don't see how we matter anyhow. But once in a while we are thrown a nationalistic bone on which to chew: we growl collectively and work ourselves up; the crisis fades; we retreat into privatization once more. But the strong nationalist always dreams of a perfectly unified society—highly mobilized and ready to battle.

Nationalism is so pervasive we must work to disenthrall ourselves, to detach ourselves long enough to take a hard look at its genealogy and its stranglehold. We can excise neither the term nor the phenomenon. An act of deconstruction, therefore, takes the form of weakening nationalism and showing the ways in which it is at odds with patriotism. For the task of critical separation between nationalism and patriotism we must call upon exemplary thinkers and political activists and, as well, resurrect some among the all too many monsters of nationalism.

First, several examples of rapacious nationalism. What emerges clearly is how nationalist concepts of statehood turn on the presence of enemies within and without. This was true, for example, of both Mussolini's Fascism and Hitler's Nazism. Mussolini proclaimed that "the Fascist conception of life stresses the importance of the State and accepts the individual only in so far as his interests coincide with those of the State. . . . The Fascist conception of the State is all-embracing; outside of it no human or spiritual values can exist, much less have value." The State, he insists, creates the nation-conferring volition on an otherwise inert people. The State is the masculinized form giver, shaping feminized matter. Without the State, no country, no people, exist. Imbued with this statist nationalism, a revitalized nation will go forth and, from its aggressive energy, take from the weak for the strong shall inherit the earth.

We usually think of Nazism in much the same way—a militant and narrow nationalism—and certainly many Germans experienced it as such. In Albert Camus's wartime "Letters to a German Friend," for example, he contrasts two attitudes. He loves his country too much to be a nationalist, he says. "You said to me," Camus writes to his friend:

"The greatness of my country is beyond price. Anything is good that contributes to its greatness. And in a world where everything has lost its meaning those who, like us young Germans, are lucky enough to find a meaning in the destiny of our nation must sacrifice everything else." I loved you then, but at that point we diverged. "No," I told you, "I cannot believe that everything must be subordinated to a single end. There are means that cannot be excused. And I should like to be able to love my country and still love justice. I don't want just any greatness for it, particularly a greatness born of blood and falsehood. I want to keep it alive by keeping justice alive." You retorted, "Well, you don't love your country."

Later on, Camus laments tenderly, "You speak of Europe, but the difference is that for you Europe is a property, whereas we feel that we belong to it."

The theory of Nazism included but went beyond militant nationalism, valorizing one of the most pernicious notions of twentieth-century thought—not so much nationalist as supranationalist, the insistence that blood or race is the biological basis for human collectivities. Hitler is quite clear in *Mein Kampf*, "We, as Aryans"—not Germans—"are . . . able to imagine a State only to be the living organism of a nationality." This transnationalism respects neither state nor national frontiers. For the highest purpose of the bio-State is preservation of "those racial primal elements which, supplying culture, create the beauty and dignity of a higher humanity." Hitler suggested that the word "nation" had been perverted through its links to nineteenth-century ideals of nationhood. Hitler's supranationalist aims, as Hannah Arendt points out in *The Origins of Totalitarianism*, looked for a dominating superstructure that would destroy all "home-grown national structures alike," for the body-politic, the *only* civic home for a patriot, was too narrow and modest a compass for Hitler's form of "über" nationalism.

These brief comments on hyper- and supranationalism of the sort that have terrorized our century unearths a central feature of nationalist discourse as compared with the discourse of patriotism. The nationalist specializes in global abstractions and declarations of absolutist principle. George Orwell, in "Notes on Nationalism," marks the drastic simplifications and overwrought evocation of competitive prestige in which the nationalist, one who uses all "his mental energy either in boosting or in denigrating," indulges. Orwell calls nationalist thought obsessive and indifferent to reality— persisting on a plane far removed from the concrete truths of everyday social life. Orwell is insistent that although the words, patriotism and nationalism, get used in vague ways, they involve opposing ideas.

The nationalist classifies people like insects and assumes that "whole blocks of millions or tens of millions of people can be confidently labelled 'good' or 'bad' "; as well, he insists that no other duty must be allowed to interfere with duty to the nation-state— hence the dismal, distorting blindness of Oceania's nationalist Newspeak in Orwell's 1984, a language that functioned to prevent historic knowledge, particularly memory of what had once been Britain, as well as to corrode particular loyalties to friends, families, lovers. The patriot, on the other hand, is devoted to concrete loyalties as well as to a homeland and way of life that "he has no wish to force upon other people." The nationalist evokes power as force—we need more of it, we can never have enough of it, somebody else is creeping up on us and may soon have more than we do—and sinks his own individuality into an overreaching identification with the collective.

By contrast I have in mind two men, both of this century, the one a disenfranchised son of America struggling to make the dream of American democracy a reality—Martin Luther King—the other, the well-educated son of a respected upper-class German family, an innovative theologian who struggled with and against love of country in the dark days of World War II—Dietrich Bonhoeffer. There is no time to tell you of Bonhoeffer's tale. Suffice it to say that he was a young man of great gifts who might have played it safe, lasting out the war on America's shores in residence at Union Theological Seminary in New York. Bonhoeffer had come to New York in June of 1939. But by July 1939, he decided, "I have made a mistake in coming to America. I must live through this difficult period of our national history with the Christian people of Germany. [He refers here to those of the confessing church, and all others who had not made peace with Fascism.] I will have no right to participate in the reconstruction of life in Germany after the war if I do not share the trials of this time with my people. . . . [We] face the terrible alternative of either willing the defeat of [our] nation in order that Christian civilization may survive, or willing the victory of [our] nation and thereby destroying our civilization." Bonhoeffer returned from security to danger and, as a German patriot as well as a believer committed to an international *oikumene* who knew that discipleship may bear enormous costs, he worked for the defeat of his own country, joining the anti-Nazi resistance to assassinate Hitler and to overthrow his regime. "You can't be universal anywhere except in your own backyard," he wrote. He was executed by the Gestapo Easter Day, 1945. A strong nationalist could never consider Bonhoeffer's course—it would not be within the range of his thoughts—that to preserve his country he must fight, and pray, for its defeat. Bonhoeffer's life and martyrdom exemplify a profound acceptance of his culture's gifts as well as responsibility for its excesses.

We all have some sense of what is at stake when we describe Martin Luther King as a "great American patriot" who had the courage to criticize his *"beloved country"* in time of war even as he affirmed his ties to that country. It would make no sense to think of King as a "great American nationalist." His "I have a dream" speech is a vision of a multinational, racially and regionally diverse, plural democracy united in a covenant for essentially pacific purposes. But it is King's "Beyond Vietnam" sermon (Easter, 1967) that I want to focus on briefly. He begins by reminding his listeners that "men do not easily assume the task of opposing their government's policy, especially in the time of war." He tells us he was concerned that the civil rights movement might be deflected should he speak out on Vietnam. But the time had come to "make a passionate plea to my beloved nation. This speech is not addressed to Hanoi or to the National Liberation Front. It is not addressed to China or to Russia . . . I wish not to speak with Hanoi, but rather my fellow Americans who, with me, bear the greatest responsibility in ending a conflict that has exacted a heavy price on both continents." These are the words of a patriotic—not nationalist—citizen, as well as a Christian. As Hannah Arendt reminds us, nationalist concepts of citizenship "depend to large extent upon the presence" of foreign enemies, and King undercuts explicitly any such construction.

King challenges America's evocation of enemies, *without*, in his words, turning "North Vietnam and the National Liberation Front" into "paragons of virtue": there is no reverse demonology in his plea.

Linking the war to the domestic economy, to a war upon the poor; noting the injustices committed in the pursuit of the war; insisting that external violence promotes inner decay; King proclaims there are means that cannot be excused. As one concerned with the "integrity and life of America today," he cannot ignore the war. "I speak as an American to the leaders of my own nation. The great initiative in this war is ours. The initiative to stop it must be ours." America remains a land of hope—we can, he insists, recapture a patriotic dream and revolutionary spirit, we can fuse love of country and an ethos of concern for all, we can and must struggle against a "negative anticommunism" and for democratic affirmation. He quotes Langston Hughes: "Oh, yes, I say it plain, America never was America to me, and yet I swear this oath—America will be!"

It would be pleasant to end the story here—with the evocation of a patriot's compassionate dream. But there are complexities in this picture. I shall discuss just one, women and the discourse of patriotism, offering intimations of a more complex story. I begin with that great celebrant of demanding patriotic citizenship, Jean Jacques Rousseau. Teasing apart patriotism from nationalism is but a first step; a second is to take the measure of various *patriotisms*, asking if we can or should aspire to be patriots for our time within the frames these diverse visions offer.

Rousseau's views on "love of fatherland and mother's milk" rush over the reader in a torrent of vivid portraits of civic virtue and morality. Rousseau has had many critics but one who specifically demurred, seeing in his tight linkage of civic virtue and stalwart soldiering a recipe for civic disaster, was the feminist foremother, Mary Wollstonecraft. I take up Rousseau's side of the story first.

Virtuous policies require virtuous families, Rousseau argues; children must imbibe love for the *partrie* with their mother's milk. Thus Rousseau in *Emile*:

The first education is the most important, and this first education belongs incontestably to women; if the Author of nature had wanted it to belong to men, He would have given them milk with which to nurse the children. The laws—always so occupied with property and so little with persons, because their object is peace not virtue—do not give enough authority to mothers. . . . There are occasions on which a son who lacks respect for his father can in some way be excused. But if on any occasion whatever a child were unnatural enough to lack respect for his mother—for her who carried him in her womb, who nursed him with her milk, who for years forgot herself in favor of caring for him alone—one should hasten to strangle this wretch as a monster unworthy of seeing the light of day.

Similarly, Rousseau finds the citizen in whom love of the homeland as a civic *mother* does not beat steadily and true, a monster, an unworthy wretch. Just as treason to the mother warrants strangulation, treason to the *patrie* calls for Draconian punishment, public shaming, and execution. Mothers figure centrally as the mothers of to-be citizens and of to-be mothers of citizens. Mary Wollstonecraft balks at this, insisting that women must be active citizens if they are to pass on civic virtue to their young. Why does Rousseau preclude direct female political participation? The answer lies in the terms of his civic republicanism. Rousseau offers a tautly drawn nexus between being a citizen and bearing arms, a sex-linked civic difference. Men alone have the bodies of defenders. Women, absorbed with caring for vulnerable infants, cannot go forth to defend the polity through force of arms. But they are nonetheless patriotically defined. He describes the female citizen, in a terrifying passage from *Emile*, Book I, as follows: "A Spartan woman had five sons in the army and was awaiting news of the battle. A slave arrives; trembling, she asks him for the news. 'Your five sons were killed.' 'Base slave, did I ask you that?' 'We won the victory.' The mother runs to the temple and gives thanks to the gods. This is the female citizen." In her critique, Wollstonecraft indicts a patriotic motherhood that looks solely to Sparta and disdains the loss of one's children.

Rousseau is a defender of the freedom and autonomy of bodies-politics. I have located this freedom, or the desire for it, as central to patriotism. The widespread use of mercenaries, of soldiers paid to fight, is one indication for Rousseau, following Machiavelli, of a loss of *virtú*, or civic virtue, and a sure sign the republic is on the wane. For republican virtue and freedom to flourish, citizen soldiers are required. To this end, women play a central role but must be kept in their (honored) place.

The glorious republicanism of the ancient world was lost, Rousseau argues, in part because of a loss of masculine vigor, an effeminizing of social life, and the acceptance of a specifically devirilizing religion, Christianity. Rousseau's free republic requires standing armies. Wollstonecraft will have none of this; better, she wants civic virtue without Rousseau's martial overtones. If a nation were forced into war, she argues, women too would be aroused and do their part. She shares a vision of civic duty for men and women. But Rousseau, in her view, celebrates not virtue but barbarism. He idolizes the Romans who conquered and destroyed but did not extend "the reign of virtue."

In his rush to rescue virtue from vice, Rousseau misidentified virtue. He missed the truly "gigantic mischief" of arbitrary power in social or private life that, together with a "standing army," are "incompatible with freedom." She warns that subordination is a chief sinew of military discipline and that "despotism is necessary to give vigour" to the military enterprise. Romantic notions of honor may be apt for the commanding few but the vast majority of soldiers are swept along by coercion and fear. How can this possibly stand as a model of virtue? It may be a tragic necessity but it cannot serve as *the* exemplar of civic probity. Wollstonecraft's recognition that the tradition of civic republicanism from Machiavelli through Rousseau assimilates civic and martial virtues and, in so doing, guarantees the civic incapacity of women remains salient today as we think about what political equality between the sexes implies or requires by way of responsibilities as well as rights and privileges.

War has always created history's greatest gender gap. But that gap has narrowed in the era of total war when distinctions between the front lines and the home front are obliterated; when no one any longer is safe or can be protected; when the women move in to do the men's work short of the actual business of killing and dying in combat, though some women have proclaimed that, too, as a civic duty and right.

The watershed separating innocence from irony in this matter, for Europeans at least, (it has taken us longer to lose our innocence) was World War I, the Great War. In World War I, male disillusionment with war and female enthusiasm for the freedom and liberation wartime duty meant for women is dramatically evident, reversing the usual cultural expectations. In a provocative essay, "Soldier's Heart: Literary Men, Literary Women, and the Great War," Sandra Gilbert, following Paul Fussell's masterful, *The Great War and Modern Memory,* observes that World War I "fostered . . . modernist irony in young men . . . by revealing exactly how spurious were their visions of heroism, and—by extension—history's images of heroism. Mobilized and marched off to the front, idealistic young soldiers soon found themselves immobilized, even buried alive, in trenches of death."

Gilbert contrasts the ironic and pessimistic discourse of men with examples of the upbeat literature and fevered rhetoric of women writers and feminist activists. *The Suffragette,* the newspaper of the Women's Social and Political Union, was renamed *Britannia* "and dedicated to king and country. . . . Bernard Shaw describes young

women handing white feathers to all young men not in uniform."
May Sinclair "described 'the ecstacy' of battle in *The Tree of Heaven*.
Rose Macaulay in her 'Many Sisters to Many Brothers' expressed
envy of the soldier's liberation from the dreariness of the home front:
'Oh it's you that have the luck, out there in blood and muck.' " Says
Gilbert: "In the words of women propagandists as well as in the
deeds of feather-carrying girls, the classical Roman's noble *patria*
seemed to have become a sinister, death-dealing *matria*." While male
writers "associated the front with paralysis, many female writers
imagined it as a place of freedom" and they wrote of the delight of
female mobilization. To be sure their experiences, not on the front,
were "very different from that experienced by entrenched combatants."

There was, as well, a female politics of pacifism and antimilitarism
in this period that didn't succumb to war fervor. But I note this
reversal to indicate that war's gender gap is by no means so simple as
male bellicosity on the one hand and female pacifism or antimilitarism
on the other. And among female pacifists there are important
differences. Take, for example, the reactions of two great women
who, during World War I or in its aftermath, evoked an active
citizenship, a politics to combat wartime excess, on the one hand, or
embraced a vision of female withdrawal into an indifferent society of
outsiders, on the other. I refer to the distinction between a pacifist
feminist citizen like Jane Addams and a pacifist feminist noncitizen
like Virginia Woolf. Although Woolf's ex-patriotic plea, *The Three
Guineas*, was written in 1938, and most of Addams's writing on the
war occurred during the war or immediately after, I will take up Woolf
first.

Collapsing patriotism into nationalism and disdaining both, Woolf
advocated the "use of indifference." Women who had made their
own inner withdrawal from anything to do with political life must
become part of an "anonymous and secret Society of Outsiders"—so
anonymous and secret its extent could not be known even to those
who were in it. We—this Society of Outsiders—"experiment not with
public means in public but with private means in private." The citizen
recedes in her story for women must free themselves from all
"unreal" loyalties including national loyalty. The only true loyalty is
to oneself. "As a woman my country is the whole world." Two short
years later, framed by aggressive Nazism, Woolf's words seem the
manifesto of a pale aestheticism. As Elaine Showalter argues in *A
Literature of Their Own*, the language of *Three Guineas* "is all too

frequently . . . empty sloganeering and cliche," offering an eerie memesis of that which Woolf opposes, the discourse of nationalism, which exhibits rhetorically these very same qualities.

Different indeed is Jane Addams, who brought patriotism to bear *against* nationism, using the ideals of democracy to critique the blindness of national excess. She describes movingly the plight of the antiwar citizen in the time of war, "sick at heart" from the violence but also at the estrangement from her fellow citizens. She knew that women do have countries. Women will not, no more that did socialists and the working classes, forsake their homelands *en masse* in the name of a thin, supranationalist ideal. Addams's solution was political: concerned men and women in each country must fight militarism; peace is a social form that must be struggled for in the name of democratic values. In celebrations of male action in wartime, Addams sees moments of patriotic devotion and honor, yes, but she also sees a centuries-old trail of tears and that is the image that must come to prevail in our thinking.

To combat war enthusiasms, Addams determined that an identity with a nonstatist ethic, as well as patriotic love of country, was required. She found hers in a social gospel and in a network of activists, most of them women, many of them pacifist. Family and state do not suffice as bases for ethical life, she decided. One requires communities of conscience, associations, and movements, many concrete, social possibilities. As well, experience with those unlike us is vital, affording an angle of vision from which one can view one's own nation and its institutions afresh. Without these multiple loci of meaning and identity construction, especially in times of crisis, the state may be all that remains standing—the state of nationalist excess—and we will be compelled to love it, as Simone Weil chillingly wrote in *The Need For Roots*, because nothing else exists. Between Woolf's call to indifference and Addams's call to citizenship lie two different ways of being—the one explicitly abstracted from politics; the other specifically called to critical and dissenting citizenship in the name of a generous vision of humanity and a deeply felt love of country.

Can we be patriots in our time? Patriotism is neither a program nor a policy but a way of being in the world. I shall conclude with a sketch of the *chastened patriot* in contrast to the strong patriotism of civic republican lore. The chastened patriot—chastened in the sense of stripped of the excesses of nationalism—has learned from the past. Rejecting a counsel of cynicism, she modulates the rhetoric of high patriotic purpose by keeping alive the distancing voice of ironic remembrance and rueful recognition of the way patriotism can shade into rapacious nationalism, recognition of the fact that patriotism in the form of Rousseauian armed civic virtue cannot be reconstructed for our time. A major task of the chastened patriot "is to work to weaken the principle of nationalism" with its sacralization of state sovereignty.

The chastened patriot is both committed *and* detached: enough apart so that he or she can be reflective about civic ties and loyalties. This patriotism cannot go back to an innocent time before the murderous excesses of twentieth-century nationalism. Chastened patriots cherish many loyalties and speak in many voices: a reclaimed patriotic choir is polyphonic. Diversity in commonality is not only tolerated but cherished. A view of ourselves "devoid of all utopian and universalistic pretensions . . . a view that takes account of the element of relativity in all antagonisms and friendships," that is the view of the chastened patriot and the words are George Kennan's.

In an essay on "Karl Jaspers," Hannah Arendt argued that "nobody can be a citizen of the world as he is a citizen of his country. . . . No matter what form a world government with centralized power over the whole globe might assume, the very notion of one sovereign force ruling the whole earth, holding the monopoly of all means of violence, unchecked and uncontrolled by other sovereign powers, is not only a forbidding nightmare of tyranny, it would be the end of all political life as we know it. . . . A citizen is by definition a citizen of a country among countries."

As a citizen among citizens in a country among countries I am prepared to make a few modest suggestions. A civic life animated by chastened patriotism bears implication for our attitude towards centralized state power and the historic closure of political space beneath the level of the state. With her high estimation of civic activity, the patriot is one inspired to consider ways to reverse the political drain upward. The chastened patriot dissents as she considers our current strategic doctrine for the nationalist imperatives imbedded in that doctrine commit us, if it should come to that, to the wholesale slaughter of civilian populations. But the chastened patriot has no illusions. She recognizes the limiting conditions in international politics and refuses to embrace utopian fantasies of world federations or unilateral disarmament.

From strength not weakness, the patriotism I here evoke urges us to take bold initiatives in order to break symbolically cycles of vengeance and fear. Given her recognition that the action of a citizen, or group of citizens, can rupture the frozen surface of an unacceptable status quo, the chastened patriot extends that imperative beyond the domestic arena, holding forth the hope that action from a single state, especially a dominant and powerful one, reverberates throughout the international system. Knowing peace on earth is not at hand, the chastened patriot believes that the world can be a less dangerous and deadly place and works to diminish its dangers, to make gentler its ways.

In his book on *Solidarity*, Timothy Garton Ash notes that the dissenting Poles, as they created a truly working-class movement, kept alive a tradition of resistance, and worked to attain basic freedoms, also evinced love of country and a desire to see their country free from foreign domination. Some among the dissenters raised with their fellow protestors, who are becoming free citizens, the question of what kind of country an independent Poland might be. Would she be a Poland nursing wounded nationalism, and turning her injuries against internal and external foes, or would she be a Poland of the sort that once served as a beacon of political freedom in a largely autocratic surround. "Polska tak," these thought-ful patriots affirmed and then they asked, "ale jaka?" Poland yes, but what sort of Poland?

I conclude with a similar affirmation and a question. America yes, but what sort of America?

Notes

Index

Notes

Preface

1 Cited in Norman Malcon, *Ludwig Wittgenstein, A Memoir* (London: Oxford University Press, 1972), 39.
2 Hannah Arendt, *Men in Dark Times* (New York: Harcourt Brace Jovanovich, 1968), viii.

Introduction

1 Karen Offen, "The Use and Abuse of History," *Women's Review of Books,* vol. VI, no. 7 (April 1989): 15–16, 15.
2 Martha Nussbaum, *The Fragility of Goodness: Luck and Ethics in Greek Tragedy and Philosophy* (Cambridge, Mass.: Cambridge University Press, 1986), 258.
3 Joan Wallach Scott, *Gender and the Politics of History* (New York: Columbia University Press, 1988), 7.
4 Hannah Arendt, *Men in Dark Times* (New York: Harcourt Brace Jovanovich, 1968), vii.
5 Eric Schmitt, "Changes Asked on Child Societies," *New York Times,* February 7, 1989, 26.

Chapter 1. A Return to Hull House

1 Allen F. Davis, *American Heroine: The Life and Legend of Jane Addams* (New York: Oxford University Press, 1973), xi. Addams is not among the many women rediscovered in our time and restored to her presumed rightful place in history by feminist social historians and political thinkers. Outside the mainstream feminism of her day, Addams remains an ambivalent figure for contemporary feminists, one not easily appropriated to any particular cause save that of antimilitarism.
2 Daniel Levine, *Jane Addams and the Liberal Tradition* (Madison, Wis.: The State Historical Society of Wisconsin, 1971), x.
3 Henry Steele Commager, *The American Mind* (New Haven: Yale University Press, 1959).
4 Ralph Henry Gabriel, *The Course of American Democratic Thought* (New Haven: Yale University Press, 1956), 360.
5 Richard Hofstadter, *The Age of Reform* (New York: Vintage, 1955).
6 Christopher Lasch, ed., *The Social Thought of Jane Addams* (Indianapolis: Bobbs-Merrill, 1965), xv, and *The New Radicalism in America 1889–1963* (New

181

York: Vintage, 1965). The chapter devoted to Jane Addams is entitled "Jane Addams: The College Woman and the Family Claim," 3–37.

7   Interestingly, John J. McDermott, editor of *The Philosophy of John Dewey* (Chicago: University of Chicago Press, 1981), states that much of Dewey's "range of interests" in addressing public issues "can be traced to Jane Addams and her work at Hull House in Chicago." This appears in footnote 13 to the "introduction," xxxiii. McDermott here counters the received view that Addams is, at best, a pale, derivative Deweyite who popularized a simplified version of his philosophy. The story of Addams as an intellectual influence on Dewey has yet to be told. This lacuna no doubt reflects Dewey's stature as a philosopher and his seminal influence. But my hunch is that the somewhat condescending treatment of Addams as a thinker has other roots. One may be the fact that her role as social activist and interpreter rather than career academic meant she never acquired the automatic legitimacy we accord to credentialed scholars; in fact her interpretive, storytelling social theory is easily viewed as personalistic and subjectivist by those who prefer bloodless abstractions; and no doubt, by the presence of the old-fashioned sexist canard that posits a tacit Manichean dualism between man the thinker and woman the feeler.

8   I worked from three published editions of *Twenty Years at Hull House* at various points: a 1968 edition published in New York by Macmillan; a New American Library paperback published in 1960; and the one-volume combined edition of *Twenty Years at Hull House* and *The Second Twenty Years at Hull House,* the final installment of Addams's autobiography, published originally in 1930, republished as part of *Forty Years* by Macmillan in 1935, the year of Addams's death.

9   Davis, *American Heroine*, xi. Addams could never have seen herself reflected from the mirror as a tough-minded *realpolitiker*. This is not a piece of dissimulation; instead, it is her honest awareness of the fact that the trajectory of her life and the response of a particular public at a particular time to her evocations of moral suasion were of a piece. Given that Addams repudiated a power definition of politics, a repudiation fully compatible with a realistic assessment of who has force, who controls, who manipulates, etc., for her to have embraced a tough-minded, calculating image of herself is unthinkable.

10 Addams, *Forty Years at Hull House*, 66.

11 I do not see the American chauvinism Davis covers in *Twenty Years*, which most often includes a heavy dose of arrogance towards other ways of life. As a social activist Addams resisted overidentifying her public life with a narrow nationalism that might preclude criticism of state policy. She broke openly with the mission of America to "make the world safe for democracy" in World War I. This undercuts, at least in part, Davis's collapse of Jane Addams's personal calling with America's mission.

12 Addams, *Forty Years at Hull House*, 66.

13 Jane Addams, *Democracy and Social Ethics* (New York: Macmillan, 1902), 1.

14 Addams, *The Second Twenty Years*, 6.

15 Ibid.

16 Her first published book was a collection, *Democracy and Social Ethics*.

17 *Twenty Years* (Macmillan ed.), 122.

18 Ibid., 126.

19 Ibid., 174–75.

20 Ibid., 247.
21 Addams implies but never develops fully a theory of the child's developmental emergence as a moral being. She recognizes that early neglect may lead the individual to remain forever impervious to life's gentler aspects, and that compelling a child to complete tasks beyond his or her "normal growth" is cruel and often disastrous. She poses a concept of sublimation, urging that blind appetite be transformed into worthy psychic impulses by the moral motives. For Addams, child development was a *Bildung*, an evolving education of the heart.
22 Jane Addams, *A New Conscience and an Ancient Evil* (New York: Macmillan, 1912), 137. This attack on prostitution and paean to chastity is described by Walter Lippman as a "hysterical book." It is not one of her finest efforts.
23 Jane Addams, *Twenty Years* (Macmillan ed.), 85.
24 Ibid., 91.
25 Ibid.
26 Ibid., 121–22.
27 Ibid., 111–12.
28 Addams, *Forty Years*, 132.
29 Ibid, 150–51.
30 See Lasch, *The New Radicalism*, 157. Addams's ambivalence is also traceable to the fact that she saw in the social forces of industrial production a political potential for the spread of industrial democracy.
31 Discussion of aesthetic impulses and the necessity of social space for free play are themes that run through her work.

Chapter 2. The Vexation of Weil

1 Simone Weil, *The Need for Roots* (New York: Octagon Books, 1979), 51.
2 Simone Weil, *Oppression and Liberty* (Amherst, Mass.: University of Massachusetts Press, 1979), xi.
3 Staughton Lynd, "Marxism-Leninism and the Language of *Politics* Magazine: The First New Left . . . and the Third," in *Simone Weil: Interpretations of a Life*, ed. George Abbott White (Amherst, Mass.: University of Massachusetts Press, 1981), 111.
4 All three essays are reprinted in Weil, *Oppression and Liberty.*
5 Ibid., 3–4.
6 See the discussion in Herbert Lottman, *The Left Bank* (New York: Houghton Mifflin, 1982).
7 Weil, *Oppression and Liberty*, 4.
8 Ibid., 5.
9 Ibid., 9.
10 Ibid., 10.
11 Ibid., 108. Cf. the discussion of work "set over against" the human person in John Paul II, "Laborem Exercens," or "On Human Work" (Boston: Daughters of St. Paul, 1981).
12 Ibid., 115.
13 Weil, *The Need for Roots*, 114. Weil sometimes fails to distinguish, and sometimes confusingly distinguishes, state, nation, collectivity, community. Here her reference is clearly "the" state, the hegemonic centralized power in a nation-state society.

14 Ibid., 116.

15 Simone Weil, *Lectures on Philosophy* (Cambridge, Mass.: Cambridge University Press, 1978), 128. Weil understands "reason" in a formalistic, Cartesian sense here, as a kind of mathematical certainty.

16 Weil, *Oppression and Liberty*, 48.

17 Ibid., 79.

18 Simone Weil, *Gravity and Grace* (New York: Octagon Books, 1979), 212.

19 Ibid., 55.

20 Weil, *Oppression and Liberty*, 39.

21 Ibid., 108.

22 Ibid., 67.

23 Weil, *Gravity and Grace*, 222.

24 Ibid., 86.

25 The dramatically different metaphysic and epistemology of early Christian doctrine is detailed, eloquently, in two books: Margaret R. Miles, *Fullness of Life* (Philadelphia: Westminster, 1981) and Peter Brown, *The Cult of the Saints: Its Rise and Function in Latin Christianity* (Chicago: University of Chicago Press, 1982).

26 Weil, *Gravity and Grace*, 130.

27 Ibid., 162.

28 The "best place" to look for Catholic social doctrine remains the great "social encyclicals": John Paul, II *Laborem Exercens*; and *Mater et Magistra* and *Pacem in Terris*, both of which appear in John Paul XXIII, *The Encyclicals and Messages (Washington, D.C.: TPS Press, 1964), among others.*

29 Quoted in Simone Petrement's biography, *Simone Weil: A Life* (New York: Pantheon, 1976), 499. Cf. Robert Coles, *Simone Weil: A Modern Pilgrimage* (Reading, Mass.: Addison-Wesley, 1987.)

30 Richard P. McBrien, "Roman Catholicism: E. Pluribus Unum," *Daedalus*, vol. III (Winter 1982): 77.

31 Hannah Arendt, *The Human Condition* (Chicago: University of Chicago Press, 1958), 247.

Chapter 3. Eleanor Roosevelt as Activist and Thinker

1 Peggy Reeves Sanday, *Male Dominance and Female Power* (Cambridge, Mass.: Cambridge University Press, 1981), 133, 155.

2 Eleanor Roosevelt, *The Moral Basis of Democracy* (New York: Howell, Soskin and Co., 1950), 76.

3 Abigail Q. McCarthy, "Eleanor Roosevelt as First Lady," in *Without Precedent. The Life and Career of Eleanor Roosevelt*, eds. Joan Hoff-Wilson and Marjorie Lightman (Bloomington, Ind.: Indiana University Press, 1984), 214–25, 216–17.

4 Emily Jones Putnam, *The Lady: Studies of Certain Significant Phases of Her History* (Chicago: University of Chicago Press, 1969; first published 1938), xxvii.

5 Anne Firor Scott, *The Southern Lady: From Pedestal to Politics 1830–1930* (Chicago: University of Chicago Press, 1970), x.

6 Ibid., 160.

7 Ibid., 180, 181.

8   Tamara Hareven, *Eleanor Roosevelt: An American Conscience* (Chicago: Quadrangle Books, 1968), 7.

9   Duncan Crow, *The Victorian Woman* (London: George Allen and Unwin, 1971), 62–63.

10 Archibald MacLeish, *The Eleanor Roosevelt Story* (Boston: Houghton Mifflin, 1965), introduction.

11 Joseph P. Lash, *Eleanor and Franklin* (New York: Signet Books, New American Library, 1973), 27.

12 Eleanor Roosevelt, *This Is My Story* (New York: Harper and Brothers, 1937), 3–4.

13 Ibid., 34.

14 Ibid., 103.

15 Ibid., 171, 173.

16 Personal communication to the author. Thanks also to Ms. Phelan for some bibliographical research and summarizing and to my son, Eric, for note-typing.

17 Lash, *Eleanor and Franklin*, 616.

18 Susan Ware, "ER and Democratic Politics: Women in the Postsuffrage Era," in *Without Precedent*, 46–62, 49.

19 Hareven, *Eleanor Roosevelt*, 271.

20 Lash, *Eleanor and Franklin*, 146.

21 Roosevelt, *This Is My Story*, 67.

22 Lash, *Eleanor and Franklin*, 258.

23 Eleanor Roosevelt, *This I Remember* (New York: Harper and Brothers, 1949), 175.

24 Roosevelt, *This Is My Story*, 260.

25 Joseph P. Lash, *Love, Eleanor: Eleanor Roosevelt and Her Friends* (Garden City, N.Y.: Doubleday, 1982), 67.

26 Mrs. Franklin D. Roosevelt [sic], *It's Up to the Women* (New York: Frederick A. Stokes, 1933), 36–37.

27 Ibid., 87.

28 Lash, *Eleanor and Franklin*, 417–18.

29 Roosevelt, *The Moral Basis of Democracy*, 42.

30 Ibid., 81–82.

31 Lash, *Eleanor And Franklin*, 42–43.

32 Ibid., 140.

33 Ibid., 466.

34 Ibid., 548.

35 Ibid., 74.

36 Roosevelt, *This I Remember*, 330.

37 Oscar Romero, "The Political Dimension of Christian Love," *Commonweal* (March 1982: 169–172), 169.

38 Ibid.

39 Ibid, 171.

40 Ibid., 172.

41 Hareven, *Eleanor Roosevelt*, 23.

42 Ibid., xii.

43 Jill Conway, "Women Reformers and American Culture," *Journal of Social History* (Winter 1971–72): 166.

44   Eli Zaretsky, "The Legacy of Jane Addams," unpub. ms., 1984.
45   Conway, "Women Reformers," 168.
46   Zaretsky, "The Legacy of Jane Addams."
47   Eleanor Roosevelt, *The Autobiography of Eleanor Roosevelt* (New York: Harper and Brothers, 1958), 412–13.
48   Ibid., 420.
49   Jane Addams, *The Long Road of Woman's Memory* (New York: Macmillan, 1916), 129. See also Jean Bethke Elshtain, "Women as Mirror and Other: Toward a Theory of Women, War and Feminism," *Humanities in Society,* vol. 5 (Winter–Spring 1982): 29–44. In *Women and War* (Basic Books, 1987), I pretty thoroughly undercut arguments that flow too easily from "women's peace" to international harmony.
50   Susan Wave, "ER and Democratic Politics," 49.
51   Roosevelt, "It's Up to the Women," 243, 263.

Chapter 4. The Family and Civic Life

1   Plato, *The Republic,* Book 6, 500c–501b. Bloom translation (New York: Basic Books, 1968).
2   Shulamith Firestone, *The Dialectic of Sex* (New York: Bantam Books, 1972).
3   Anne Donchin, "The Future of Mothering: Reproductive Technology and Feminist Theory," *Hypatia,* vol. 2, no. 2 (Fall 1986): 121–37, 130.
4   Alison Jagger, *Feminist Politics and Human Nature* (Totowa, N.J.: Rowman and Allanhead, 1983), 132.
5   Martha Nussbaum, *The Fragility of Goodness* (Cambridge, Mass.: Cambridge University Press, 1960), 40.
6   Ibid., 135, 141.
7   Ibid., 214.
8   This is not to say that all features of these ontologies are, in principle, no longer available to us. Many continue to structure their lives primarily in and through such ontologies of faith, but not, I would argue, without conflict.
9   Hobbes's version of this story fuses absolutism with consent in all spheres, including the family, and accepts coerced "choice" as legitimate.
10   On this subject, see Mary Lyndon Shanley, "Marriage Contract and Social Contract in Seventeenth-Century English Political Thought," in *The Family in Political Thought,* ed. Jean Bethke Elshtain (Amherst, Mass.: University of Massachusetts Press, 1982), 80–95.
11   John Locke, *Two Treatises of Government,* ed. Peter Laslett (New York: New American Library, 1965), 357.
12   John Stuart Mill, *The Subjection of Women* (Greenwich, Conn.: Fawcett, 1970).
13   Not even Mill took the argument for consent to its *reductio ad absurdum* as in some recent versions of "children's liberation." See Richard W. Krouse, "Patriarchal Liberalism and Beyond: From John Stuart Mill to Harriet Taylor," in *The Family in Political Thought,* 145–72.
14   Alexis de Tocqueville, *Democracy in America,* vol. 2, ed. Phillips Bradley (New York: Vintage, 1945), 223.
15   Ibid., 209. There is an echo of Rosseau in this.
16   Ibid., 203–4.

17 William E. Connolly, in "Modern Authority and Ambiguity," *Politics and Ambiguity*, (Madison, Wis.: University of Wisconsin Press, 1987), 127–42, argues that ambiguity is necessary to a defense of authority in modernity.

18 Mary Midgley, *Beast and Man: The Roots of Human Nature* (Ithaca, N.Y.: Cornell University Press, 1978), 291.

19 Connolly, "Modern Authority and Ambiguity," 138.

Chapter 5. The Family Crisis, the Family Wage, and Feminism

1 Jean Bethke Elshtain, "Feminism, Family and Community," *Dissent* (Fall 1982): 442–49.

2 Ibid., 448.

3 Barbara Ehrenreich and Jean Bethke Elshtain, "On Feminism, Family and Community," *Dissent* (Winter 1983): 104–5.

4 Eleanor Rathbone, *Family Allowance* (London: George Allen and Unwin, 1924), x.

5 Ibid., 1.

6 Ibid., 6.

7 Ibid., 10.

8 Ibid., 29.

9 Ibid., 52.

10 Paul Douglas, *Wages and the Family* (Chicago: University of Chicago Press, 1925), ix.

11 Ibid., 199.

12 Ibid., 223.

13 Ibid., 255.

14 Nancy Cott, *The Grounding of Modern Feminism* (New Haven: Yale University Press, 182.

15 Ibid., 207.

16 For a discussion of radical, liberal, socialist, and psychoanalytical feminisms on the family see my *Public Man, Private Woman: Women in Social and Political Thought* (Princeton: Princeton University Press, 1981).

17 Betty Friedan, *The Feminine Mystique* (1963; reprinted, New York: Dell, 1974), 353.

18 Michelle Barrett and Mary McIntosh, "The 'Family Wage': Some Problems for Socialists and Feminists," *Capital and Class* 2 (1980): 59–71.

19 Ibid., 57.

20 Ibid., 59.

21 Ibid., 69.

22 See Jane Humphries, "Class Struggle and the Persistence of the Working Class Family," *Cambridge Journal of Economics* 1, no. 3.

23 Martha May, "The Historical Problem of the Family Wage: The Ford Motor Company and the Five Dollar Day," *Feminist Studies* 8 (Summer, 1982): 398–424.

24 May, "The Historical Problem of the Family Wage," 401. May refers here to the laissez-faire notion that poverty was the fault of the individual worker.

25 Ibid., 404.

26 Nadine Bozan, "Former Wives: A Legion of the Needy," *New York Times*, July 29, 1987, sec. 3, pp. 1, 4.

27   See Sylvia Hewlett's discussion of "The Wage Gap" in *A Lesser Life* (New York: Warner Books, 1986), 70–100. Hewlett's book was much attacked by feminists representing the dominant discourse.

28   Ibid., 71.

29   "In 1980 only 10 percent of all women aged forty to forty-four were childless. Women are having fewer children, and they are having them later, but more women are having at least one child than ever before." See Hewlett, *A Lesser Life*, 177.

30   Reverend John D. Callahan, S.T.L., *The Catholic Attitude Toward a Familial Minimum Wage*, (Washington, D.C.: The Catholic University of America, 1936), 13.

31   Ibid., 13.

32   Bishop's Pastoral, published by *Origins*. NC Documentary Service, 432.

33   How we do that is another question. Tax credits for dependent children, so the degree of benefit isn't proportional to one's income, is a start. A child allowance for families with a household income less than thirty thousand dollars a year is another possibility. John Buell has suggested taking a hard look at the forty-hour work week as the length of the work week, which has remained virtually unchanged since New Deal days, makes it more difficult for both parents to engage in child care and nurture. The sad truth is that an estimated five million children under the age of ten come home to empty houses in the afternoon. This is a disgrace that cries out for imaginative attention.

34   Nancy Fraser, "Women, Welfare and the Politics of Need Interpretation," *Hypatia* (Winter 1987): 103–21.

Chapter 6. The Family Crisis and State Intervention

1   And those patterns have often been under stress at particular points. For example, the Homestead Act depleted the male population of most New England towns, making it very difficult for fifty years or so for women to find anyone to marry. (Thanks to Jane Mausbridge for this historic footnote.)

2   Pamela G. Hollie, "Study Urges a U.S. Family Policy," *New York Times*, September 12, 1977, 1, 54.

3   Diane Ravitch, "In the Family's Way," *The New Republic* June 28, 1980, 18–24, 19.

4   Ibid., 24.

5   Brigitte Berger and Peter L. Berger, *The War over the Family: Capturing the Middle Ground* (Garden City, N.Y.: Doubleday/Anchor Press, 1983), 172.

6   See John Scanzoni, *Shaping Tomorrow's Family: Theory and Policy for the 21st Century* (Beverly Hills, Calif.: Sage, 1983).

7   This may be a bit strong. There have been cycles of interest in issues of child abuse and neglect and private violence. But the coalition of interests surrounding such questions at present is a new phenomenon.

8   Barbara J. Nelson, *Making an Issue of Child Abuse* (Chicago: University of Chicago Press, 1984), 2.

9   Nelson tells this story in detail.

10   Nelson, *Making an Issue of Child Abuse*, 15.

11   The number of young male victims of rape is also consistently understated and invisible—not constituted as a social question—this despite the fact that

adolescent male reaction to sexual assault is a much higher suicide rate than among young female victims.

12   "Changing Patterns of Family Violence," *New York Times*, November 14, 1985, C–9.

13   Evan Stark, Anne Flitcraft, and William Frazier, "Medicine and Patriarchal Violence: The Social Construction of a 'Private' Event," *International Journal of Health Services*, vol. 3 (1979): 461–93, 479–80.

14   Ibid., 480.

15   Challenged on its figures, Child Fund currently estimates that there are fewer than 600 cases of missing children per year. According to the *Boston Globe*, June 14, 1985, of the 1,080 children currently listed as missing in Massachusetts, 75 percent are runaways and the remaining 25 percent are cases of parental abduction.

16   Poor or lower-middle-class children are more readily removed from the home and placed in foster care. For middle- and upper-middle-class families, preferred intervention is to send the child away to school, or to reintroduce either child or offending parent back into the family but under terms of therapy and surveillance.

17   See Deborah Fallows, *A Mother's Work* (New York: Houghton Mifflin, 1986).

Chapter 7. The New Eugenics and Feminist Quandries

1   Ann Dochin, "The Future of Mothering: Reproductive Technology and Feminist Theory," *Hypatia*, vol. 2, no. 2 (Fall 1986): 121–37, divides up feminist positions into noninterventionist moderate interventionist, and radical interventionist. Our take on these issues is somewhat different, my approach being more philosophical and explicitly lodged in moral concerns than Dochin's. But her discussion is helpful, and each of us rounds up many of the usual suspects.

2   For the next few pages I draw upon an earlier essay, "The Liberal Captivity of Feminism: A Critical Appraisal of (Some) Feminist Answers," which appeared in *The Liberal Future in America. Essays in Retrieval*, ed. Philip Abbot and Michael B. Levy (Westport, Conn.: Greenwood Press, 1985), 63–84. As about two dozen people in the world seem to have discovered this book I don't feel too badly about recycling several arguments.

3   Charles Taylor, "Atomism," *Possessions and Freedom: Essays in Honor of C. B. McPherson*, ed. Alkis Kontos (Toronto: University of Toronto Press, 1979), 39–61, 39.

4   Ibid., 41.

5   Ibid., 48.

6   Ibid.

7   Laurie Bobskill, "Couples in Western Massachusetts Offered 'Gender Preselection'," *Springfield Union News*, Friday, December 4, 1987, B–7.

8   Interestingly, the higher the education level the more the Sterns were favored over Mary Beth Whitehead. The same held for income level, of course, as education enjoys a strong positive relation to income. Also, using gender as a differentiating category, more women than men favored the Sterns (61.3 percent to 54.8 percent), indicating, I believe, how strongly the "best interests of the child" argument has taken hold—and that the character assassination of Mary Beth Whitehead by Judge Harvey Sorkow had some effect.

9   *Episteme* is a concept drawn from Michael Foucault that refers to "the total set of relations that unite, at a given period, the discursive practices that give rise to epistemological figures, sciences, and formalized systems." See his *The Archeology of Knowledge,* trans. Alan Sheridan (New York: Harper Colophon, 1972), 119.

10 See Jean Bethke Elshtain, *Public Man, Private Woman: Women in Social and Political Thought* (Princeton: Princeton University Press, 1981), for a complete discussion.

11 John Stuart Mill, *The Subjection of Women* (Greenwich, Conn.: Fawcett, 1970), 18.

12 Ibid.

13 Ibid., 141.

14 See Jean Bethke Elshtain, "Existentialism and Repressive Feminism," in *Liberalism and the Modern Polity,* ed. Michael J. Argas McGrath (New York: Marcel Dekker, 1979), 33–62.

15 Shulamith Firestone, *The Dialectic of Sex* (New York: Bantam Books, 1972), 201. See also Elshtain, *Public Man, Private Woman,* 205–28.

16 Dochin,"The Future of Mothering," 130.

17 Peter Singer and Deane Wells, *Making Babies: The New Science and Ethics of Conception* (New York: Scribner, 1984), 157–58. Indeed, Singer and Wells use Firestone to insist that feminists support their position.

18 Jean Bethke Elshtain. "A Feminist Agenda on Reproductive Technology," *The Hastings Center Report,* vol. 12, no. 1 (February 1882): 40–43.

19 Cited in Genoveffa Corea, "How the New Reproductive Technologies Could Be Used to Apply the Brothel Model of Social Control Over Women," *Women's Studies International Forum,* vol. 8, no. 4 (1985): 299–305, 299.

20 Gena Corea, *The Mother Machine* (New York: Harper & Row, 1985), 2, 134, 233. One reason the new reproductive technology could burst upon the scene with such apparent suddenness is the fact that many decades of intrusive and cruel experimentation on animals went unmarked. Animals' bodies for decades have been violated as part of a quest for scientized production and control. There is a direct line between laboratory experiments on animals; farm factory production; and the new eugenics. See also Renate Klein, ed., *Infertility* (Winchester, Mass.: Unwin Hyman/Pandora, 1989).

21 I oppose the invasive technology of in vitro fertilization because it deepens the atomistic world view; it enhances the demand for technological solutions as well as the power of those who proffer such solutions; it disentangles human intimacy and reproduction; and it promotes the view that human beings have an absolute right to their *own* child rather than sustaining them in accepting limits to their own fertility while, at the same time, encouraging a loving relationship to children who are not their direct biological offspring. But women and men who seek, often desperately and repeatedly, to reproduce biologically deserve empathy, not contempt. To call such women prostitutes is cruel. Cf. Christine Crowe, "Women Want It: In-Vitro Fertilization and Women's Motivations for Participation," *Women's Studies International Forum,* vol. 8, no. 6 (1985): 547–52. Crowe questions "choice" and shows the ways in which IVF provides the technological intervention in procreation in ways that mirror power relations between males and females as groups.

22   Maria Miles, "Why Do We Need All This? A Call Against Genetic Engineering and Reproductive Technology," *Women's Studies International Forum*, vol. 8, no. 6 (1985): 553–60, 559.

23   Andrea Boroff Eagan, "Baby Roulette," *The Village Voice* (August 25, 1987), 16–21, 16.

24   Ronald S. Cole-Turner, "Is Genetic Engineering Co-Creation?" *Theology Today* (October 1987): 338–49, 344–45.

25   Ruth Hubbard, "Prenatal Diagnosis and Eugenic Ideology," *Women's Studies International Forum*, vol. 8, no. 6 (1985): 567–75, 568.

26   *New York Times*, March 24, 1987, 26. Lipset, an assistant professor of anthropology, was pretty clearly out of his depth on this one.

27   James Barron, "Views on Surrogacy Harden After Baby M Ruling," *New York Times*, April 27, 1987, 1,16, 16. Of course, at one point the denial of the personhood of women got lodged by Friedan and others in the assumption that a necessary bond existed linking biological and social motherhood: how ideological worms turn!

28   Katha Pollitt, "The Strange Case of Baby M," *The Nation*, May 23, 1987, 1, 682–88, 688. Pollitt even had a few good words about the Vatican instruction on reproductive technology. The Vatican was right, she claimed, in insisting that you "don't have a right to a child, any more than you have a right to a spouse. You only have the right to try to have one."

29   Ellen Willis, "1987. Feminiso," *Village Voice*, January 5, 1988, 21.

30   Patricia Spallone, "The Warnock Report: The Politics of Reproductive Technology," *Women's Studies International Forum*, vol. 9, no. 5, (1985): 543–50, 544.

31   Oliver O'Donovan, *Begotten or Made* (Oxford: Clarendon Press, 1984), 90.

Chapter 8. Relying on Nature

1   Unless otherwise noted, all quoted material is drawn from *The Closing of the American Mind* (New York: Simon & Schuster, 1987.) Portions of the first few pages of this essay are drawn from my book review of Bloom's tome for *Cross Current*, no. 4 (Winter 1987–88): 476–79.

2   See, for example, Alasdair MacIntyre, "The Essential Contestability of Some Social Concepts," *Ethics*, 84, 1 (October, 1973): 1–9.

3   I draw upon my discussion in *Public Man, Private Woman: Women in Social and Political Thought* (Princeton: Princeton University Press, 1981), here.

4   There are some real issues at stake here. My point is that Bloom makes matters too easy for himself by arming himself with Nature as if this settled things by fiat.

5   Again, there are genuine matters to be debated. My complaint is that Bloom stops the discussion before it ever really gets a chance to start by heavy-handed use of such fraught categories as "the good."

6   Nussbaum's book, *The Fragility of Goodness: Luck and Ethics in Greek Tragedy and Philosophy* (Cambridge: Cambridge University Press, 1986), is must reading for anyone concerned with the self and schemes of value.

7   Ibid., 40.

8   Ibid., 135.

9   Ibid., 258.

10 Jean Bethke Elshtain, *Public Man, Private Woman*, 351.

Chapter 9. Pornography Politics

1 A similar ordinance was subsequently passed in Indianapolis given an alliance of radical feminists, conservative Republicans, and right-wing antismut activists. It was declared unconstitutional, null, and void on November 19, 1984, by Judge Sara Baker Evans, U.S. District Court Southern District, Indiana, in the case *ABA v. Hudut*.

2 The stress on cause is understandable but dubious. The classic literature on free speech (J. S. Mill) and such Supreme Court cases as *Schenck*, the Holmes dissent, assume cause as an acceptable standard. This sets the horizon for debates in our political culture. (Thanks to Jane Mansbridge for her helpful notes on this question.)

3 The most recent Court decision, the so-called Dial-a-Porn case (Sable Communications of Cal. v. F.C.C., 1989), satisfied almost nobody but especially offended antiporn forces. The statute in question, according to the Court, denied adults access to telephone messages "which are indecent but not obscene," thereby exceeding what was necessary to limit the access of minors to such messages.

Chapter 10. The Power and Powerlessness of Women

1 Kathleen B. Jones, "Aspects of Citizenship in a Woman-Friendly Polity," 9 (unpub. ms.).

2 See, for example, Seymour Martin Lipset, *Political Man: The Social Bases of Politics* (Garden City, N.Y.: Doubleday Anchor Books, 1963), 216–17.

3 In *Public Man, Private Woman: Women in Social and Political Thought* (Princeton: Princeton University Press, 1981), I offer the unabridged story.

4 Dorothy Emmet, "The Concept of Power" in *Power*, ed. John K. Champlin (New York: Atherton, 1971), 78–106, illumines these many meanings.

5 Peggy Reeves Sandy, *Male Dominance and Female Power* (Cambridge, Mass.: Cambridge University Press, 1981), 155.

6 From Stimpson forward to Powers's book (Chicago: University of Chicago Press, 1987), xii.

7 See, for example, Martine Segalen, *Love and Power in the Peasant Family* (Chicago: University of Chicago Press, 1983).

8 Julie Taylor, *Eva Peron: The Myths of a Woman* (Chicago: University of Chicago Press, 1971), 13.

9 I am not suggesting that the Romans had this in mind explicitly; rather, I am claiming that the weight of ethnographic evidence pushes towards these contrasting definitions and locates males lopsidedly inside one, females the other.

10 See the full discussion in Jean Bethke Elshtain, *Women and War* (New York: Basic Books, 1987).

11 Vaclav Havel et al., *The Power of the Powerless: Citizens against the State in Central-Eastern Europe* (Armonk, N.Y.: M. E. Sharpe, 1985), 59.

12 Ibid., 72.

13 See Adam Michnik, *Letters from Prison and Other Essays* (Berkeley: University of California Press, 1985), 169.

14 Hannah Arendt, *The Human Condition* (Chicago: University of Chicago Press, 1958), 247.

Chapter 11. Realism, Just War, and the Witness of Peace

1 "*Hamlet*, a Mirror of the Times" from the *New York Times*, Wednesday, November 2, 1988, 27.

2 Michael Howard, *The Causes of War* (Cambridge, Mass.: Harvard University Press, 1984).

3 Jean Bethke Elshtain, *Women and War* (New York: Basic Books, 1987).

4 Immanuel Kant, *Perpetual Peace and Other Essays*, trans. Ted Humphrey (Indianapolis: Hackett, 1983).

5 Jean Bethke Elshtain, "Problems with Peace," unpub. ms.

6 Stanley Hauerwas, *Against the Nations: War and Survival in a Liberal Society* (Minneapolis: Winston Press, 1985), 132–55, *passim*.

7 St. Augustine, *The City of God*, ed. David Knowles (Baltimore, Md.: Penguin Books, 1972).

8 Elshtain, *Women and War*, 252–58.

9 St. Augustine, *The City of God*.

Chapter 12. On Patriotism

1 John Schaar, "The Case for Patriotism," in *Legitimacy in the Modern State* (New Brunswick and London: Transaction, 1981); Alasdair MacIntyre, "Is Patriotism a Virtue?" University of Kansas, Philosophy Department, The Lindley Lecture, 1984; Stephen Nathanson, "In Defense of 'Moderate Patriotism'," *Ethics* (April 1989): 535–53; Lewis H. Laphan, "Notebook. The New Patriotism," *Harpers*, June 1984, 7–8; R. W. Apple, Jr., "New Stirrings of Patriotism," *New York Times Magazine*, December 11, 1983, 43–47, 87–96, 128–40); D. E. D. Beales, "Mazzini and Revolutionary Nationalism," in ed. David Thomson *Political Ideas* (New York: Penguin Books, 1982), 143–54; Simone Weil, *The Need for Roots* (New York: Octagon Books, 1979); Albert Camus, *Resistance, Rebellion and Death* (New York: Knopf, 1961); Jane Addams, *Peace and Bread in Time of War* (New York: Macmillan, 1922); Virginia Woolf, *Three Guineas* (New York: Harcourt Brace Jovanovich, 1966); Edmund Wilson, *Patriotic Gore* (New York: Oxford University Press, 1962); Dietrich Bonhoeffer, *Letters and Papers from Prison*, ed. Eberhard Bethge (New York: Macmillan, 1967); George Orwell, "Notes on Nationalism," *The Collected Essays, Journalism and Letters of George Orwell*, vol. 3, *As I Please 1943–1945*, ed. Sonia Orwell and Ian Angus (New York: Harcourt Brace Jovanovich, 1968), 361–79; Hannah Arendt, *The Origins of Totalitarianism* (New York: Harcourt Brace Jovanovich, Harvest Books, 1973); J. J. Rousseau, *The Emile*, trans. Allan Bloom (New York: Basic Books, 1979); Mary Wollstonecraft, *A Vindication of the Rights of Woman* (New York: W. W. Norton, 1967); Sandra Gilbert, "Soldier's Heart: Literary Men, Literary Women, and the Great War," *Signs: Journal of Women in Culture and Society*, vol. 8, no. 3 (1983); Paul Fussell, *The Great War and Modern Memory* (New York: Oxford University Press, 1975); Elaine Showalter, *A Literature of Their Own* (Princeton: Princeton University Press, 1977); Hannah Arendt, *Men in Dark Times* (New York: Harcourt Brace Jovanovich, 1986); Timothy Garton Ash, *Solidarnösc: The Polish Revolution* (New York: Scribner, 1984).

Index